Who D

CW01507200

"Inspirational, nuanced and wise—Dana Williams' engaging sociology of trust is a rich and timely wake up call to re-imagine social structures through cooperative action and mutual aid, beyond the multiplicity of forces that seek to divide us."

—Jonathan Purkis, author of *Driving With Strangers: What Hitchhiking Tells Us About Humanity*

"Through trust, Williams offers a compelling framework with which to analyze the possibilities and obstacles for transforming our lives for the better. After digging deep into the sociopolitical definitions and theories of trust, Williams thoroughly examines all the permutations of trust and distrust in the organization of state, capital, and society. In the end, he offers inspiration for practical ways to build the needed trust to overcome those obstacles we are accustomed to and seize the possibilities that we are trained to think are utopian."

—Shuli Branson, author of *Practical Anarchism: A Daily Guide*

"In this timely examination of trust, mistrust, and distrust, Williams offers a critical analysis of the forms of trust practiced by groups across the political spectrum, along with a radical exposition on how we might become individually and collectively more discerning. A powerful engagement with a core building block of any healthy society: the thoughtful practice of trust."

—Matthew T. Lee, PhD, Professor of the Social Sciences and Humanities, Baylor University

Who Do We Trust?

Power, Solidarity, and Anti-Authoritarianism

Dana M. Williams

First published 2025 by Pluto Press
New Wing, Somerset House, Strand, London WC2R 1LA
and Pluto Press, Inc.
1930 Village Center Circle, 3-834, Las Vegas, NV 89134

www.plutobooks.com

British Library Cataloguing in Publication Data
A catalogue record for this book is available from the British Library

ISBN 978 0 7453 5064 6   Paperback
ISBN 978 0 7453 5066 0   PDF
ISBN 978 0 7453 5065 3   EPUB

This book is printed on paper suitable for recycling and made from fully
managed and sustained forest sources. Logging, pulping and manufacturing
processes are expected to conform to the environmental standards of the
country of origin.

Typeset by Stanford DTP Services, Northampton, England

Simultaneously printed in the United Kingdom and United States of America

EU GPSR Authorised Representative
LOGOS EUROPE, 9 rue Nicolas Poussin, 17000, LA ROCHELLE, France
Email: Contact@logoseurope.eu

Contents

CONTENTS

Acknowledgments

These ideas were previously presented and deconstructed thanks to conference organizers and fellow presenters Richard Simon, Erek Smith, David Michael Orenstein, and Tom Hochschild at the Mid-South Sociological Association; Jeff Shantz and P. J. Lilley at the North American Anarchist Studies Network conference in Kwantlen; Carl Stempel, Kristin Haltinner, and Isaac William Martin at the Pacific Sociological Association; Valdosta State University's Science Seminar Series; and Chico State University's College of Behavioral and Social Sciences research colloquium and the Humanities Center brownbag forum. Portions of a study that appeared in *Social Science Quarterly* have been used selectively, and editors Simon Springer and Richard J. White supported a focused, thematic chapter on confidence in police within their volume *Towards Anti-Policing* (Lexington). I appreciate the support of Alex Prichard and Pluto's editors, including Ken Barlow, and reviewers Cayce Jamil and others. Some of these ideas were originally incubated in decade-old faculty learning communities, formed by two different centers for excellence in learning and teaching, one by the late Kathe Lowney and a second coordinated by Kate McCarthy, that included David McCoy and Julie Holland. Also, amazing thanks to those who provided comments and constructive criticisms on the manuscript at different stages, especially Mark George (for his extensive notes, crucial suggestions for refining the argument, multi-year-long conversations about topics contained herein, and general friendship). Suzanne Slusser helped immensely with every stage of this project—to simply express trust in her would be this book's greatest understatement.

Introduction

This book has a simple argument: We humans do best when we trust each other but also have a healthy distrust for the hierarchical systems that privilege some and dominate others. We have a promising future with this combination of trust relations. Thus, it's incumbent upon social movements that aim for long-term, systemic, and radical change to emphasize activities that develop fertile communities and social tendencies of trust, while inoculating larger and larger swaths of society against the manipulative and seductive pull of hierarchy. The chapters that follow introduce considerable complexity and nuance to this argument, but this is the book's main thesis.

The concern over misplaced trust or the absence of trust is important and pressing, as America (like many other places across the world) has become—with some merit—a rather distrusting place. Granted, some historians make the not-terribly-controversial argument that America has positioned distrust at the center of its societal ethos from its very origins in the American colonial period—distrust of King George III, distrust of central government, and distrust of other individuals—and thus the current situation is more of a change of degree rather than a true change in form. Regardless, it's impressive, even surprising, that society continues to "function" regardless of the substantial level of distrust that many people profess for each other. Most notably, many Americans don't simply lack trust in each other but also in major institutions and even the future. It's impossible to know—but still worth asking—if this disaffection resembles empires like Babylon or Rome in their waning years?

Whether we individually trust or distrust, American society and its dominant institutions try to pull us in unhealthy and destabilizing directions. While surveys don't exist to comprehensively demonstrate longitudinal changes in public opinion prior to the last few decades, it's highly likely that Americans have become more distrustful—of each other and "the system"—in the years following the 1960s and 1970s. Since then, less than half the population has claimed most people can be trusted, a trend that has declined over time according to the General Social Survey (GSS): 46 percent trusted in 1972 but only 25 percent by 2022.[1] The radical movements targeting the unequal American system during the 1960s was clearly positive in many regards—it generated considerable anti-imperialism, an undermining of systems of gender and racial privilege, the appearance of ecological consciousness, and a loosening of puritanical and conformist norms—but it also introduced a great malaise and a sense of existential threat to the traditional forces that initially created America.[2] These changes promised to send society spinning out of control. And it's not just in the United States either.[3]

While some of these developments are scary, others are undeniably good. The anti-authoritarian movements that have often propelled these changes—while contentious and apparently chaotic—have not only brought about some of the most admirable and worthwhile features of modern society but possess the best potential for transforming the world for the better. But such movements—which are dependent upon social trust and solidarity—and the change they seek are neither guaranteed nor simple. The lure of social distrust and the authoritarianism encouraging re-establishment of political trust are tempting and infectious. For example, the anti-police uprising in the US during the summer of 2020 brought out militant solidarity and anti-authoritarianism, pushing cities to take both reformist and occasionally more progressive steps to change policing policy. The largest changes surely involve gently shifting public opinion in the direction of abolition. Such developments are almost inconceivable in the absence of large-scale protest and radical trust. Those fighting for justice also know to distrust authority figures who promise results via blue-ribbon committees to "look into the matter", particularly when such committees are composed of the community's most well-heeled members (including members of law enforcement), who tend to promise much but deliver little. Another common trend is a bifurcation in attitudes between traditional defenders of hierarchical power and dissidents seeking wider justice and freedom.

The US and many other societies in the modern era are torn between an individualistic impulse of all-against-all, fascist authority-worship, liberal system-defenders, and an organic anti-authoritarianism that finds common ground in horizontal solidarity with our fellow social equals. That the former is so seductive to large swaths of society and the latter seemingly chaotically decentralized and inconsistent suggests the challenging contours of the struggle facing us today. It also illustrates the challenges faced by past anti-authoritarian movements to more fully realize their goals, let alone gain wide traction.

We can see potential trust landmines by investigating suggestive examples of archetypal dis/trusters. First, Trump and his coterie of authoritarian Trumpists; second, the detached and paranoid nihilist; and third, the usually liberal and rosy-eyed optimist. In rejecting these orientations toward trust in turn, it's clear something is problematically amiss in each. Trump, as with all narcissistic strongmen, wants trust to flow-upwards toward the strongman at the top; the paranoid nihilist has no patience, interest, or capacity to trust those who are deserving of it; and the rosy-eyed optimists seem to think that most everyone has good intentions, including hierarchical institutions that have a demonstrable record of violence and injustice. These optimists either don't understand critiques about hierarchical authority or are just hopeful they can get "better" people into those positions (e.g., nicer cops, better bosses, more competent politicians).

These three caricatures of trust pitfalls warrant additional exploration. First and most notably, the 2016 election of Donald Trump was *not* interesting because of Trump's own pathologies but due to the vast reservoir of toxic impulses it revealed within the American populace's hearts and minds. Trump—the elite scapegoater-extraordinaire—contrasted himself in 2016 with an "insider" opponent, politician Hillary Clinton. Despite his innumerable untrustworthy characteristics, his initial popularity seemed inconceivable, almost magical. Trump capitalized on American distrust for Clinton, who was widely viewed (even by many "liberal" Democrats) as untrustworthy due to her impersonal approach, politician-like calculation, and toxic association to her husband, former President Bill Clinton, who was widely viewed as untrustworthy himself, having been impeached for lying about his predatory sexual relationships with female subordinates.

While Trump implores people to trust him, he also blatantly lies, "gaslighting" people by attempting to throw off our perceptions of reality and thereby keeping all eyes fixed on him as he continuously hijacks the daily news-cycles. Part of the magic of Trump's lying and gaslighting is that liberals and Democrats became convinced that Trumpism was new, beginning only with the 2016 election.

Indeed, Trumpism's origins go back much deeper in American history and the American consciousness, as does the Clintonian neoliberalism that seeks to placate radical aspirations echoed in earlier political movements while globalizing the strength of capital and diversifying the wealthy's mobility. In the latter case, performative moves of "inclusion" can pretend to replace actual equity: Now Black men or white women can become president or a CEO. Both Trumpism and neoliberalism seem like dramatic changes from the mid-century status quo but cynically retain the same powerful institutions, leaving intact the greatest threats to justice and freedom. Hierarchy and its authoritarianism are not new, although Trump inspired a new collection of shock-troops to fight in defense of it.

Behind Trump are his assorted bootlickers—the much-discussed alt-right that attempted to gather "IRL" (in real life) away from 4chan's more toxic sewers, as well as even vaster legions of acolytes marinating in small towns and suburbs across America. The young disaffected white men of America can now gather in the streets of American cities to antagonize their cultural enemies ("woke liberals", LGBTQ+ peoples, "social justice warriors", and others).[4] Their vulgarity and willingness to insult anyone is on full display— they rarely even trust other factions of their movement, just the occasional charismatic leader or savior, professing to worship an idealized past and future.

4

The 2024 presidential contest between Donald Trump and the hastily picked Vice President Kamala Harris (replacing President Joe Biden) was rife with distrust themes. Unsurprisingly, Trump's ethos remained hierarchical—his singular message was "trust *me*". More than most modern politicians, Trump demands a particularized trust in him rather than a general trust in wider institutions, including his party. He paired this with the central theme of "distrust *them*", which included innumerable social enemies, ranging from the Democratic Party and other elite political institutions (e.g., "the deep state"). This even extended to others within the Republican Party, which he had managed to turn into "the Party of Trump". His critique of real and imagined competitors was accompanied by a vindictive attitude promising retribution once he reclaimed presidential power. Trump's 2024 campaign was more openly vitriolic than his prior two presidential runs, featuring sweeping condemnation of disadvantaged or demographically small social groups like immigrants, queer and trans people, educators, the left, and others.

According to Trump, the "radical Left" (apparently Marxists circa 1936 and a Hollywood-esque caricature of "anarchists") was driven by the Democratic Party—an allegation that shows just how far from reality Trump can be. His extreme but simplistic solution to deport immigrants (even legal residents and naturalized citizens), incarcerate political opponents, and even have police or the army kill "criminals", screamed social distrust. It turned out that many Americans either possessed similar distrust or were easily led to such fears—more voted for Trump in 2024 than 2020, and he won the popular vote for the first time.

Contemporary Trumpism initially arrived to power in the vacuum created by an "oppositional" liberal left that mostly gave a pass to eight years of a drone-bombing, National Security Agency (NSA) spying, immigrant-deporting, and Wall Street-enabling moderate Democrat. The current anti-Trumpers instead placed trust in "the system", which upon closer reflection, was completely uninterested in anti-imperialism, civil liberties, and anti-capitalism.[5] The 2016 and 2020 enthusiasm for democratic socialist Bernie Sanders can partially be explained by disappointment in Obama (and Hillary Clinton). During the first years of the Trump presidency, the Democrat Party mainstream embarrassingly rebranded itself "the resistance", indignant that their insider candidate was "robbed" of "her" presidency by a loud-mouthed usurper. These party moderates and mainstreamers also blamed the party's small progressive faction (i.e., Sanders supporters) for "dividing" the party into an alleged "Bernie or no one" hostage demand. Their "trust" in the electorate apparently only extended to those willing to do its bidding; dissident voices critical of the party's corporate allegiances and imperialist posturing were attacked. Moreover, these Democrats only trusted their party's process when it resulted in the nomination of moderate, corporate-friendly presidential candidates (i.e., Al Gore, John Kerry, Barack Obama, Hillary Clinton, Joe Biden).

Surveys on support for political institutions reflect an oscillation in the electorate depending on who is in office—Democrats strongly "trusted" the presidency from 2008 through 2016, while Republicans were unsurprisingly strongly "trusting" following 2016. Still, there is deep distrust in the *institution* of the presidency itself, as well as other major institutions. The consistency of this distrust is not partisan but systemic. In the US presidential elections of the modern era, rarely has much more than 60 percent of the eligible adult population even bothered to vote. And those who do vote often place higher priority on voting *against* a candidate than voting *for* the one they ultimate cast a ballot for. This speaks to the dissatisfaction and alienation felt toward the dominant order, as well as available options in the voting booth. Even though record numbers of people voted in the 2020 election, voters still represented just under two-thirds of all eligible American adults.[6] With Trump's 2024 victory, he convinced Republican voters that the untrustworthy electoral system from 2020 became, somehow, trustworthy—a change from two in ten Republicans confident in vote-counting prior to the election, to six in ten confident afterward.[7]

So, where does the mass of dissident, disaffected people turn? Some turn toward demagogues and populist scapegoats, while others may seek out stronger allegiances with the disparate left, which has no viable third-party options given the structural limitations of the

US's first-past-the-post electoral system. These two populations are on opposite poles, but both risk burnout, becoming ever more apolitical and depressed in a world they feel less and less able to rely upon. Without institutions or individuals to trust, how do people continue with their lives? Trumpism, authoritarianism, and even mainstream Democrat Party propagandists share the desire for a unified populace under the leadership of a strong leader, directing the country according to their unique, even divine, designs.

In many ways, Harris's 2024 campaign was the inverse of Trump's. She and the Democratic Party asked voters to *distrust Trump*, correctly noting that he is a dangerous demagogue, wannabe-dictator, and so forth. In addition, however, Harris advocated for trusting in the hierarchical, representative system of the US state. Where Trump advocated distrust in wide-ranging institutions (e.g., the media, judiciary, executive branch regulatory agencies, and Federal Bureau of Investigation [FBI]), Democrats argued for *more* trust in those institutions. While Trump could often barely articulate his critiques of those institutions beyond his own personal grievances, Harris lacked specificity as to why such trust would be well founded. Indeed, those institutions are, arguably, highly unworthy of popular trust.

The Democratic Party's lack of interest in engaging with the US's left, and its routine condemnation of third parties like the Greens as "spoilers", has provoked wider distrust in the party's motivations. Fewer examples better demonstrate this unprincipled bad faith than the Harris campaign openly bragging about garnering Republican supporters opposed to Trump. Endorsements from former Vice President Dick Cheney and his daughter Congresswoman Liz Cheney were meant to make Harris appear to have broad support. But many saw Harris embracing the endorsement of a war criminal like Dick Cheney as an open abandonment of any critical values differentiating Democrats from Republicans. It was reminiscent of Hillary Clinton's 2016 declaration of affinity with, and tutelage from, another Republican war criminal, Henry Kissinger.[8] Democrats like the Clintons, Obama, Biden, and Harris have been stronger advocates of trusting conservative opponents than trusting the left and its values, providing mere lip-service to progressive causes that would appeal to a large electorate. Leading Democrats like Harris could have convinced a skeptical, disengaged adult population to turn out to vote by supporting abortion legalization, drug decriminalization, military shrinkage or de-funding, increases in the minimum wage and taxes on millionaires, or universal health care—positions much of the world considers not only reasonable but banal and uncontroversial. Tenuous trust can evaporate quickly in the wake of such disappointments.

Beyond the Trumpists and authoritarians—and those who cynically oppose them (most notably Democrats)—there are the paranoid nihilists, who feel disillusioned by their past misplaced trust. They feel harangued by telemarketers and pushy salesclerks. Landlords and employers place unreasonable demands on their daily lives. Experts and scientists—and the corporations they often work for—do not have their concerns at heart (whether by their creation of genetically modified organisms or immunizations) and their findings stymie the potential to respond. For instance, it is not only Big Oil that is to blame for climate change, as some people are quick to scold, but everyone who drives a car and eats meat. Why recycle when the world is going to shit? Why place trust in people when they will just let you down or stab you in the back? For many, experience and everyone else's warnings tell them that people are not to be trusted—perhaps, they believe, untrustworthiness is an essential feature of *human nature*.

And it's not just the average person: Institutions have let them down at every turn, while bureaucracies are infuriating and devoid of human compassion. These nihilists' social distrust toward others inhibits any optimism regarding the potential for collective collaboration within social movements. Popular cultural perceptions tell them there's just as little value in trusting their fellows as in trusting officials, leaders, and the state. The US political climate—driven by endless election cycles—generates distrust in almost every social actor and social problem, from at least one side's perspective. But, if no one can be trusted, what prospects exist for uniting to fix those problems?

The paranoid nihilists are extreme with their distrust yet embody the same simplistic vision that the final, third archetype does: rosy-eyed optimists. Just as modernists and liberals see "progress" as an ever-present, slow march toward a better world, optimists presume the best from everyone they meet. Since, for them, the general arc of the world seems to bend toward progress, most social actors they meet are assumed to be working toward that better world. This is seen in the mass support—through use and advocacy—of innumerable powerful organizations. Google has made the world better through access to the internet and Uber makes transportation easier. Obama made everything and everyone nicer, and more reasonable. Food companies provide us healthy grocery choices and the Environmental Protection Agency makes sure that no one pollutes. They look upon the Democratic Party not as the "lesser of two evils" or Corporate America as a primary source of economic hardship but upon both as forces for good in the world. It does not matter that these claims can be easily falsified; the optimist has faith in their fellow humans, but most importantly in the large systems of control that have evolved, presumably for the common good, to keep humans on the straight and narrow.

These rosy-eyed optimists see the supposedly benign "gifts" of Facebook's interactive potential but ignore its intended design (to sell advertisements), as well as its malevolent uses for union-busting, sexual harassment, state suppression of movements, and manipulation of consumer desire and political opinion. While the government is "not perfect", it is surely the best solution to any of our challenges, right? Thus, we ought to turn out to vote for Democratic candidates (or moderate Republicans) who are *reasonable* and take the center lane. "Slow and steady wins the race", and we're on track so long as we can beat back distrust. Such simplicity can be found in the optimistic—and naive—plea by Democrat Pete Buttigieg in *Trust: America's Best Chance*.[9] If we only place our trust in each other and the system, then the City Upon a Hill is within reach.

What is most dangerous about the rosy-eyed optimist's extremism is their tendency to place trust in the powerful. The tempting reaction is to put trust in a "savior", who will deliver the masses—

or at least us as individuals—from the problems we face.[10] Here, it's common for people to look to wealthy or celebrity donors or politicians who can create private-sector solutions or laws that fix "problems". But such saviors tend to be dodgy and turbulent, whether in the White House, corporate boardroom, or nongovernmental organization (NGO) office. The "great man of history" thesis is not only flawed but bad politics. If there's a better world to make, we all need to be involved in achieving it. Seeking a savior implies the *need* to be "saved". Essentially, without a savior, we are weak, impotent, or incompetent. This is flawed logic: While we surely need larger, organizational collaboration to work with others, this doesn't require a savior or hierarchical institutions.

It's important to consider why people believe they can't "save" themselves or each other. Maybe it's helpful to first ask: What is the thing we need to be saved *from*? As it turns out, most of the personal troubles we face are structured by dominant institutions that actively wreck our lives. Sociologically speaking, individual salvation is not only difficult but inefficient. If the problems we face have social origins and affect people en masse, this suggests a need for collectively designed solutions.

The authoritarians, nihilists, and rosy-eyed optimists don't see much benefit in collective action and lack a critical orientation toward trust. Even the distrustful nihilists aren't critical enough of trust's *constructive* power, if wielded by everyday people. But collective action, while commonplace in many countries, has been denigrated and made to look alien to Americans. American culture—whether media, schools, or other popular narratives—does an incredibly poor job of providing examples of successful collective action, especially that which doesn't rely upon charismatic authority figures. Even the most popular, iconic, subversive, and revolutionary science fiction characters of the last generation, from *The Matrix* to *V for Vendetta* to *Mr. Robot*, feature individualistic characters or those beholden to charismatic hierarchies, who aim to save others who cannot save themselves. Mainstreamed mythological narratives about the civil rights movement of the 1950s and 1960s that dominate US culture place a few heroes (Martin Luther

King, Rosa Parks) at the center.[11] This in no way reflects the reality of radical movements, which typically eschew both charismatic and legal-rational leaders, and involve wide participation. From the French Revolution to the Spanish Revolution, American civil rights, or the autonomous zones of Zapatista-controlled Chiapas, Mexico to Rojava in Western Kurdistan, it is typically the poor and powerless, often women and disadvantaged minority groups, who aspire and often succeed (even if temporarily) to create a better world for themselves.

It often seems *easier* for folks to find a single trustworthy, convincing charismatic person to trust, rather than putting their trust in large swaths of humanity. Celebrity pop culture, American-style elections, and even religion are based on the premise that a charismatic authority figure whose divine lineage or impressive message will provide salvation. For celebrities, the deliverance they provide may come in the form of distraction and entertainment, or their charitable contributions through a federally registered 501(c)(3) nonprofit organization (the US government's tax-exempt status for such organizations). An American politician running for office begs for the electorate's trust based on their promises, personalities, and the story told about them; if we identify with their lives, they must be good people, worthy of trust! And most religions are based around the past lives of individuals remembered for their impressive deeds and radical ideas, their breaking with traditions. The assumption that charismatics are trustworthy rests on acceptance of the expressed intentions of those authorities, as they launder historical contradictions and engineer more convenient narratives to fit each era's sociopolitical needs. People think they choose who they believe and trust, but that's unlikely. Those with the greatest number of followers (in the biblical-sense as well as the Facebook or Twitter-senses) and those who wield the most institutionalized power are likely to receive the masses' trust (and *mis*trust), not the non-conformists.

A significant swath of the American population seems to be placing their trust in fear-stoking, hierarchical authority figures and institutions; in this day and age, it's politicians like Trump (or the less-offensive Joe Biden), the police, right-wing media personalities on Fox News, or anybody else willing to spin a tale that *those other people* are to blame. So, do you volunteer your time and offer extra money to those who need it most, perhaps with one of the hundreds of mutual aid collectives across the US, or do you make a "run" on certain commodities like toilet paper, flour, and beans? Here, "preppers"—who stockpile goods so they and their families can survive an apocalypse—seem mostly uninterested in creating *social* support and safety nets or building mutual aid networks for collective survival. Their "drawing boundaries", focused on developing a superior identity to those unable to "survive", presumes survival pathways come from competitive behavior, not compassion.[12]

Here, it's instructive to look at the impulses of various groups during times such as the coronavirus pandemic that began in 2019. If you fear your world is collapsing around you, who do you rally around? One-half of the population—people who express goodwill in solving problems collectively—seems to answer: "my neighbors" and "my community".[13] As a reflexive target of trust, it makes sense to critically interrogate what "community" actually means, as understandings of the word vary wildly from person to person. Communities may not be as universally positive as flippant claims imply: Substantial hierarchy or even violent abusers may reside within them. Community isn't "naturally" occurring, it's a social construction. Therefore, when people say they trust "community", their perception may be far more *aspirational* and idealized than grounded in actual, messy conditions.

It's for these reasons that I argue that we need more social trust and less trust in hierarchical systems, an orientation I call "radical trust". This thesis emphasizes why we should care about issues of trust: We need it for the common good, for a civil society, functioning social movements, and progressive revolution. Central to this is the collective capacity to think clearly and critically about what kinds of trust are good—and which are bad—and how to build this radical trust over time.

Radical trust is horizontal and assumes: (1) hierarchical institutions are harmful, and (2) peers can be beneficial. This might not seem like a "radical" position to take; in fact, it may seem safe, even conservative. But it is "radical" in the sense that it "gets to the root of" a major dilemma: Trust is not universally warranted while still absolutely necessary. Radical trust is a strategy of distinguishing between trust targets: distrusting hierarchical institutions, while trusting social peers. It requires strong anti-authoritarianism—critique of major, hierarchical institutions in all their manifestations despite people having to, by necessity, sometimes participate in and interact with them. Radical trust also requires active social solidarity—collaboration with and mutual aid for less powerful, socially disadvantaged groups, and all other social equals.[14]

Incidentally, radical trust is an implicitly anarchist orientation—a tradition I identify strongly with. In fact, the "quality of mind" that orients radical trust is akin to James C. Scott's "anarchist squint", wherein the initial appraisal of all situations is channeled through this rough, ideological lens.[15] But this trust orientation is not exclusive to anarchist traditions alone; similar sentiments can be found in many other critical traditions and movements, including radical feminism, antifascism, little-c communism, liberation theology, decolonialism, and others. One need not personally identify with these traditions or movements—or even care about their details—in order to practice radical trust. What's important is the ethos: Don't trust authority, trust each other. As Charles Tilly notes, this involves creating a non-institutionalized trust, which anarchists (like Proudhon) have long pursued.[16]

This book disputes the dominant liberal narrative that presumes all trust is good. This narrative isn't just spun by politicos and media: Nearly all social science extols the virtues of increased trust, whether social, general, political, or otherwise. Contrary to the mantra conveyed by defenders of "civility" and "democracy" (meaning representative systems of statecraft), hierarchies ought to be distrusted. Most of our human ancestors would have easily identified the truth of such a statement. And despite the all-to-common fearmongering of media, popular culture, advertisers, and popular "common sense", most people *can* be trusted. This is particularly relevant to those belonging to groups regularly targeted for distrust, despite no rational cause for distrust being present: the poor, immigrants, women, LGBTQ+ people, people of color, and so forth. Additionally, hierarchical societies impose difficult conditions on people that make it hard to trust, including a rough economic climate, growing nationalist arrogance and capitalist-fueled climate chaos.

People who have power—whether they identify as liberals or conservatives—would like nothing more than to pervert our natural impulses to trust. They may not publicly express this, but their work becomes easier and their status stronger when we rely on them more than our peers. Indeed, wide social trust and solidarity would make their power unnecessary and their privileges irrelevant. Liberals want us to trust the modern system, with its far-flung, bureaucratic state apparatus, its impersonal but smiley capitalism, and the comforting notion that more-civilized economic exploitation will bring us closer to utopia. Conservatives sell a different trust message: We must fear the other and venerate those in power, even leaders who profess illiberal, antidemocratic sentiments (as we are weak without them). Both groups are wrong: We have much to lose by not trusting our fellow peers and little to gain by believing the promises offered by hierarchical systems.

Recent trends around trust in the US have involved demands for institutional trust in one political party (and distrust of the other), and especially in the self-anointed saviors at the top of each party. Additionally, virulent distrust of disadvantaged groups appears to be a core platform of the Republican Party. "Both" sides advocate for political trust in themselves and their side. Trump followers express hierarchical trust in their leader, while Democratic voters adhere to trust in a hierarchical system of state and capitalism. These are symptoms of serious problems in the American body politic.

Instead of prioritizing horizontal solidarity and the transformative potential of democratic, cooperative social movements, trust is demanded in the institutionalized levers of elections and representatives. A consistent refrain repeated every four years is that progressives and the left—to say nothing of apolitical people—must unite behind a Democratic Party to defeat an ever more right-wing Republican Party. Needless to say, these patterns pose serious threats to personal safety and health, peace and justice, and freedom. The logic for investing much trust in either side seems foolhardy: Yes, there's a lesser-evil "available" to voters, but it doesn't deserve our trust, per se. Voting for lesser-evils is merely harm reduction, not the means for building a better society.

The past three election cycles involving Trump reveal changing, but also consistent, patterns of trust, distrust, and mistrust. This suggests formidable challenges stand in the way of those struggling for justice and freedom in the US and, incidentally, most everywhere else too. Predictably, neither of the US's dominant political parties are headed in encouraging directions, but social movement activity and popular resistance to authoritarianism indicate an encouraging horizontalism that can stymie the Republican Party's hierarchical-ism and deflate the boastfulness of the Democrat's truster-ism. This book dives deep into these issues, focusing on the contemporary malaise facing America and many other societies, and the histori-cal processes underlying it. Here, it is worth noting that while this book focuses primarily on the US, it includes innumerable examples from elsewhere and is intended to shed light on hierarchical trust dynamics across many societies. Regardless of where lines might be drawn on a map, we all need solidarity and anti-authoritarianism, although the specifics will vary geographically.

I want us to consider how we can impulsively trust or distrust—with good and bad consequences—and how hierarchical institutions benefit from our unreflective orientations. Innumerable powerful actors benefit from trust disorientation; this book aims to clear up this deliberate obfuscation. I articulate a radical vision for social struggles, movements, and revolution that nurtures a "trust" wary of its socio-organizational requirements but that is also reasonable about the adversaries who attempt to limit and stymie these nec-essary phenomena. Our radical trust can defend against hierarchy and domination, as well as serve as a collective means in the struggle for greater freedom and justice. The way forward is a social—not an individualistic—path rooted in movements, rebellion, and wide-scale social transformation. While trust is not the only necessary ingredient for these processes, it is a central one, that we ignore at our peril.

I wrote this book to grapple with what I consider to be the central questions of our era: In hard times, where can we look for help? Who can we rely upon for accurate information and a fair representation of reality? And what social forces reinforce the status quo and what social forces can overturn that status quo?

In seeking answers, I kept returning to the matter of trust. Incidental discoveries made pouring through quantitative datasets kept showing the relevance of trust, not just in the US, but internationally. But that impact of trust varied by kind and impact. As a scholar of social movements, I was intrigued by how protest seemed to be enhanced by generalizable social trust, but also depressed by political trust. People who seek to dispute something about society—who expend effort to publicly protest—tended to trust each other, while also distrusting the political order. Countless positive features of the modern era, that people in many countries (but crucially not all) often take for granted, were first demanded by social movement protest, ultimately resulting in reforms that blunted the more violent edges of capitalism, patriarchy, white supremacy, and the state—they still make life *better*. And countless millions have dedicated themselves, over years and decades, in struggles for these advances, and have even died in their pursuit. Given the centrality of movements to our lives, this combination of social trust and political distrust I kept finding seemed significant and worthy of further exploration.

1

Us and Other People: What Trust Is

When most people consider *who* they trust, they think of friends. Friends are the family you choose. I trust them to not trash-talk me to others. They reach out when something serious is going down, if they think it may affect me. We can loan each other things without care and never worry about them being returned. This kind of trust flowers within community and feels supportive, and empowers us beyond our usual capabilities, extending our individually endowed power. Trust would be a straightforward, simple subject if this was the only existing kind of trust. Of course, things are rather more complicated.

PARADOXES OF TRUST

Even though trust is often considered an essential feature in society, its "taken-for-grantedness" conceals serious paradoxes. The following two problems deserve serious reflection and require experimentation to figure out how they can be overcome.

First, social change (to say nothing of revolution) demands social trust, while counterrevolution encourages social distrust. The forces that support the status quo are unlikely to advocate in support of revolutionaries. But the better future we need requires a very different present to get there. We need trust *now* to get more trust *later*. In a sense, this is a chicken-versus-the-egg conundrum. Trust creates solidarity, and solidarity creates trust. This reciprocal relationship requires we start somewhere—but what to do when both are in short supply? A transitional political distrust and social trust is necessary for a future in which leveled hierarchies and vibrant social solidarity reign. Prefiguration is a way to practice some of those values in the present, with the hope that transformative and liberatory norms can be expanded as we proceed forward.[1] This can be called the "you need some to get more" paradox.

Second, the people who could most benefit from social trust (e.g., the poor and working classes, people of color, women, etc.), and those it would aid in resistance and movement building, actually tend to have the most reasons to distrust others due to their many disadvantages living in what bell hooks perceptively calls a "white supremacist capitalist patriarchy".[2] They have found themselves, in various ways, at the receiving end of these systems of domination. In a world filled with people who look like their villainous employers or landlords, police and others who offer them bigoted stares and comments, or harassing and bigoted men, they'll find it hard to trust. Despite the many benefits of social trust, experience has taught them a different, yet seemingly reasonable, lesson. This ought to be called the "most disadvantaged" paradox. If those who face multiple forms of domination in their lives are motivated to develop greater social trust, they may take risks and try to trust more people. But if, due to systemic inequality, the people they reach out to and invest trust in are, in fact, untrustworthy then the likely let-downs and abused promises they encounter may cause them to slide into even further distrust. Thus, the most disadvantaged paradox reflects the compounding, multiplicative character of social domination. Distrust in hierarchy—or at least its on-the-ground agents—can also translate into distrust in other individuals not highly placed in social hierarchies.

To better understand the challenges faced, consider the example of how white Americans—a group with a lot of social privileges—are the ones who most trust the police; white people feel comfortable calling "911", police officers mostly look like them, and they can rely on (even if unintentionally) this centuries-old system to protect white interests. However, people of color in the US have a very different set of expectations when encountering police officers, also rooted in long-term experience and history, that lead them to distrust cops (just as poverty and neighborhood instability generates distrust in large numbers of other people in their communities too). But since police are solidly representatives of the hierarchical state, a more illustrative example would be how patriarchy and misogyny has led considerable numbers of women to distrust not only men who are known to be untrustworthy but men in general. Later chapters will more fully outline how police (and other powerful, hierarchical social institutions, such as patriarchy) keep power concentrated, promote societal distrust, and thus stymie the pursuit of justice and freedom. But for now, it's enough to remark that the "most disadvantaged" paradox makes it harder for people of color (or women) to place trust in general (including those white people or men who could be allies), while the "you need to some to get more" paradox makes it difficult to build social trust within and for anti-police or anti-sexism movements.

Of course, there are numerous reasons for the average white person to *also* be suspicious of the police—including the pro-elite class biases, patriarchal attitudes, and authoritarian interpersonal styles of police. But people of color have their own very reasonable motivations for distrusting the police and are thus more easily recruited into anti-authoritarian movements (like those seeking to defund the police) once these paradoxes are individually and collectively overcome. White people must be recruited differently to the project to build a radical, alternative society.

Thus, the difficulties for movement organizers or even unaffiliated individuals are formidable: To be an agent in one's own liberation implies struggling against the many inclinations, personality preferences, and disagreeable experiences that have played a part in those very people's immiseration. To address these paradoxes means to push against deeply entrenched features of societies—generations of history and the punitive lessons taught in our own lifetimes.

WRITTEN IDEAS RELEVANT TO TRUST

In this book, I argue for a particular version of radical trust that combines horizontalist solidarity with anti-authoritarianism.[3] As such, there are a variety of relevant theoretical insights, definitions, and contributions to survey that come from intellectuals, radicals, and activists. The following helps to frame my ideas, contributing to the overall project of radical trust, while also serving to connect my concerns with a long-established social science tradition. While the review is not intended to be comprehensive, it will selectively present the ideas I most heavily draw upon in the remainder of the book.

It wouldd be impossible to talk about trust and social order without mentioning French sociologist Émile Durkheim. He presented a crucial conceptualization of solidarity—splitting its structure and purpose into two dialectical versions. Mechanical solidarity presumes similarity between people, even an interchangeability between individuals. With this kind of solidarity, there is strength in commonality. In such a society, where everyone is mostly like everyone else, they are connected via those characteristics. Organic solidarity, however, features dissimilarity, interdependence, and strength in difference. Our vast specialization and differences from each other—in skills, values, labor—mean that we *need* each other, thus creating durable bonds. Durkheim contrasted these two, arguing that mechanical solidarity is the prevailing form of social order in simpler, earlier societies that are small in scale. Mechanical has been replaced by organic solidarity in complex, industrial societies where there is a stark division of labor and mere associational ties between individuals. But modern societies continue to have both features, of course. We live part of our lives in more homogeneous, mechanical spheres, while other parts in heterogeneous, organic spheres. Durkheim's observations about Europe's transition from mechanical solidarity to organic solidarity were intended to describe some of the changes taking place in the heart of the British industrial revolution. By disconnecting peasants from their role in the feudal system (as general agricultural laborers) and integrating them into the rising workshop and factory system in major cities (as the urban proletariat) required a wider range of tasks and skills.

The key feature of solidarity for Durkheim resides in the ties between individuals that integrate them into a collective whole (of whatever variety). Rejecting the abstracted "ethical" view of morality, he observed that morality pertains to the commitment and support people have toward each other and society. We are able to relate to each other and build solidarity because we are moral beings.[4] Durkheim inspired an important question: What truly supports morality (and thus social solidarity), and what could help create more egalitarian social relations as opposed to simply perpetuating an unequal status quo? Solidarity fuels social trust, and the moral imperatives for solidarity help inspire trust when there is no existing evidence to suggest it is possible. Durkheim even argued that crime could be a functional force for solidarity, as it unites the majority of the population in outrage against transgressions of commonly held morality—this shock and offense appears to be as unifying for corporate criminality as it is for murder.

Friedrich Engels's contribution to trust comes from an indirect, passing reference penned in a private letter, in which he described class consciousness.[5] This is an important feature in Marxian thought: Individuals in a capitalist society tend to be either class conscious—aware of the class position they occupy and how their fates are tied to others of their class—or falsely conscious, wherein individuals misunderstand that class position and work against their own class interests. Usually, wealthy capitalists are highly class conscious: They understand they are rich and need to collaborate with each other (even while they economically compete in the market) in order to protect their class interests from the masses who would otherwise seek economic redistribution, class warfare, or revenge. A central task of the labor movement is the awakening of class consciousness within working-class people, helping them see that they need each other and shouldn't fruitlessly compete.

It's hard to say just how many people (even those I call "hierarchicalists") are falsely conscious—perceiving an affinity with their bosses, elite politicians, and the like. In the US, individualism and the "middle-class model" compel many working-class people to disavow their class standing.[6] Engels's idea only really seems to work with social class; the logic of consciousness extends rather poorly to ascribed statuses like gender and race. Class consciousness helps illuminate how aware we are of our self-conceptualizations and our relations to others—factors essential for trust. The notion of false consciousness is also key to understanding why people do or do not resist capitalism. Having a class-conscious society—like the UK more than the US—affords average people the means to articulate who is worthy of trust and who isn't, whether they do so via labor unions, the Labour Party, or as individuals.

A core premise of what is usually called conflict theory comes from erstwhile sociologist Georg Simmel. He described cohesion found in, and created by, conflict.[7] We create strong social bonds in our unified opposition to others (e.g., via ethnic conflict, nationalism, sports). Thus, conflict breeds distrust of "the other" but concurrently promotes trust among those who also oppose those others (cf., the enemy of my enemy is my friend).[8] Following Simmel, we might not even need to consciously pursue trust with others, since our opposition to the enemy will automatically unite us. Therefore, trust and its contradictions are the glue of society (although it still relies on a leap of faith). While being in league with our peers against various hierarchies can be immensely unifying, however, unity can lessen when conflict diminishes. For example, in a broad societal conflict—say, between large numbers of people and the police—if those in power make concessions to protest demands, this will divide some of the dissidents (e.g., reformist elements may believe politicians' promises to reform the police, while radicals will remain skeptical and want to keep pushing in the streets). Trust and distrust are both important, just as with unity and conflict.

Another social scientist who emphasized the relationship between conflict and cohesion was Peter Kropotkin. In his famous study entitled *Mutual Aid: A Factor of Evolution*, Kropotkin demonstrated how societies survive (and maybe even "evolve") because of interpersonal cooperation, not competition.[9] Despite social Darwinist interpretations from Thomas Huxley and Herbert Spencer, competition is less important for the survival of people (and other animals), than finding ways to collaborate. The only real life-and-death struggle in a community is usually against outside forces (e.g., invaders) or the environment (e.g., "natural elements" like cold, starvation, disasters). Societies that cooperate survive longer and can advance. Kropotkin argued that modern, bureaucratic hierarchies superimpose themselves upon our impulses to cooperate, trying to dull our natural inclinations. Thus, narratives of "competition" are primarily beneficial to those who seek to maintain their power, which undermines the basis for social trust among those lacking power.

Utilitarianism has had a substantial impact on the science of trust. For example, sociologist James Coleman argued in *Foundations of Social Theory* that trust is the willingness to risk.[10] For Coleman, this is best understood in what is often called "rational choice" or "exchange", wherein trust exists within relationship markets. Trust is mathematically modeled—a somewhat controversial approach for many sociologists, but a perfectly reasonable approach for economists—and trusting relationships include three important characteristics. First, by having trust placed in them, a trustee's action that wouldn't have otherwise been possible is enabled. Second, if a trustee is trustworthy, then the placement of trust benefits the truster and the withholding of trust negatively impacts the truster. And, third, trust voluntarily places resources at the disposal of a trustee without a real commitment from the trustee.

What does all this really mean? Let's assume we're talking about a legally defined citizen (i.e., not an immigrant) trusting a police officer. Coleman's propositions suggest that the police have a wider range of possible action with a citizen who trusts them; they will be able to patrol more widely, be less questioned or challenged, and can use force more effectively (and legitimately). Being able to trust a cop means the citizen can get something from the cop they otherwise wouldn't be able to, while distrusting the cop will likely hurt the citizen somehow (perhaps by denying them the ability to report victimization of a crime). If trust is the willingness to risk, we should ask whether citizens trust (risk) because they want to or whether there are no better options. And is this risk evenly borne? Or do institutional employees (e.g., police) not have to risk as much as those they rule?

Also, in the rational choice tradition, Richard Emerson described what he called power-dependence relationships. Power is based on "ties of mutual dependence". Thus, the powerful require people's dependence on them.[11] Dependence occurs due to restrictive control over some kind of resource or rewards needed by, for example, the spouse of an abusive, patriarchal partner. Applying this logic to trust, it's pretty clear that positive, nurturing, and mutually beneficial trust relationships don't involve power over one partner or dependency (at least in this subordinate sense). Rather, trust flourishes in conditions where neither party *unequally depends* upon the other for something. By contrast, citizens "need" police for certain resources (a sense of security or safety) and thus are dependent on them, which gives police power. Workers "need" employers and are dependent upon them for jobs and wages, thus giving employers power. Citizens (or workers) can only trust police (or employers) insofar as such people keep providing the things that keep them dependent, like security (or a job).

Left philosophers and activists have theorized extensively about trust and its related concerns. For example, Erich Fromm's *The Art of Loving* offers an empowering interpretation of "love" highly sympathetic to radical trust, stripping it of its mystique, unpredictability, and abstraction. Fromm ultimately views love as a skill that can be taught and performed for others; romance and infatuation are essentially irrelevant, as are blood ties or marriage. Love involves the basic elements of care, responsibility, respect, and knowledge. As such, anyone can love anyone else and anyone can learn to practice love for others. This framing of love is significant: Love is not a random emotional or psychological state of mind but a chosen set of actions to care for others' lives.[12] Understood as such, to truly love someone means extending them solidarity and accepting who they are comes before one's own demands of that person. Love is arguably the engine of Durkheim's social solidarity, the consciousness of Engels, and the mutual aid of Kropotkin. For Fromm, true love necessitates love for oneself, as well as all of humanity.[13] Not only do loving relationships necessitate trust, but love is the natural out-growth of trust. In order to love others in the way advocated by Fromm, we must first be able to trust them and be ourselves trustworthy.

In their book *Joyful Militancy*, Nick Montgomery and carla bergman define trust and responsibility as flexible "common notions" that grow out of relationships. The "twin pitfalls" of individualism and conformity are not simply opposites, as both are equally problematic for trust. Anti-authoritarianism doesn't imply individualism (and its liberal ideology) any more than solidarity implies conformity (found in the obedience-demanding Marxism of sectarian leftists). Montgomery and bergman argue that trust and responsibility are practiced in indigenous struggles, anti-violence, and transformative justice movements, as well as deschooling and youth liberation movements. Trust has a defensive capacity, to "resist Empire and defend ... insurgent forms of life".[14] They suggest that there is potential for trust "up-front", but lots of pre-existing oppressions and divisions make this unreasonable. As such, to trust is "to undo fear and control".[15]

Finally, as social trust is symbiotically bound to solidarity, Markus Kip's etymological exploration of the word "solidarity" in *Radical Keywords* is essential. He locates the word's origins in the French Revolution, where fellowship trumped kinship (in other words, voluntary association, rather than association predetermined by blood). Thus, trust could be invested beyond one's family to larger circles of people chosen freely by each individual. This was exemplified in France's new national slogan: liberty, fraternity (i.e., solidarity), and equality.[16] Solidarity replaced the primarily feudal significance of fraternity often found in kinship, with the logical reasoning and fellowship of solidarity. The means of solidarity can be found in the state (top-down) or a popular movement (bottom-up) and can be transmitted individually or collectively.[17] As such, solidarity can be institutionalized into either the norms or laws of a society or be freely chosen by people on a daily basis. Movement solidarity can be seen as both a process of radical activism and an outcome of organizing.[18] Thus, trust is something transmitted hierarchically or horizontally, via powerful institutions like the state or social movements, respectively.

In light of this substantial body of ideas, there are some specific theoretical directions that this book pursues. Sociologists David Wagner and Joseph Berger argued that there are various ways to build social theory.[19] I use two of their strategies in regards to trust;

I *elaborate* upon and *proliferate* the theory of radical sociopolitical trust. Elaboration involves making a theory either more general or more specific. Thus, this book seeks to elaborate how radical trust can be applied to various institutions, across micro- or macro-conditions, and across space and time. Proliferation of theory generates new or different sociological problems. Here, I aim to complicate trust's locus of concern within a hierarchy, rejecting the common assumption that social status, position, or rank has no bearing on whether one should trust or distrust.

WHAT DO WE MEAN BY "TRUST"?

Trust is ultimately an expectation about people's future behaviors and is best when it improves sociality. In other words, trust is social, not individualistic, and cannot be detached from either the truster or the trustee. The looseness that often accompanies discussions of trust does us a disservice, as such looseness turns trust into something guaranteed, fixed, or magical—which it is surely not. Or loose conceptualizations of trust can overlook how unidirectional trust usually relies on hierarchy, and is thus, more often than not, bullshit mistrust.

Before we go too far, it's helpful to distinguish trust from a variety of things that seem like trust, but in fact are *not*. Meaning matters and the slipperiness of casual definitions can get us confused and in trouble. First, trust is not the same thing as *happiness*. Although happiness can result from many forms of trust, we can trust and be trusted under conditions that bring us no joy. Second, trust is not simply an *attitude or opinion*. Attitudes are just what people think about things, while trust should be embedded much deeper in our impulses and in our social relationships. Third, trust is not *overly formalized*, like an official contract. Indeed, if you need to sign a contract with someone, that implies the parties involved don't fully expect each other to live up to their verbalized promises, at least without the threat of a lawsuit.[20] For decades, rock music labels like Dischord Records or Touch-n-Go Records have done business on a "handshake", viewing this as what *should be* done among those who trust each other. To further disconnect trust from an official contract, consider anthropologist David Graeber's observation that bartering or exact trades usually occurs among strangers who don't expect to see each other again or who deeply distrust.[21] Finally, trust is not—despite the regular use of the word—*faith*. Believing something suggests there is no evidence for it; while trust should be backed by past experiences that constitute decent evidence for future expectations. Belief and faith tend to be religious or spiritual in character, and thus ideological or idealized, rather than practical or grounded. Faith is evidence-less "trust", while trust is "faith" with evidence. The former is speculative and dangerous, while the latter ought to be sound judgment.

As seen from these examples, we must be cautious in what we label as "trust". The danger of slippage is real. Despite the inherent sloppiness of the above associations, it's important to resist the lure of these conceptions when we analyze trust, which in fact is much more radical, meaningful, and complicated.

Trust exists throughout society, often without any acknowledgment of its existence. For example, many people use public roads despite the alleged existence of "crazy drivers", suggesting people implicitly trust each other every time they drive. Despite occasionally being rude or inconsiderate, other drivers can generally be trusted to at least be competent and not endanger our lives. While accidents do happen, they are the exception to the rule. The same is true for most examples of public interaction: We're a pretty trustworthy species and mostly benign toward each other.

The issue of scale indicates two different kinds of trust. First, *generalized trust* is focused on most people in general. A common survey question that generates this variable asks: Can most people be trusted or can you not be too careful? Thus, without specifying any singular person or group of people, could "someone" be trusted? Generalized social trust is one of the most common kinds of trust that social scientists study, despite its incredible abstraction. It's probably pretty difficult for the average person to randomly conceive of "someone" for whom the above survey question would pertain, without mentally picturing a particular kind of person.

Second, *particularized trust* involves trust for a certain type of person (e.g., women, immigrants, or the disabled). This kind of trust isn't really about an individual person who has a certain characteristic but about "all" those who share that characteristic. If your trusting partner were a woman (or an immigrant or a disabled person), would her gender reduce the likelihood that you would trust her? There are as many types of particularized trust as there are social groupings in society. Thus, trust can be general or particular, and can involve social equals as trusting partners, or political and other hierarchical institutions, as shown in Table 1.1.

Table 1.1   Forms of Trust

	Social	*Political*
General	"Most people can be trusted"	Political trust
Particular	e.g., neighbors	e.g., confidence in the army
	Non-institutional	**Institutional**

Sometimes generalized trust is the most important thing to consider, while other times it's particularized trust. An example can help highlight the difference here. Police usually trust each other (one narrow category of particularized trust); consequently, there's a "blue wall of silence" in which cops trust each other not to speak out when accusations of police misconduct surface. Silence prevails even when numerous officers witness an infraction or even personally dislike a perpetrator cop. This is in stark contrast to the distrust that police typically have for the populations they patrol. In general, police suspect that the average person cannot be trusted[22]—especially trusted to tell the truth to a cop—so they remain suspicious and distrustful. This generalized social distrust is about "most people", not a particular type of person (although cops, like most people, often have *greater* distrust for particular groups, like Blacks or Latinos).

Trust can exist in a mediated or unmediated form—this refers to whether we experience trust indirectly or directly, distantly or intimately. Institutions get in the way of intimate relationships, a communalism which Ferdinand Tönnies referred to as *gemein-schaft*.[23] Large hierarchies epitomize *gesellschaft*, imposing rationalist conditions and distant mediation between individuals. A customer who wants to ask questions of a chain store clerk is really interacting via a mediated corporate culture, with the clerk reduced to a go-between or "middleman". Mediation means that someone else tries to manage the relationship, spinning or directing it in a way that is unnatural (and likely benefits the spin-doctor). This derails the potential for organic, meaningful relationships. If trust can exist in such instances, it is strained and feels artificial.

By contrast, unmediated trust—just like unmediated democracy, unmediated justice, and unmediated freedom—places us in direct contact with those whose trust we would most benefit from. We work with our neighbors directly, as opposed to a city official who tries to organize such relationships from the top-down. Peter Kropotkin argued in *Mutual Aid* that the state gets in the way of these organic relationships, supplanting our natural impulses to aid our fellow humans: calling the cops instead of breaking up a fight ourselves or pointing a homeless person to a food shelter instead of feeding them ourselves.[24] One conclusion implied by the distinction between mediated and unmediated is the benefit of operating (and thus trusting) within small groups (prioritized more by unmediated trust). Nevertheless, we can still work with large numbers of people if the relationships we construct are horizontally configured, directly democratic, and value-based.

The motivations for trusting also matter a great deal. Political scientist Russell Hardin argues that trust is actually "encapsulated interest".[25] This means that trust depends on the assessments we make of the motivations others have toward us. When there is a co-alignment of interests (i.e., our interests are "encapsulated"), we trust more easily. Thus, the "trusting partner" is very important. It's rather demanding to ask an individual to trust an institution, especially if someone's interests benefit from that institution only as a marginal client or customer, rather than a more central actor, like an investor, powerbroker, or manager. Can communities—especially poor communities of color—"trust" the police if they do not share co-aligned interests? If police seek to control a neighborhood or punish residents they view as deviant, while the residents want security and stability (but not at the expense of broken-up families and mass incarceration), then how could we expect anything except distrust to result? It's actually against the interests of such a community to trust police, because if they do, they'll experience higher arrest rates and little improved safety.[26]

Hardin's encapsulated trust presumes that we are *able* to distinguish between our interests and others' interest. But this is sometimes pretty difficult. Not all working-class people perceive their conflicting interests vis-à-vis their bosses or the wealthy, and thus often side with pro-wealthy policies and individuals due to their confusion (i.e., Engels's false consciousness). Unless we're perceptive, we could incorrectly interpret our interests as aligned with forces that will abandon the relationship whenever they like. For example, the Democratic Party (a bourgeois party from its early nineteenth-century origins) has been adopted by some progressive movements as "their" party, and therefore tends to *lean* "left" more than the Republican Party. Thus, the Democrats seek out leftists to support them (electorally only), arguing that the interests of voters and the party co-align. Millions of leftist voters—by definition, critical of capitalism—are necessary for the Democrat Party to stay in power; and if the party is unwilling to move its platform to the left, then it's simply manipulating voters' perceptions of encapsulated interest for the party's own benefit. If trust is encapsulated interest, it requires being able to accurately understand a trusting partner's motivations, commitments, values, and past actions. In an era of public relations firms, mass media, and spin-doctors, that's rather challenging to do, and therefore a hard-sell for grassroots progressives or the left to seriously trust the Democratic Party. Indeed, party elites rely heavily on wealthy donors for financial stability and don't embrace the redistribution efforts its left wing seeks.

Understanding trust as encapsulated interest illustrates *who* can best collaborate. When we share things in common with people "like us" or share similar positions of power and authority, trust is more easily placed and such people *are* more trustworthy. For example, trust is easier among immigrant groups than between immigrants and native-born groups, just as trust is more easily fostered among working-class people than between workers and employers. And women often find it easier to trust each other than to trust men. Encapsulated trust is central to numerous immigrant and refugee rights organizations, movements, and communities throughout Europe (including in large cities like London, Paris, and Athens), as well as in autonomous worker-organizing projects and worker cooperatives.

Finally, trust can take the *form* of trust, distrust, and (as I will soon argue) mistrust. The *type* of trust pertains to the nature of the trusting partners, often social and political—although I expand on the latter to include all manner of hierarchies, not just the state.

HISTORICAL INTERPRETATIONS OF TRUST

While social science doesn't provide clean, consistent definitions of trust, there are a few historic working models that offer helpful insight. First, communalist trust results from peoples' close relationships and regular interaction. Everyone is very similar and shares common reference points. Émile Durkheim points to a form of mechanical solidarity in which our commonality is the key social bond. Others can be trusted because we are able to predict everyone's decisions and actions, as well as presume we share comparable interests (thus a highly encapsulated form of trust). A unified, even hegemonic, culture informs everyone's values and minimal deviance is tolerated, thus making trust possible. A real-world community's day-to-day functioning generates and sustains this communalist trust. This form is most likely to appear in pre-modern periods, with social simplicity.

Second, centralized states and the Enlightenment ushered in a presumably neutral guarantor of trust: the social contract. According to figures like John Locke and Jean-Jacques Rousseau, the social contract illuminated a set of mutual expectations between people and the state; the rights and freedoms gained by individuals, in exchange for subordination to state jurisdiction. While the social contract is usually considered an agreement between people and the state (as how the earlier Magna Carta aimed to protect certain groups), it also can be seen as a set of reasonable expectations between individuals and society, thus constituting a civil society autonomous from the state.[27] In fact, trust is a consequence of this contract as well as its precondition. We all must understand what is expected of us— our social or legal obligations—and our common interests. There is a "document" (even if unwritten) that stipulates what we can expect of each other. We can trust the contract because we trust the underlying system that contracts require; this is addressed in the concept of "civil liberties", wherein all are granted certain rights. The social contract is enforced via an appeal to rules and norms, as well as via coercive state power. That said, such contracts are likely to benefit those in the best position to create and enforce them. Additionally, as the age of Enlightenment was also an era of colonialist expansion and rapidly expanding inequality under industrial capitalism, the social contract was most readily enforced for good-standing citizens, especially male property owners. Non-citizens—including people of color, slaves, indigenous people, immigrants, and women—were not considered entitled to fair treatment under the law due to their reduced status.[28] Consequently, the Enlightenment's "neutrality" is up for debate; it may generate trust in the abstract principles of one person, one vote, and equal rights. Or, it may legitimate the veneer of such abstractions, under the surface of which inequality thrives, thus demanding "trust" in an untrustworthy system.

Relatedly, third, a modern, capitalist form of solidarity and trust results from a need for each other. Thus, trust appears because we must rely on each other (typically in the context of a market) to get our needs met. As previously mentioned, Durkheim referred to this as organic solidarity. Trust in factories, for example—what they abstractly represent and what they practically do—are what makes the entire productive enterprise function. Graeber calls such relationships "communist" (with no small irony) even when it happens within capitalist enterprises, as it requires extensive cooperation.[29] Such trust allows people to collectively produce products, provide services, and do the logistical work necessary to provide for needs, even within a complex industry and production process. This trust system mirrors a bureaucracy—all the functioning components serve each other and benefit the overall whole. Workers (and consumers) do different things in the economy, thus creating a complex division of labor wherein everyone must rely on nearly everyone else for society to function properly. Additionally, the notion of a "liberal" world-order in which global capitalism spreads throughout the earth, linking all countries together by shared, mutual economic interest, thereby "eliminating" war, is a form of this trust. A radical variant of this is a cooperatively pursued mutuality, that circumvents the profit motive and privately owned capital; the division of labor is based around values and needs of peers.

Finally, a parochial form of trust is found in nationalism. The belief in the sanctity, innate goodness, or even infallibility of *your* people, ethnic group, or the state can solidify trust. In fairly homogeneous societies (e.g., Scandinavia), trust is higher, presumably because there are very few "outsiders" who weaken people's trust in each other or their shared emotional commitments. This is a common explanation for the cultural compatibility with social democracy throughout Scandinavia: Fellow Scandinavians are the recipients of society's collective generosity, not "others" from outside the nation. It's uncontroversial to support the welfare state when it provides a safety net for people like you. Trust exists in your kin only and excludes those who don't "belong". Similar ideas emerge about racial tolerance of others, insofar as they are "close" to us—compare this with Emory Bogardus's theory of social distance, where people are more willing to trust and thus participate with "closer" people.[30] This interpretation of trust mirrors the critical view of the Enlightenment's social contract, which introduced the modern, post-monarchical European state system, in which not everyone benefits equally. Rural dwellers are usually presumed to be rather suspicious of outsiders, especially national authorities, but, empirically, the opposite is true—city dwellers possess significantly more political distrust than their rural neighbors, a pattern that's also affected by level of human development.[31] Table 1.2 depicts these four historic trust trends, categorized by their emphasis and execution.

Table 1.2   Typologies of Historic Trust Trends

| | | *Emphases* | |
		Similarities	*Dissimilarities*
Execution	**Cooperative**	Communalist (1)	Organic (3)
	Coercive	Parochial (4)	Social contract (2)

THE MULTI-LEVEL MEASUREMENT OF TRUST

These traditions and systems, whether offering mediated or unmediated trust, illuminate how trust is practiced at various levels throughout a society. The dynamics of trust are structured up and down in these levels. The macro-level (e.g., societal-wide) is premised upon the aggregation of individuals in meso-structures, which are aggregated into the macro. The patterns of trust at the micro-level occurs because of order imposed upon individuals at both the meso- and macro-levels. Let's consider each in order.

The micro-level is an interactive scale in which trust and distrust are exchanged and shared between individuals, in the context of interactions, and sometimes even within the "self". For example, individual co-workers may trust each other (or not), may trust a manager (or not), just as friends and family members may trust one another. This is the intimate field upon which trust manifests and feels most real; it is unmediated and contextual. When people think about "trust", they often envision trust at this level: between individuals. While trust at the micro-level is practical, it's "typically ineffective as a source of macro-level social order" as it is too difficult "to know whom to trust in a large complex organization or community".[32] For this reason, radical trust can guide people with a political distrust orientation.

The meso-level is a higher scale of human groupings. The most common form of meso-level groupings includes small groups or formal organizations. Trust and distrust exist within and between those groups or organizations. Even though these structures can be witnessed at the micro-level, their importance is submerged there, while salient and foregrounded here. Organizations may either trust (or distrust) other organizations—which is to say, usually, that there is a rough consensus among the participants, members, or leaders of such organizations about what their collective attitude and practice of trust should be vis-à-vis other organizations.

The same is true in small groups that lack formal organization structure. The kinds of organizations that may trust or distrust include workplaces, departments, neighborhoods, corporations, and many others. For example, one company may trust another enough to create a shared marketing campaign; although under most conditions, capitalist firms distrust each other greatly. The same is true for far-right organizations, like Nazi skinhead gangs (e.g., Hammerskins), or other ultra-nationalist and white supremacist groups, in regard to disadvantaged racial or religious groups, immigrants, or leftists (including antifascist collectives).

Finally, the macro-level is the most abstract level at which social analysis occurs. Here, trust and distrust occur among major institutions: They either trust each other and their mutual contributions, or they suspect that one has a greater advantage and is a threat. For example, police not only follow the lead of political elites, but reflect the common interests of economic and cultural elites. Militaries and wealthy interests (the rich and their corporations) often implicitly work hand-in-hand, and trust that they will all benefit from belligerent policies against foreign adversaries. Macro-level trust (or distrust) can also include entire societies: Wealthy, Western countries may sometimes bicker among themselves, but their immense shared interests (and financial investments) prevent deep distrust from breaking out (e.g., in the G8). However, great distrust exists between countries of the Global South and the wealthy countries of North America and Europe.

Cross-level trust is arguably more difficult: that is, for particular individuals to trust large institutions (and vice versa). However, those large institutions seem intangible, while individuals have an immediate presence whose behavior can easily be witnessed. Additionally, individuals typically are the face of great bureaucracies—teachers of large school districts, police within local polities, a salesperson employed at a multinational corporation—and thus someone we can identify with (perhaps even empathize with), even though they represent something huge, hegemonic, and often destructive. At the same time, individual next-door neighbors are representatives of a wider "public" or other general group. Thus, while this kind of multi-level analytical framing helps a bit, it is not always straightforward that institutions are easily distrusted and individuals quickly trusted. It's probably more informative to think about the interests represented and how power works (and in whose favor).

Which is more common and what is more practically helpful: to trust individuals or the institutions they represent? In other words, is it more reasonable to trust an individual priest or the Catholic Church, a single officer than the unified military command, or an upper-level manager than the entirety of corporate capitalism? Trusting individuals is more reasonable, but individuals are the ones who often do bad things. In all the above examples, individuals may sexually assault subordinates—while the larger institution scrambles to cover it up and marginalize critics. Thus, are individual actors the problem or the systems they are part of? Recent years have seen shocking public disclosures about the horrendous acts of certain men in leadership positions. While these men find themselves outed, it is often difficult to hold them accountable, let alone fix the flawed institutions they work in. We shouldn't simply distrust individuals like Harvey Weinstein but the elements of the entertainment industry who facilitated and concealed their crimes. Capitalism and states constrain individual, organizational, and institutional action, and thus compromise their trustworthiness. Ideally, our trust could be reserved for those who are independent of hierarchical pressures and are accountable in meaningful ways to the communities such individuals influence.

Before moving on, it is helpful to assess the differences between some of these macro-phenomena (i.e., structures, bureaucracies, hierarchies, and institutions), which are often conflated with each other. First, structures are any enduring social systems that humans

create. They need not be bureaucratic, hierarchical, or institutionalized, but easily can be. Inertia often pushes people to make structures
as complex as an entire economic system or as simple as a single corporation's charter or decision-making processes within an activist
group. Bureaucracies are regimented, formalized social structures
that possess a division of labor. Given enough time, bureaucracies
may become institutionalized. They are often implicitly hierarchical, yet not the most efficient kind of hierarchy. Possible varieties
of bureaucracies include organizations which distribute monthly
social welfare, a university's faculty senate and subcommittees, or
a corporation's research-and-development division. Hierarchies are
social systems featuring relations of command and obedience. They
are not always bureaucratic but tend to have at least some bureaucratic form or residue, such as the US Army, a corporation's chain of
command (from the CEO to mail-room clerk), and apartheid-based
(or apartheid-derived) race relations. Hierarchy is a prevalent way of
delivering trust, but it's not the kind argued for in this book. Finally,
institutions are long-lasting structures that need not be bureaucratic
or hierarchical but often are. They reflect established social norms
and stable group relations, such as the patriarchal family, Catholi-
cism, and market relations.

All these macro-level distinctions, while seemingly minor, are
important. Hierarchical trust does not require trust in all institutional actors or even all institutions, just trust in the hierarchy. Since
not all institutions (e.g., families) are explicit hierarchies, institutional distrust is not really what should be advocated. There are ways
of restructuring institutions—and *maybe* certain bureaucracies—so
that they are nonhierarchical and thus worthy of trust. For example,
making families less patriarchal would be a positive transformation.
Handling community defense without police would mean creating
social structures that permit safety without having to subordinate
oneself to armed government bureaucrats (i.e., police). Or, transforming cultural or religious rituals to be decolonialist, anti-racist,
and liberatory rather than dominating would necessitate providing
for important social-psychological and emotional needs without
hierarchy. Some bureaucracies could be trustworthy, to the extent

that they avoid hierarchy—in theory, a *fair* and democratic bureaucracy could avoid inequality and domination of some over others. However, since this is unlikely to be the case for most bureaucracies, they deserve active distrust.

WHY TRUST MATTERS

At this point, some readers may wonder: Why give trust so much emphasis? I argue trust is the DNA behind our social relationships, networks, and communities. And, implicitly, trust is also in the DNA of social movements and all efforts at resisting domination. Trust is what makes life interesting and enjoyable. On the other hand, the world of pure individualists—who lack fundamental trust in each other—would be a non-society. Like their Ayn Rand fantasyland, ultra-individualists ignore how they are co-dependent upon those around them. This is distinct from other threads of individualism, like philosopher Max Stirner's "union of egoists", which acknowledges the legitimate need for relationships.[33] Trust is also an important subject because it can also facilitate "the great con" that authority pulls on us, misleading us to trust in hierarchy.

Trust matters because it allows us to care for those younger and weaker than us. In the case of the former, society must defend children if it wishes to see the species continue. Elders also have value in communities long after their bodies lose their strength, reproductive capacities, and other energies—they are a source of cultural memory, moral strength, and wisdom. Such "weaker" individuals often contribute many things to communities, in terms of their emotional, intellectual, psychological, and social efforts. Abandoning those groups to the whims of selfish and violent individualism would do direct harm to those middle-aged and stronger. A society in which youth/elders and the weak cannot trust the middle-aged and strong would effectively cripple its functioning.

Trust matters because it binds us together over time. A key to sociability is the social "debt" we owe to each other. Anthropologist David Graeber describes our lives as replete with exchanges—monetary and otherwise—that are not one-to-one trades and that rightfully lack a balancing ledger. People do things for and give things to each other, without immediately expecting anything in return. We willingly go into debt with each other because we want to continue these relationships. We both want to stay in each other's debts and do nice things for each other. This give and take, without the need to always be "fair" in exchange, is the foundation of our relationships. We like having friends who are generous and families that don't expect every debt to be immediately repaid. We expect immediately "settled" exchanges or barter with people we don't trust—we don't really care if we see them again. Debt is a valuable social feature of our relationships and is enabled by trust.[34]

Trust matters because it creates a valuable potential in our social ties, and thus its attrition is tragic. As trust, social capital, and community have measurably declined in the US over many years, the weight of those losses has become clearer. Many things that people value have been adversely affected by this phenomenon and all sorts of quality-of-life measures, like democracy, well-being, safety, and even the planet's future, to say nothing of satisfaction and happiness, have decreased in recent decades. Political scientist Robert Putnam's study *Bowling Alone* (2000) attributes responsibility for social capital decline to a variety of factors. For example, the advent of unidirectional, hegemonic, mass entertainment like television has modified how people in the US spend their time; TV viewing is an individualistic behavior, and encourages distrust due to TV's content and implicit consumerist values.[35]

Rising inequality and increases in women's employment have removed some of the primary agents of civil society from volunteer, charitable, and organizational labor, relocating them to the (mainly lowly) paid economy. Women struggle to create social networks in communities when they work two part-time jobs and have to manage a house full of kids.[36] And the dominance of car culture and suburbanization of human settlements has disrupted more natural patterns of land use and movement. Suburbs disrupt diverse, organic land use, separating residents from their workplaces and other community affairs. People cannot as easily develop trust in their neighbors if they rarely see them or others on the street. Having to drive long distances to attend a job or shop means long periods of time not spent building trust with other people.[37]

Finally, the consequences of distrust can extend across multiple generations. Revolutionary movements that attempt to pursue justice and freedom can be stymied in their tracks. For example, no historical conflict in the modern era among the left is as contentious, personal, and long-lasting as the Marxist–anarchist schism dating from the 1870s. At the First International congress in the Hague, a massive fissure erupted between socialist followers of Karl Marx and anarchists grouped loosely around Mikhail Bakunin. The General Council which "guided" the International was dominated by Marx and his acolytes, who implicitly distrusted the motives of Bakunin and his Social Democratic Alliance, who wanted membership in the International. Bakunin wanted to set the International on a non-statist path, while Marx wanted to replace the capitalist state with socialists like himself. Thus, Marx had the council engineer Bakunin's expulsion from the International along with his anarchist adherents.[38] As anarchists constituted the majority of the International's sections (especially in southern Europe), this move decimated the revolutionary labor movement. Marx moved the International's office to New York City, where the anarchists of southern Europe could not easily reach or travel. This prevented their participation, but also killed the organization's vitality.

This schism continues to the present day; socialists distrust(ed) anarchists' strategy, as well as their passionate sway over workers, while anarchists simply distrusted the socialists' intentions and were critical of how socialists would (and did) act once they got into power (especially within political parties and the state). While the distrust between the groups doesn't always prevent collaboration, the scars are still visible. Distrust should be seen as both the consequence of incongruent values and political strategy, as well as the cause of a weakened, dis-unified labor and working-class movement still today. This is one example of many of how trust and distrust can affect generations of human experience.

TRUST AS DEPENDENT VERSUS INDEPENDENT VARIABLE

Depending on one's concern, trust can be analyzed as a cause or as an effect. In fancy, methodological terms, this is a way of asking if trust ought to be considered an independent or dependent variable. Ultimately, the difference depends on what is more interesting to us. Clearly, trust is *both* a cause and an effect. Thus, this book assumes "both" is our response to the question above, as it's crucial to understand the *dynamics* of trust.

First, consider trust as a dependent variable (as an effect): What causes trust? Surely all sorts of things, like people's past experiences and social positions, the context of an encounter, sociopolitical ideology, and who the trusting partner is. In the past, "liberals" (maybe also a proxy for leftists?) are over-represented as social trusters, while conservatives are over-represented as political trusters. Additionally, one's class and race impact trust. People with greater socioeconomic status and white people tend to express greater social trust, while people subscribing to fundamentalist and authoritarian beliefs are less likely to socially trust but more apt to trust hierarchical institutions.

Next, consider trust as an independent variable (as a cause): What consequences result from trust? There's a laundry list of such social phenomena, some of which have already been mentioned. To start with, trust impacts happiness, stable communities, social movements, and social integration. Trust impacts the choices we make, the assessments we make in certain situations, and our long-term visions. Regardless of its position in a model, the target of trust is key—trust in everyday people is likely to result in positive results, whereas trust in elites will likely have other results. For example, years ago I noticed a pattern across dozens of diverse countries: Greater social trust and lower political trust was collectively associated with protest. In 2020, I wrote in greater depth about this pattern in a case study of the US, where I again found this relationship but also noticed that voting was associated with *greater* political trust. Thus, while social trust is crucial for both forms of political action, varying levels of political trust predict whether someone either protested or voted.[39] Further, individuals with higher in-group (i.e., family, neighbors, acquaintances) trust are more apt to vote, while those with higher out-group (i.e., people of other religions or nationalities, new acquaintances) trust are more apt to protest.[40]

A more sophisticated approach to cause and effect involves sketching-out some path models, featuring trust as exogenous and endogenous variables. (Exogenous variables are anything that serves as a *cause* for something else, while endogenous variables are anything that are an *effect* of something else.) This can get rather complicated, especially when separating social trust from political trust, and distinguishing between trust, distrust, and mistrust. However, Figure 1.1 could be a reasonable, yet simplistic, step forward in this regard. A path model—which depicts how one phenomenon works to influence something else and, in turn, has subsequent consequences—shows how there are reciprocal relationships at work. Things that predict or cause trust (like education) are also outcomes of trust. This is a recursive "feedback loop", in which effects become causes. For example, social trust is generally associated with well-being—especially in individualistic countries, where personal preferences and autonomy matter more, whereas social trust in collectivist societies derives more from conformity to norms.[41] Generalized social trust is associated with greater physical and psychological health, too, although more so in wealthy countries.[42] It's incredibly difficult to confidently demonstrate that it's social trust which results in well-being and health, when the opposite argument (that well-being and health results in social trust) is equally compelling.

Finally, it's important to mention that quite a bit of scholarly ink has been spilled trying to determine the relationship between social trust and political trust—in other words, which is an independent variable and which a dependent variable? Numerous studies have attempted to establish both patterns, with mostly convincing results. Simply, both forms of trust are reciprocal. Social trust may create the societal consensus necessary to found a state (in which political trust can occur), just as some claim that social trust stems from the establishment of a modern state in which rules are established determining what individuals ought to expect of each other. I'm a bit more swayed by the former argument, but there's evidence of the latter too.[43]

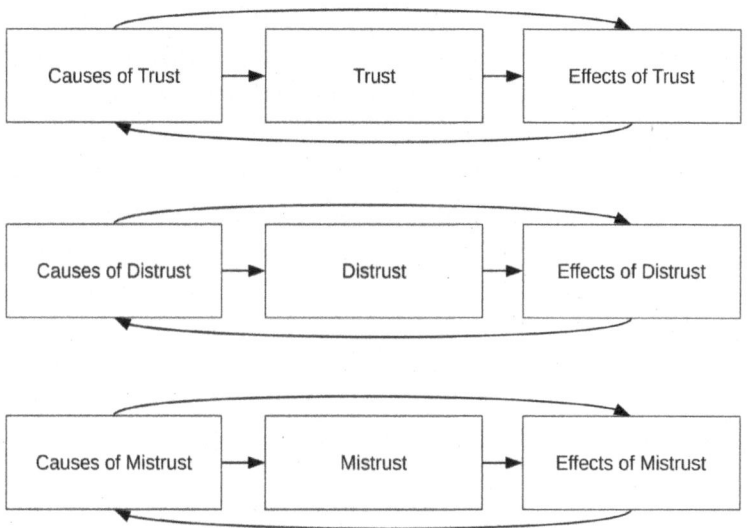

Figure 1.1   Causal Paths for Trust, Distrust, and Mistrust

SOCIOPOLITICAL TRUST

To further conceptualize the intersection between social trust and political trust—that is, trusting orientations toward everyday equals versus presumed political elites—I've created a simple, idealized two-by-two typology.[44] The many existent and possible contradictory orientations toward social and political trust indicate that a typological model for sociopolitical trust is warranted. In Table 1.3, I contrast those who socially trust or distrust with those who politically trust or distrust.

Social and political trusters can be called "trusters". Equally unsurprisingly, social and political distrust combines for "distrusters". More curiously, those who socially trust, but politically distrust will be called "horizontalists". Finally, those who socially distrust and politically trust are hereafter "hierarchicalists". These are, of course, "ideal type" categories in the Weberian sense; such categories don't necessarily map perfectly onto reality but conceptually provoke us to consider how ideas work together. Thus, in reality, many people may have *some* social trust alongside their much greater reservoir of social distrust—for this typology their higher degree of social distrust is what matters for whether they are a distruster or hierarchicalist (itself contingent on their political trust). Sociopolitical trust may be conceived of as the intersection between social (e.g., trust in comparable, "average" people) and political trust (e.g., trust in the state and its agents).[45] Theoretically, any individual can be located somewhere on this two-axis measure.

Table 1.3   Sociopolitical Trust Typology

	Political trust	*Political distrust*
Social trust	Truster	Horizontalist
Social distrust	Hierarchicalist	Distruster

Trusters and distrusters possess congruent trust, where social and political trust are positively associated; this is indicated by a weak statistical correlation. Horizontalists and hierarchicalists possess stratified trust, where social and political trust are negatively associated, and for whom differences in power result in divergent trust relationships. Socially pessimistic and optimistic positions (or, anti-solidarity versus pro-solidarity) are suggested by the social trust axis, implying a presumption of negative versus positive, respectively, outcomes for placing trust in fellow non-state actors. Authoritarian and anti-authoritarian positions are suggested by the political trust axis; the former involves trusting state authority over society, while the latter distrusts a state's authority. These four positions describe unique orientations toward people of varied social rank, associations with prominent political and economic positions, and orientations toward social change.

First, trusters (high social trust, high political trust) have a generally positive view toward everyone, independent of their position. Implicitly optimistic, this is a liberal, social democratic position that argues that both everyday people and the state can be trusted.[46] Supportive of a civil society,[47] trusters have confidence in political systems they believe benefit others (and are constitutive of everyone), and therefore social change comes from the manifested "will of the people" working through government. Thus, social support systems represent a state's efforts to support its citizenry who speak for and through such policies. Trusters are most apt to vote regularly and maintain an interest in politics.[48]

Second, distrusters (low social trust, low political trust) have a generally negative view of everyone, regardless of the target's position. Implicitly cynical, this is a neoliberal, libertarian,[49] or ultra-individualist orientation that considers no one worthy of an individual's trust.[50] While family, friends, and others sharing one's culture are trustworthy, general others are not, nor are major institutions that aren't perceived to represent them[51]—thus social change is seen as improbable. For these anti-authoritarian and socially pessimistic people, the only real change is personally initiated, with social movements and voting inherently ineffective. Paranoia of all manner of social actors—whether founded or not—leads distrusters to attempt to manage their own affairs without assistance, protect against potential criminals (including institutionalized versions found in federal, "big government"), and generally suspect the worst in others' intentions.

Third, horizontalists (high social trust, low political trust) are skeptical of those in power, while considering most average people to be generally trustworthy. Trust is extended toward social equals but withheld from authority figures, thus indicating an anarchist or libertarian-socialist orientation.[52] People can freely cooperate with others and do not need (or greatly benefit from) the state. Anti-authoritarian in orientation, horizontalists limit their trust to those who lack dominant power in society, and consequently believe that social change occurs from the bottom-up, most dramatically via social movements. Their peers are more trustworthy collaborators (since they lack "power over") than the state and movement participation implies social optimism. Thus, horizontalists would be most apt to protest and engage in extra-institutional actions. Horizontalists' social trust constitutes a belief in "the will of the people", although that will is polluted once subsumed within an untrustworthy political state—thus voting is a less desirable action than movement participation.

Fourth, hierarchicalists (low social trust, high political trust) hold a generally favorable view of those more powerful than "average" people. Social equals are not afforded trust, while those who hold power over others are, thus indicating an authoritarian or fascist orientation.[53] Hierarchicalists focus their trust on the political system, suggesting an obedience to authority and a belief that change occurs from the top-down.[54] Thus, while political trust might imply an endorsement of electoralism, their social pessimism suggests a belief that fellow voters are unreliable partners in a political system. Instead, trust in strong leadership—those who possess total political power, whether charismatic or technocratic—is most important and (perhaps) even empowering to hierarchicalists.

Trust is important for how individuals participate publicly. Those who have great political trust in the system act differently than those with lower political trust. Yet, possessing social trust also impacts how political trust or distrust operates. Only with social trust are individual non-elites capable of social action. Diverse patterns of obedience, institutionalized action, apathy, or extra-institutional action (to name a few) can result from these combinations. In the public sphere, trusters will be able to choose institutional action that distrusters—who are wracked with apathy or antipathy—will not be able to. On the other hand, horizontalists will have the ability or preference for extra-institutional action outside the state. Hierarchicalists, lacking social trust, will be disabled and only enjoy the possibilities available via political obedience. In general, this mixture sets up each category for either revolutionary or reformist orientations: Trusters and hierarchicalists will seek more reformist changes (trusters perhaps less cynically than hierarchicalists), while distrusters and horizontalists seem more positively oriented toward revolutionary change (distrusters more nihilistic or individualistic than horizontalists).

The critical implications of this sociopolitical trust typology and its hypotheses for political participation vary depending on the audience. Presumably, autocratic states seek to reduce their subjects' social trust, while increasing political trust (enhancing its own political capital and diminishing others' social capital), thereby bolstering *gesellschaft*. Hypothetically, but perhaps not always in practice, democracies seek to improve citizen's political trust, and maybe social trust, too, insofar as it enhances the state's legitimate authority (e.g., voting).[55] Ultimately, as Weber would remind us, states possess the monopoly on violence—even "democratic" states can be militaristic, unequal, and repressive. For social movements, it is crucial to mobilize supportive populations who are disposed to distrust and resist elite authority (i.e., lower-case-L libertarian), yet who possess social trust and value collective action (i.e., socialist). For civil society advocates, determining what factors—micro as well as macro—facilitate greater trust (of whatever variety) is crucial to establishing or strengthening pre-contractual solidarity.[56]

To just focus on Americans, we can use data available from the World Values Survey to assess what kinds of people are more likely to trust or distrust each other and political institutions (i.e., Congress and the police). In 2011, both women and white people were most likely to be trusters, while men and people of color were most apt to be distrusters. Older Americans and those with a higher level of education attainment were more likely to be horizontal-ists, while younger people and those with the least education were hierarchicalists. Interestingly, liberals were most apt—although not significantly—to be distrusters, while conservatives were likely to be hierarchicalists. Crucially, people who regularly voted were trusters (and non-voters were distrusters), while those who protested were horizontalists (and non-protesters were hierarchicalists).[57] Thus, horizontalists and trusters are likely to be people of privilege (white, older, more educated), while hierarchicalists and distrust-ers are more likely to be disadvantaged (people of color, younger, less educated). Generally this confirms past research showing that people who have lived privileged lives tend to be more trusting of others like them.

SOLIDARITY AND ANTI-AUTHORITARIANISM

Since solidarity and anti-authoritarianism are central to my radical trust approach, they warrant some introductory description. I consider solidarity to be collective and proactively horizontal, while anti-authoritarianism is proactively anti-vertical. Solidarity is the energy propelling the radicalism of modernity's socialism, while anti-authoritarianism is the energy behind the classical liberalism of libertarianism; together they bind us together for cooperation, while also orienting us against hierarchy. There's an extensive literature on each; what follows is a brief sampling.

Foundationally, a sense of "we" underlies group processes and is strongly associated with trust, openness, and social bonds.[58] Solidarity tends to emerge in reaction to negative emotions stemming from perceived injustice and suffering.[59] Traditional Russian views of solidarity, cooperation, and altruism (which emerge in an engagement with both Bakunin and Kropotkin) differ notably from Western notions. Solidarity of the latter variety ensures social structure's stability, but the former serves as a necessary grassroots prerequisite for social change.[60] The social and political contexts that foster solidarity are important. To truly understand solidarity requires engaging with these dynamics: the basis and *foundation* of solidarity, the *objective* or function of solidarity, how *inclusive* solidarity is, and, how strong is its *collective orientation* and the degree of individual freedom.[61] Solidarity incorporates two motivations: helpful, supportive, and cooperative behavior between individuals and collectivities, and behaviors based on and associated with obligation and value commitments (e.g., radical anti-authoritarianism).[62] Social order that promotes such "geographies of trust" rely upon mutuality without hierarchy.[63]

In their overview of solidarity, Leah Hunt-Hendrix and Astra Taylor contrast transformative solidarity against reactionary solidarity. Transformative solidarity exists only in action, is the fuel behind social movements (e.g., abolitionism) that seek to overturn hierarchies and eliminate inequality, and has a distinctly social character differing from individualist altruism, benevolence, or allyship.[64] Such solidarity can appear quite militant, as in Cindy Milstein's description of "having each other's backs" and "putting oneself at risk to create barriers so that many others might feel safer and get away".[65] Thus, for anarchists, solidarity helps to maintain equality and freedom between individuals and groups, and two different versions (instrumental and principled) have existed: (1) individuals cooperating with each other to pursue a common goal; and (2) individuals' caring relationships to ensure ongoing equality and freedom.[66]

Generally, anti-authoritarianism involves, first, the rejection of unquestioning obedience to authority, and, second, resistance to that illegitimate authority.[67] Uri Gordon points out that the term shares a common meaning and sentiment with autonomism, anarchism, and horizontalism.[68] According to sociologist Marina Sitrin's analysis of popular Argentinean movements in the aftermath of the 2001 popular uprising, horizontalism is anti-authoritarianism pursued as creation, rather than as reaction.[69] Revolutions— including those against entrenched dictatorships—succeed due to anti-authoritarian cultural and political innovations by small communities of "humanist outliers", who pursue compassionate social emancipation.[70] Finally, Chris Dixon defines four core principles of anti-authoritarianism: (1) struggle against all forms of domination, exploitation, and oppression; (2) developing new social relations and forms of social organization in the process of struggle; (3) linking struggles for improvements in ordinary peoples' lives to long-term transformative visions; and (4) organizing that is grassroots and bottom-up.[71]

REDEFINING TERMS: MISTRUST ≠ DISTRUST

Before we branch out to explore critical matters related to trust and distrust, it's important to investigate the language we casually use.[72] And, although sometimes awkward, term redefinition and re-specification can be liberating. Here, I'd like to propose changing the common definition of "mistrust" away from its currently dominant, essentially analogous definition with "distrust". According to traditional dictionaries (e.g., the *Oxford English Dictionary*[73]), mistrust and distrust are nearly identical. But this makes little sense given how the prefix "mis-" is typically employed. For most other words—like mistrial, misuse, misprint, misplace, misdiagnosis, mislead—the prefix implies mistake, inaccuracy, or accident. People who misjudge are actually judging others, just doing so incorrectly. Thus, the word "mistrust" suggests it's possible to trust in a way that objectively hurts you, does not advance your position or capacities, or inhibits your life. "Distrust" on the other hand, bearing the prefix "dis-", is more plainly linked to words like disbelief, dislike, disjointed, disconnect, displeasure, discontent, or disability, implying without, apart from, or negative. To disassemble means to *not* assemble—in fact, it means to take apart. And disagree means to *not* agree. Distrusting means not only lacking trust, but a strong resistance to potentially trusting something.

This semantic redefinition clearly suggests that distrust is a lack of trust, while mistrust is mistaken and misplaced trust. Distrusters *don't* trust, while mistrusters *do* trust (although *wrongly*). This is a healthy adjustment to the legions of authors, advocates, and research that proclaim the indisputably good benefits of trust and point negatively to the perils of distrust. Anthropologist Matthew Carey's distinction between distrust and mistrust is better than most. He argues that "mistrust describes a general sense of the unreliability of a person or thing". But mistrust is broader than unreliability—it is trust placed in an unreliable and untrustworthy target.[74] I argue that distrusting (especially those in authority) is sometimes good, while mistrusting those same actors and institutions can be very dangerous.

I suspect that "mistrust" is so commonly substituted for "distrust" because contemporary liberals who influence language's use can't conceive of why trust would be bad. Why would it be a mistake to trust someone, when trust is good? Such naivete illustrates the problems with trusting hierarchical systems—not only do they not care about individuals who are subordinate to them but their power relies upon unquestioning trust (or, rather, mistrust). In fact, hierarchical institutions ought to be starved of our trust and actively distrusted. This same skepticism is not as warranted when focused on our social equals.

Finally, in the context of redefining terms, I think it makes good sense to speak of trust as relational, rather than instrumental. Trust as a relationship involves multiple people, while trust as an orientation involves just one person. In other words, while it is common to speak of "trust in" or "trust for" others or an institution, this implies a simplistic—and unrealistic—one-way street. Trust is relational and multidirectional, placed and shared in by multiple partners concurrently. Ideally, trust ought to be reciprocal, as this is most helpful for those experiencing structural disadvantages. To have a relationship of trust *among* the poor, working class is a better way to describe trust—people trust each other. In contrast, having singular, one-way trust in powerful institutions is problematic, parasitic, and unjust, as that institution doesn't have much incentive to trust the lowly individual who has—perhaps naively—placed trust in it. Citizen "trust" (or rather mistrust) in Congress—which is filled to the brim with lawyers and millionaires—is not reciprocated. There is no horizontal, bidirectional relationship of trust here. Instead of the word "trust", words like "obedience", "faith", or "worship" are more accurate.

IN SUMMARY…

This chapter has not only defined trust but made a case for its importance. It's clear that there are many conceptualizations of trust, pulled from a wide variety of theoretical traditions and sources. Some of the most robust elements of trust—encapsulated interest, risk-taking, exchange, or even love—help us to understand why trust can be such a powerful force in society. The ways in which people trust, mistrust, and distrust can have incredible, far-reaching impacts. It will soon become clear why the trust situation is so dire in the US and so many other places.

In the next chapter, we'll explore where trust can be found in the US and where it's generally absent, as well as dive deep into the intricacies of the phenomenon of trust.

2

Who Do You Trust? Some of the Ways That Trust Works

SAFE GROUPS TO TRUST

When I think about the groups I tend to trust, I'm drawn toward those I have shared interests with. People like librarians, rank-and-file grocery store workers, or those who attend peace vigils come to mind. I trust them because they lack power over me, they are trustworthy because their work supports things that align with my values, and because I can easily see myself in their shoes (because I often *have been*). Power has not corrupted them in their roles and I easily see the solidarity we share in our common existence—we need each other and want to have a meaningful connection. We help each other out, and even when we don't have to, a pleasant mutual exchange permeates our encounters. This solidarity is especially clear in juxtaposition to the powerful, with whom we share less in common.

In more general terms, the people who are most important to trust, easiest to trust, and most often trusted are family, friends, and intimate partners. This is fairly predictable, as the blood ties and long history of families (especially families-of-origin) connect us by shared experiences, "tradition", and familial obligations. Our friends, by definition, we self-select. We generally pick with whom we want to affiliate and with whom we choose to share ourselves and our lives. If our biological families include violent, abusive, or untrustworthy people, then we can create our own organic "families" of friends. And, of course, intimate partners are usually mutually attracted to each other. They are those we profess to care for (and thus "love") and this affection extends—requires—an incredible amount of trust.

The typical right-wing credo of trusting family, God, and nation is a limited, and somewhat bizarre, modification of this list of the trustworthy. Trusting family—albeit of the straight, nuclear-family variety—is not a fool-proof policy, but it's more intuitive than trust in otherworldly abstractions like "God" and "nation". Presumably, "God" is the Judeo-Christian deity that a religious authority has told them to trust, while people can conjure whatever they want to be "the nation".[1] People can generate convenient excuses when "the nation" doesn't live up to expectations, just as easily as explaining why God has chosen to punish rather than reward them. It's important to note that this triumvirate of trustworthy institutions are actually those that people have the least free will over: You don't choose the family you're born to, nor where you are born, and the existence of an omnipresent, monotheistic God forecloses the possibilities of choosing to distrust it. In other words, the right wing demands we trust those that we effectively lack any true choice *not* to trust.

Suffice to say, these groups—family, friends, and even God or "the nation"—are not whom social scientists intend by their concept of "generalized social trust". The aforementioned are *known* groups, targets of "particularized trust". To select the family as an example, it is at no risk of destruction by forces of evil, the left, or "the other". Pat Robertson's 1992 paranoid, homophobic, far-right proclamation that feminists were lesbians who opposed families (and sought to destroy capitalism, kill their children, etc.)[2] was simultaneously ridiculous and offensive: Most feminists and lesbians have their own families that are acknowledged by most other families. Thus, contrary to such fearmongering, the above relationships of trust are usually highly uncontroversial.

Ironically, the great investment in family and friends introduces us to great risk. If this trust is exploited, tragic consequences can result. Indeed, we are around these people the most and so ultimately are more likely to be assaulted, murdered, robbed, kidnapped, and abused by those we love and who "love" us. In fact, the people most scary to us—strangers—are probably the safest for us, because they are *not* our family, friends, or intimate partners. They have less motivation and spatial proximity to harm us. And our lack of proximity to strangers means we are less invested in trusting them and thus less disappointed when such trust fails. Sociologist Emory Bogardus suggested we trust in concentric circles, primarily with those closest to us.[3] While this seems plausible, we interact far more often with those in our inner circle, thus increasing the possible opportunities for abuse emerging within such relationships.

WHO DO WE (NOT) TRUST?

Social scientists have developed numerous, albeit imperfect, ways to assess via survey questions what people think about each other. For example, surveys have shown increasing support for electing a Black or female US president, suggesting a liberalization of racial and gendered biases.[4] The GSS asked Americans if they'd favor or oppose a close relative or family member marrying a Black person—only 7 percent admitted they'd oppose such a marriage in 2022, but back in 1990 it was 58 percent! Other questions have explored whether respondents would support a certain kind of "controversial" person—racists, communists, militarists, homosexuals, and so on—teaching a class, giving a public speech, or being one's neighbor.[5]

Finally, do people trust specific marginalized groups, such as Muslims, immigrants, atheists, gay people, communists, and so on? According to the GSS, support for such groups has improved over time: Americans in 1972 supported university employment of communists at only 35 percent, atheists at 42 percent, and gay people at 49 percent. However, by 2021, 70 percent of Americans were supportive of employing both communists and atheists, and 93 percent for gay people. While this improvement is encouraging, it indicates that an entrenched minority still disproves of mere *employment* for scorned groups. If data were available, the trust folks have for criminals, drug users, refugees, sex workers, and other "undesirable others" could also be assessed. Due to their marginalization, members of these disadvantaged groups typically seek the dominant society's trust or risk further alienation from it.

It's important to note that trusting or distrusting particular groups is a probabilistic not deterministic strategy. In other words, people may *tend* to trust or distrust a group but regularly find exceptions to their own rules. For example, an individual may profess to not trust Muslims generally but actually like the next-door neighbors who "happen to be" Muslim. (This often involves mentally constructing a loophole in which that person is not *really* a Muslim or is "one of the good ones".) The actual trust someone has for a specific individual who belongs to a distrusted group may vary and is not determined by pre-existing biases. Also, such forecasting advice is only marginally helpful in practice. For example, there are (probably) far more trustworthy men in the world than untrustworthy men. But seeking to avoid men in lieu of women, because men are more likely to abuse and cause harm than women, is probabilistically reasonable, as they are on average less trustworthy.

Distrusted groups become consistent targets of propaganda campaigns; the socialization efforts children endure may lead them to scorn these groups as adults. Group members are ostracized within the wider population and sometimes even segregated into ghettos. The logic of propaganda campaigns is tragically simple: During the Cold War and McCarthyism, communists were libeled. Since September 11, 2001 and the War on Terror, refugees have been accused of importing trouble into the US. Moral panics sweep up all sorts of groups with allegedly untrustworthy values and interests, like the prototypical American boogeymen, homosexuals and atheists. And, as expected, poor economic times breed hyper-nationalistic obsessions and the subsequent scapegoating of immigrants (especially non-European immigrants), the poor and homeless, and other marginal groups.

Unsurprisingly, many of these groups have themselves the greatest *need* to trust, while there is little evidence that they *are* widely trusted. Refugees are unfamiliar with the new societies in which they now reside, and are divorced from their homelands, familiar customs, and familial and supportive networks. Native-born residents often resent refugees for their allegedly disruptive presence. But, to survive, let alone thrive, refugees have to be able to create trusting relations with their new neighbors (and each other).[6] When they cannot trust, bad things are likely to result. For example, Salvadoran refugees to Los Angeles were mistreated and segregated; in response, they began to adapt Black street gang organizational strategies to survive.[7] Further in the past, evidence exists that mistreatment of Italian immigrants encouraged them to *not* assimilate, thus permitting the establishment of mafia organizations in the US. Additionally, Italian and Jewish anarchism in the US was usually not the result of European anarchists relocating across the Atlantic but rather immigrants becoming anarchists *in* America, as an understandable consequence of inequality and injustice.[8]

The European refugee crisis that started in the early 2010s illustrates numerous patterns pertinent to trust. First, official "othering" can immediately diminish trust of outsiders, especially Muslims and Black Africans. Major hierarchical institutions have propelled this crisis: American imperialism, Global North-led neoliberalism, and Western support for crony leaders and autocrats in the Middle East and North Africa. These institutions surely deserve less trust than the poor and desperate multitudes fleeing problems those institutions generate. Second, a powerful solidarity has flowered in big cities and small towns, as communities and complete strangers risk their lives, and sometimes their freedom, to help refugees. Residents on the island of Lesbos, anarchist-led squats in Athens' Exarcheia neighborhood,[9] and politicized ship captains like Pia Klemp[10] have all sought to rescue and provide solace for refugees crossing the Mediterranean Sea to Europe. Humans are able to identify the common traits they share and act on the very human impulse to offer solidarity to those in need.

The unfortunately all-too-common Western equivalency of Islam with Islamic fundamentalism (including what Edward Said called orientalism[11]) has led to considerable distrust of Muslims. Islamic fundamentalism in Europe, India, the US, and elsewhere exists within a sea of grievances related to the perception and actualities of Islamophobia and anti-Muslim policy, combined with legitimate critiques of Western policy targeting the Muslim world. Support for Arab dictators, US military presence within the Muslim holy land of Saudi Arabia, war and sanctions against countries like Iraq, and the plight of the Palestinian people have fueled fundamentalist radicalization; each of these were concerns expressed by Osama bin Laden, presumed mastermind of the September 11, 2001, terror attacks in the United States. Muslims in Mumbai, London, Parisian suburbs, and Dearborn, Michigan, are apt to perceive the non-Muslim societies they live within to be distrustful of them, of wanting to control their behaviors and lives, and maybe even expel them.[12] This forms the basis for violent resistance by some in those communities, further enhancing Western distrust of Muslims in general.[13]

Anti-Muslim attitudes are thoroughly absurd on the surface. More than 3.3 million Muslims lived in the US during the decade and a half following September 11.[14] Islamophobes deliberately avoid considering how Black Muslims have lived in the US for decades and not manifested any substantive threat (beyond "scary" rhetoric from the Nation of Islam and its most charismatic spokesperson, Malcolm X). The legions of Middle Eastern Muslims (and Orthodox Christians) who moved to the US pursuing American manufacturing jobs posed no existential threat to the American "way of life", dominated as it was by white supremacy.

Distrustworthy outsiders entering the US were and remain a major source of distrust. But American distrustfulness goes back to the very origins of the United States and its treatment of indigenous people. After the completion of conquest (i.e., military defeat, the closure of the "frontier", consolidation of the reservation system), Native Americans' culture was stolen and incorporated by white America.[15] Hundreds of American Indian nations living in the Western Hemisphere were universally libeled by invading European groups as "savages".[16] The positive-sounding praise heaped upon Native Americans today—e.g., "noble warriors"—was racist criticism in the late nineteenth century when the US Army decimated various Plains tribes.[17] Whites generally view them *now* as trustworthy (if socially irrelevant and demographically vanishing), except for the whites who live adjacent to Native reservations, for whom unflattering stereotypes of "Indian givers", government "moochers", alcoholics, and the like are popular.

More broadly, ideological minorities like communists have long been feared for the most spurious of reasons. Rank-and-file communists—more so than their Communist Party leaders—often have good intentions to improve poor people's lives. During the 1930s, they were active partisans behind unionization drives and the movement of unemployed workers.[18] Amazingly, the Communist Party vocally supported the US government in World War II, since the Soviet Union was formally aligned with the US against Nazi Germany. No real social harm can be attributed to American communists in the 1950s, when they were sociopolitical pariahs thanks to the anti-communist evangelism of American senator Joseph McCarthy. Mainstream distrust directed at leftists (e.g., communists) is generated by various American institutions (i.e., media, schools, and popular culture); these institutions don't honestly explain the left's cooptation or exclusion from the mainstream, nor its widely popular goal of eliminating inequality. If the left were better understood, and not actively obscured by right propaganda, more people would surely self-identify with it.

Mainstream and elite distrust of groups who challenge the status quo have an international character too. Anti-communist (and anti-"red") fever during the Cold War existed in the context of intense *mutual* conflict. Both the US and Soviet Union had spies and sabotage efforts targeting the other, and invaded countries in their claimed spheres of influence.[19] Thus, the "Cold" War was rather "hot" throughout the world and resulted in millions of proxy deaths—the Zapatistas referred to the Cold War as "World War III". As William Blum argues, the Cold War was fundamentally a game for the superpowers to squash the self-determination of independent countries within their sphere of influence.[20] But the US was always the most powerful combatant in this conflict. Anti-communism was so intense that it served as a motivator for the US to desegregate in order to win the propaganda battle against the Soviets, who claimed correctly, if not disingenuously considering the USSR's dictatorship, that the US was not a trusting democracy because most Black Americans could not even vote.[21]

Sometimes groups transition from being untrustworthy to trustworthy—or vice versa. At the dawn of the twentieth century, immigrants from Italy, Russia, and other places in Europe were resoundingly condemned in the US by the corporate press and the US state.[22] Whether due to their darker complexions, non-Protestant religions, or extreme poverty, immigrants found themselves discriminated against. Viewed as dangerous criminals (e.g., "the mafia") or political radicals (especially anarchists), Italians and Jewish people were considered thoroughly un-American. Indeed, the FBI's origins date back to the suppression of ethnic immigrant anarchist movements, with J. Edgar Hoover's first major victory coming during the investigation of anarchist responses to the Palmer Raids.[23]

Propaganda claimed that the presence of unintelligent and criminally minded immigrants would deteriorate the quality of life in the US and even its gene pool. Once these southeastern European immigrants *properly* assimilated into respectable American-ness—especially as *white* Americans—negative stereotypes about such groups lessened,[24] particularly once Italians and Jews began to intermarry with other white Americans.

An opposite trope of trustworthy-to-untrustworthy can be seen in the transformation of Black African slaves as "happy" and content prior to emancipation in the South. This lie justified their subjugation—despite slave owners' widespread fear and paranoia about slave revolts, they sought to keep alive the myth that slaves *liked* the status quo.[25] But after emancipation, negative stereotypes surfaced of Black people as lazy, needing white discipline and direction. No longer were Blacks considered trustworthy, despite not having changed at all. This racial differentiation reflects how white supremacy nimbly refocuses mainstream attention on racist characterizations it wants people to accept.[26] These groups have been the long-term targets of intense propaganda, slanderous mythologies, rumors, and stereotypes, as well as subject to state, vigilante, and corporate attacks. The net result has been to reduce post-emancipation white American trust in Black people.

These oft-despised groups usually have far fewer reasons to be distrusted compared to those groups concerned with convincing the majority of this claim. In other words, the people who convince us to distrust are usually less trustworthy than those they are trying to libel.[27] For example, a standard argument for why immigrants should not be trusted, and thus barred from the US, is that they are criminally inclined. In fact, the opposite is true.[28] Immigrants commit fewer crimes than American tourists abroad—a reflection of how dedicated each group is to respecting the laws of the places they are presently residing in. In addition, immigrants are disproportionately employed in the lowest-paid and most dangerous jobs (e.g., farm work, meat-processing, unskilled labor), a consistent pattern for centuries. According to historian Aviva Chomsky, there are numerous fallacious myths about immigration in the US, all of which serve to undermine solidarity and trust between immigrants and the native-born: Immigrants take "our jobs"; they drive down wages; they don't pay taxes; they are a drain on the economy; the US is being "overrun"; the US has a generous refugee policy; they don't assimilate; they don't learn English; and so forth.[29] Despite all this, immigrant communities enjoy higher levels of social capital, thereby providing solidarity against outside threats and general safety.

Atheists, perhaps the most despised group listed above (e.g., approximately half of Americans said they'd be unhappy if a family married an atheist[30]), often have clear moral codes, which are not radically different from the rest of Christian America. In fact, atheists are not more likely to violate laws or norms than anyone else, while the percentage of the religious in American prisons happens to be significantly higher than the free population.[31] Sociologist Émile Durkheim argued in *The Elementary Forms of Religious Life* that ethical behavior is independent of religious affiliation or belief; indeed, morality equates to human solidarity. Social responsibility and affinity are the essence of morality,[32] factors that are present among atheists and theists.

Digging behind standard justifications for distrust reveals a lot about how the dominant society functions—and for whose benefit. Consider "criminals", for example. While criminals are universally distrusted in modern societies, it is highly contested as to who exactly is considered a "criminal".[33] In fact, most people have violated laws during their lifetimes, but faced little consequence for those acts because they were never "caught".[34] Intensive policing of certain communities—often poor and people of color—has meant that those who are already highly disadvantaged face the greatest likelihood of capture. Stereotypes about criminals and perceptions of their criminality varies, as do definitions of criminality across time, space, and group. Certain things that are now not legal were illegal during other times. Some jurisdictions have laws against one behavior, while others do not. And some groups have been expressly forbidden to do things that others were allowed to do. To distrust someone simply because they have the "criminal" label applied to them overlooks the other aspects of their lives where they may be trustworthy and how "non-criminals" may be untrustworthy.[35]

A strong illustration of this can be seen by comparing people who have homes with those who are homeless. People who have "legitimate" homes (that they legally own or rent) are allowed to do a wide variety of activities because of their economic position. They can sleep whenever they like, hang out doing mostly anything they wish, engage in sexual behavior, and drink alcohol. The homeless are unable to do any of these things with any security and are routinely harassed and arrested by police for doing exactly what people with homes do regularly without consequence. This is not because the homeless are untrustworthy, but because laws targeting vagrancy, loitering, indecent exposure, and public intoxication have been *created* that criminalize the actions, bodies, and lives of homeless people.

Criminality's socially constructed nature can be seen by contrasting alleged criminals with police. While this may seem a simple, stark comparison, the two groups are often more similar than either would care to admit. Law enforcement has often enforced terrible things, such as slave patrols who enforced the white supremacist laws of slavery. Police have also engaged in all manner of unethical activities, like corruption, drug dealing, and physical violence against citizens and each other.[36] Due to such lower ethical standards among police, they receive low trust from heavily policed communities (especially poor people of color). The striking similarities between the values and personalities of criminals and law officers are more serious: Past studies have shown that police and prison guards are more likely than the general population to have antisocial personalities, comparable to prisoners (for example, prison employee tolerance of rape).[37] Both groups—criminals and police—act "above the law"; criminals in pursuit of profit, power, or desire, and police because they *are* law enforcers. The people who enforce rules do not usually have any incentive to enforce it upon themselves. External force is generally the only means of accountability.[38]

The distrust heaped upon many groups has an effect larger than the sum of its parts. Arguably, the greater the number of distrusted groups in a society, the lower the overall trust levels in that society. This conclusion suggests that demonization of large numbers of social groups has a negative impact on a society's ethos. The paranoid distrust of supposedly problematic, threatening, and dangerous groups indicates a broad social psychosis. Consequently, a huge coalition of hierarchical institutions are mobilized to attack distrusted elements. For example, the presence of Native Americans on the US "frontier" provoked widespread distrust between indigenous nations and white settlers, producing predictably violent consequences. While this artificially increased trust among whites and among many Native nations (à la Georg Simmel, as they unified against their common enemy[39]), it also brought the full weight of the US's new systems of domination to bear on the distrusted Natives: The US Army was mobilized, as were Christian missionaries, alcohol salesmen, scalp bounty hunters, and—once containment had been achieved—the Bureau of Indian Affairs and boarding school directors. All worked in loose concert to force the distrusted Native to submit and Americanize, disappear on reservations, or die. Many institutions of domination created to control and subjugate experience "mission creep" as they expand. For example, one of the US Army's primary original tasks was to engage in war with indigenous Americans, but over time it came to be a robust fighting force that expanded into Latin America, eventually establishing military bases throughout the world.[40]

Distrusted groups are presented via mainstream culture and media as unlikely to reciprocate any trust extended them, immoral (at least to the mainstream standard of "morality"), and anti-status quo. These orientations make distrusted, less powerful groups a "threat" to the mainstream. Anarchists are a perfect example of this; throughout the whole modern era, they have been absurdly portrayed as criminal elements, just as likely to knife a fellow worker as they were to assassinate a czar or president. In 1908, Theodore Roosevelt called anarchists "the enemy of humanity, the enemy of all mankind", while others condemned them as having mental disorders.

Anarchists' purported untrustworthiness is an odd conclusion when contrasted against those libeling them as such. Compared to other "extremists", anarchist violence is very rare, largely due to deeply held values about the sanctity of life and freedom.[41] However, those calling anarchists violent, such as US Democrats and Republicans, are unequivocally the most violent elements in society. The former dropped bombs on Hiroshima and Nagasaki, escalated the Vietnam War, bombed Kosovo, and expanded a murderous, unaccountable drone warfare program, while the latter overthrew the democratically elected Guatemalan president, bombed Cambodia to ruins, engineered a coup in Chile, funded the barbaric Contra guerrillas of Nicaragua, and invaded Panama numerous times and Iraq twice. Historian Howard Zinn noted that anarchists oppose the world of disorder, violence, and terror that nation states and capitalism sustain and promote,[42] while David Graeber claimed that "one thing anarchists will never be good at is large-scale violence".[43] Despite this, society perversely labels anarchists as violent.

All of these minority and less powerful groups have endured sustained distrust from the dominant US society for generations. But curiously, many institutions in the US have also seen a decrease in trust over recent decades. Since the start of the Covid-19 pandemic, trust in governments has declined throughout the world, according to an Edelman survey.[44] For example, in 2024, only 5 percent of

US residents reported having "a great deal of confidence" in the US Congress, 9 percent had similar such confidence in major companies; while 31 percent in 2017 professed "not very much" or no trust at all in the police.[45]

So, an interesting question is whether low levels of support for powerful institutions in the US is reflective of a recent, general crisis, or a long-standing, anti-systemic preference? Evidence suggests that the 1960s introduced changes that destabilized US society and its institutions (and the rest of the world), provoking not only distrust but systemic disaffection with America. Resistance to states like the US have arguably occurred since before they were formed— for example, indigenous resistance to European settlement, slave rebellion, and anti-colonial resistance to empire (such as in Latin America and southeast Asia). Large numbers of people have been distrustful for a very long time, although not usually sampled via survey techniques.

Most institutions have not been around quite as long as states, at least in terms of human history. One notable exception may be patriarchy, whose multi-millennia existence has evolved but remained dominant until very recently (and arguably still is). Interestingly, repeated surveys (like the GSS and the World Values Survey) have not asked about respondent confidence in *this* institution. Given how females are deeply integrated within social structures governed largely by men—and cannot really gain "independence" from them or easily remain segregated—how could women "escape" patriarchy in the manner that James C. Scott notes elsewhere?[46] And how about all the people who can't escape due to the state's power and reach, especially in the modern era where states have so much technological capacity to intrude upon our lives?

The impulse to trust is transmitted hierarchically. Usually those whom elites and dominant culture consider trustworthy are judged "worthy" of society's trust. However, this implies that largely distrusted groups have not done enough to accrue trustworthiness or have actively reduced others' ability to trust them. For example, people may believe gays offend straight people's sense of decency, atheists blaspheme sacred Christian symbols, or immigrants steal "our" jobs and are dangerous. These assumptions are easily disprovable and rest on conjecture alone. Additionally, for every "indecent" gay person we can point to, there are not only numerous decent ones but numerous indecent straight people. What is blasphemous toward a sacred symbol lies in the eyes of the accuser. And so on. Treating all group members the same is essentialist, inaccurate, and absurd. But the enduring "wisdom" of these stereotypes and dominant orientations of trust are reflected time and again in surveys, which show many Americans would not trust such people to be teachers or allow them to speak in public.

Often generalized social trust is really an out-group orientation—it focuses on how well we trust those who are unlike us.[47] In other words, the measurement of social trust really assesses othering. I'd like to argue that the "us" we're considering regarding social trust be expanded to include those typically "othered" (e.g., strangers, people of different nationalities or different religions), and that the "other" should really describe people in power and authority.

GETTING WHO-NOT-TO-TRUST WRONG

Sadly, many Americans have an inaccurate view of society and misperceive their relationship to it. In particular, many assume that they are part of the small minority who acts with principle. This rather widely held belief does not stand up to scrutiny: If most people assume this—that they are the good ones—they may well be "good", but it cannot be the case that most others are "bad". If almost everyone self-identifies as good and trustworthy but calls others untrustworthy, who are we to believe? I suspect we're generally right about our impressions regarding ourselves (that we are good) but wrong in our impressions about others (that they are bad). What's more reasonable to believe: that we are partially incorrect (about others) or that most everyone else is partially incorrect (including about us)?

These misperceptions imply a lack of trust in how others represent themselves and their experiences. People who possess false class consciousness may believe *they* are oppressed but not those other people ("I'm struggling to make it, but those other people are just lazy!"). Amazingly, this is even true of those who have incredible privileges—middle-class white males in particular. Faulty logic and ignorance is at the heart of this misperception too. Many of the same people who reject the existence of "racism" cry foul on any mention of the existence of race, claiming "reverse-racism". The thing that allegedly doesn't *exist* (racism) actually hurts *them* the most, the people who don't believe it. This doesn't mean that poor and working-class white males have no legitimate complaints— they're right that the economic system isn't necessarily set-up to benefit them. But capitalism has benefited them a bit more as a group than women and people of color. Needless to say, we're error-laden judges of other people's intentions and social standings. We have America's usual hierarchical institutions (capitalism, the state, patriarchy, white supremacy, etc.) to thank for this, in addition to mainstream media, ultra-individualistic Ayn Rand-ian fantasies, and other engines of misperception. How can we trust people—sincerely, meaningfully, lovingly, committedly—when we don't even understand the basics of their lives?

Ultimately, many accepted social phenomena, organizations, and practices are premised upon broad social trust. For this reason, they are under constant attack—things like libraries, public education, parks, and other public spaces and commons. Linguist Noam Chomsky has argued that a primary reason why Social Security Insurance (SSI) is regularly attacked by the US right wing (who have advocated for privatizing it) is because of SSI's philosophical foundation of social trust and solidarity. According to Chomsky, SSI is underwritten by the simple idea that people should care about other people, including the grandmother on the other side of town you've never met and likely never will. It is human, according to Chomsky, to care for others and this natural solidarity coincidentally gets in the way of the rich's ability to profit off the poor.[48] Since SSI has worked so well and is so popular, the right wing has tried to undermine support for it, claiming it's overdrawn, going bankrupt, funds selfish seniors, that it's *your money* and you should be able to use it whenever you want, and so on. That entire generations of right-wing activists have fought, mostly unsuccessfully, to convince people that others are not worth caring about, speaks volumes to the immense value behind such a belief.[49]

The old, perhaps original, sentiment of deep human bonds and connection has only recently come under this kind of threat. Even just a century earlier, working Americans extended class solidarity to each other. This was a common feature across working-class communities, dating back centuries to Europe's medieval-era guilds and brotherhoods. US history is replete with stories of solid unity during strikes, wherein customers would not cross picket lines where their neighbors worked, while other workers would engage in sympathy strikes (this was so ideologically repugnant to elites that the 1947 Taft–Hartley Act outlawed sympathy strikes). Neighbors minded each other's kids, often in large numbers, fewer people felt compelled to lock their doors at night, and crime prevention strategies relied on "eyes on the street", often elderly people who knew everyone and could brow-beat the teenager who stole some cash or beers out of a neighbor's unlocked apartment. While not without its problems or contradictions, such principled, objective trust allowed working and poor people to defend their interest from external threats.

Why do people remain paranoid and ill-informed of others' intentions? Sociologist Barry Glassner's *Culture of Fear* documents how mass media often exaggerates minimal risks, while ignoring some of the most dangerous things we face. Amazingly, as moral panic spread through the media about crime in the 1990s, crime rates were actually going down.[50] This suggests our perceptions of what we should fear are not always reliable, especially when those with social power (like media) encourage us to think in certain ways. Inevitably, who we trust is defined as those we *don't distrust* (a double-negative), rather than a positive form of trust. The distrusted pose a more immediate threat and loom nefariously in our minds, regardless of reality.

If we distrust the *wrong* social actors, we reduce the likelihood of seeing common cause with our peers and critique those in power. Witness the broad attack against unions and the public sector in

Europe and North America. For example, in the UK this involved an attack on class solidarity, most clearly seen by Thatcher's undermining of the miner's union and the privatization of numerous public sector enterprises (e.g., British Telecom, British Aerospace, British Gas, British Petroleum, Rolls-Royce, British Airways). Her oft-repeated claim that "there is no such thing as society" aimed to reduce social solidarity in groups like "selfish miners", labor unionists, immigrants, Londoners, and others who saw social relationships outside the market as being more important than the foolishness of selfishness.

The right-ward pitch of many European societies (e.g., far-right party successes in France, Hungary, Italy, and Poland) indicates a growing distrust in humanity, but one focused on the most disadvantaged: the poor, refugees, and non-Christian religious groups (especially Muslims). Sizable minorities of these countries have decided the primary problems they face come from "outsiders" and people suffering great hardships, rather than dominant institutions that make life difficult for everyone.

Ultimately, this means we trust only those we are unwilling to place in the distrusted category yet. Some groups of individuals are not *yet* criminals or dangerous. Here I argue it is worth designating the trustworthy and distrustworthy not simply as opposites but in terms of their relations to power. We may make a few mistakes in doing so, but on the whole this approach is far more accurate. To do so, we must consider whether trust is an outcome or a source of something else.

TRUST IN ELITES

Depending on your vantage point, the long-term destabilization of trust in ruling institutions is either a horrifying foreshadowing of things to come or a blessing in disguise. Who is "elite" or what such a change ultimately means is unclear.

Although we don't have survey data for it, most communal societies presumably had incredibly high trust in the small, localized institutions that governed their lives. Those "institutions" were immediate, reasonable, and inoculated through heavy socialization. Village communities had (and have) considerably horizontal social relations, a popular decision-making and judicial process, and few elites to cause problems. Despite the massive inequality experienced during the ancient and feudal eras, there was likely higher trust (as we're defining it here) compared to now. The interdependence of estate institutions (e.g., church, aristocracy, peasantry) may have improved trust, despite the disempowerment felt by the peasantry. The noble obligation (*noblesse oblige*, according to Max Weber[51])— of the aristocracy to provide for the peasantry in times of need and to defend against external threat—was part of an arrangement in which the three estates owed each other and had to cooperate. In other words, the more powerful were expected and ultimately required to help the less powerful.

Even acknowledging the US's ultra-individualistic origins does not deny that early American life was highly communal (the unavoidably large exceptions of slavery and indentured servitude aside) and trusting (at least among property-owning white males). Of course, the industrial revolution began to change all this. But a big nail in the coffin of elite trust occurred during the post-1960s crisis—experienced most profoundly in the West—with the disruption of the ruling consensus constructed in the US following World War II. The détente between labor and management disintegrated, the taken-for-grantedness of free domestic female labor was forever lost, and the second-class citizenship of non-whites was formally rejected. These changes, while absolutely good, paralleled a sharp decline in political trust. Stable and reliable jobs, placid families, and a polite yet violent racial order were all called into question. There was a resurgence of poor countries struggling along the periphery of the world-system through anti-colonial movements, which involved the universalizing of many opportunities and social democratic policies created throughout the world on behalf of the most vulnerable. In the US, the violent, endless Vietnam War and Nixon's Watergate scandal undermined institutional trust. Since the start of this period, universal, government entitlement programs have faced unrelenting attack by right-wing forces and Libertarian-style

Figure 2.1a   Uncivil Sphere Institutions

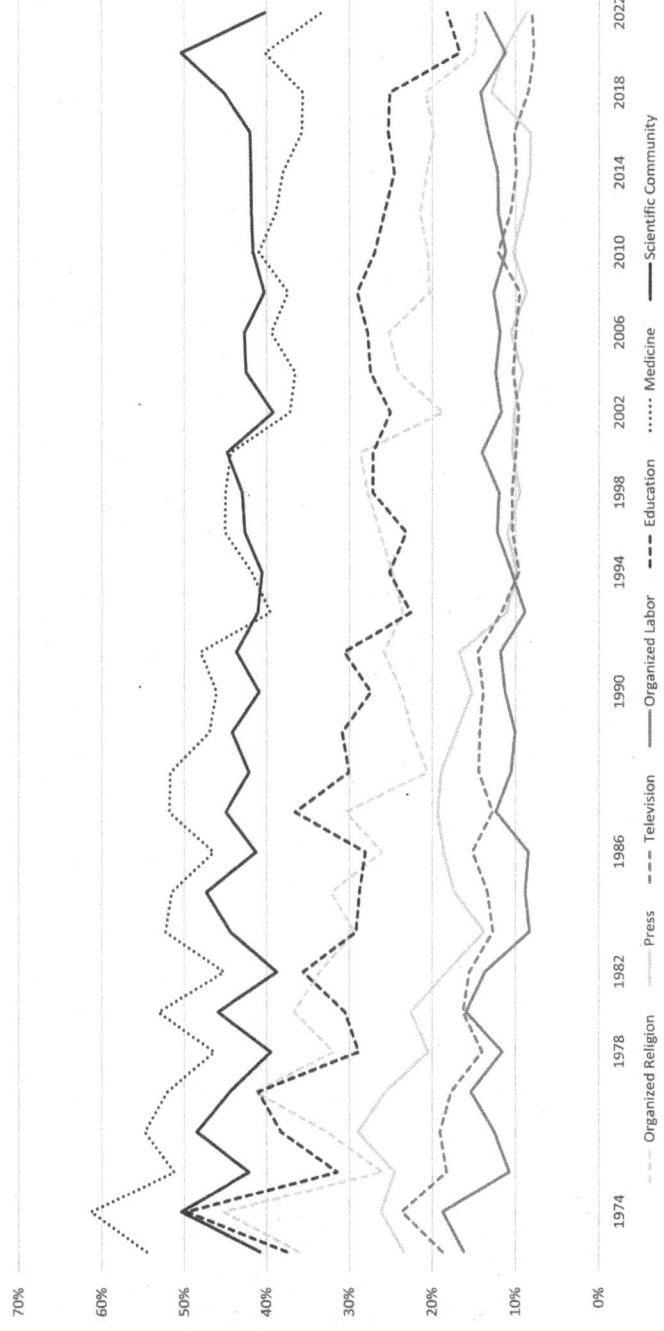

Figure 2.1b Civil Sphere Institutions

Note: Figures 2.1a and 2.1b show the state of institutional trust—contrasting uncivil sphere (economic and political elites) and civil sphere—since the 1970s.

austerity, simply because they threatened the powerful's hegemony, technological innovations, and media tools.

The decline in institutional confidence following the tumultuous 1960s is stark: Sizable drops in trust across most institutions occurred. Figures 2.1a and 2.1b show the state of institutional trust since the 1970s. Purportedly neutral institutions like medicine have experienced a 20-percentage point drop from 1973 through 2018 (partly due to perceptions of unethical behavior by doctors[52]), while education dropped over ten percentage points. The US Supreme Court did not lose much trust over time, although it has hovered around a paltry 30 percent of the US population expressing a "great deal of confidence" in it. The US Congress dropped nearly 20 points, making it the least trusted US institution (approximately 5 percent of adults had a great deal of confidence in it).[53] Notably, the military had recovered much of the confidence it lost in the post-Vietnam era, nearly doubling its support to become the most trusted institution, enjoying 60 percent confidence. Yet, the most dramatic increase in support for the military occurred in 1991 when the US invaded Iraq, thus depicting the "rally-round-the-flag effect" where public opinion is distorted by groupthink patriotism.[54]

While these survey questions—pulled from the multi-decade GSS—are often understood to embody the concept of "political trust", it is important to remember that "politics" does not simply imply states and statecraft. Although some of these institutions are clearly components of the US state, not all are. At its core, politics is about the public struggle over power to make decisions that affect society. If "politics" is democratic, rowdy, and anti-authoritarian, then politics might actually exist in opposition to statecraft. Thus, "political trust" may be an inappropriate label, simply standing in for "trust in the state (and its various hierarchical agencies and bureaucracies)".[55] Understood this way, loss of trust in "the system" implies a rejection of the state having the sole claim to political power.

Occasionally, this political distrust has been revolutionary. It helped topple the feudal systems of Europe and the Russian czardom, and it was a major force in the liberatory movements of the 1960s. There is good reason for growing political distrust—

existing state-based political systems prop up the hegemonic, bureaucratized, and structural mechanisms that propagate inequality, violence, and disempowerment. Since 1968, these systems have become better understood thanks to the actions of American social movements. These movements broke with many orthodoxies but couldn't surpass them all completely. The system was able to eventually regain control, and purchase or barter for greater political trust again. Racial or gender justice has come to mean—for many—not medical *system* change but managers of color or female bosses, or the ability to elect non-white, non-male presidents. This is surely a myopic conception of what was sought by many in those movements!

While those radical, anti-authoritarian movements have not succeeded, the developments they brought have been generally positive. There has been a broadening of civil liberties to previously unincorporated groups, a tolerance for critical speech, a liberalization of gender and sexual mores (and freedoms), and a radical critique of violence and power—especially state violence, central in war-making, policing, and prisons. The popular 1960s youth slogan "question authority" embodies these positive results, but the slightly more cynical and exclusionary slogan of the era—"don't trust anyone over thirty"—wasn't quite as helpful. Although older people were and are more likely to be *in* authority, that's not necessarily or even usually true (i.e., most elders are not "elites"). And the problems aren't due to the ages of the people staffing positions in hierarchical institutions, it's the institutions themselves and the values guiding them.

Growing political distrust is only a problem if it is not replaced by growing, strong social trust, with people simply spreading their ample distrust in "the system" to everyone else. In other words, moving to a position of across-the-board distrust implies an anti-human nihilism that isn't helpful for creating positive social change.

A comparable situation occurred in the recent past. The 1960s is presented through popular culture as a breakdown in society's moral order, as well as a disruption of political trust. By the 1970s, there were massive levels of crime, drug abuse, widely publicized atrocities, chaos, urban decay, and fear of others. People could have compensated for throwing-off their reliance and trust in the state by trusting their fellow Americans. Instead, the populace generally turned cynical against its social peers. Some of this was surely state-directed hostility against social trust—see the Nixonian reaction against Black radicals, drug use, rock music, permissive sexual mores, and general anti-authoritarianism—but it was also due to the adaptability of hierarchical American culture, as well as failures in the anti-authoritarian left.

Granted, this narrative of the 1960s is not the only accurate story, as the 1970s saw an explosion of anti-elitist, cooperative movements, along with the transference of activists and organizers from civil rights, anti-war, and other movements into community struggles and second-wave feminism. Communal living, worker and consumer cooperatives, and innumerable ecological projects all emphasized human beings' interconnection with each other—not our disconnection. But, problematically, many of these efforts *did* serve to divide the alternative activists from mainstream society (as opposed to bringing them along). In some cases, people who were influenced by these same communalist tendencies joined New Age movements, opting out on a case-by-case basis as opposed to struggling for collective, social change. The escape from scary cities to rural communes accompanied the countercultural slogan of "turn on, tune in, drop out". This escapism involved consciously willed trust focused on narrow and deliberate targets, while not having to trust anyone else. New age trust avoided directly challenging hierarchical systems, giving the latter a free pass to perpetuate the status quo.

DISTRUST WITHIN ANTI-ELITE CONSPIRACY THEORIES

We live in an era of dizzying, but also unsurprising, conspiracy theories. The US is a cauldron of such paranoias: At least half the American population endorse one or more popular conspiracy theories.[56] Conspiracy theories stem from distrust and generate continued distrust, sometimes of powerful groups and sometimes the less powerful.

Needless to say, conspiracy theories have a complicated relationship to elites and trust. While distrust in elites and their claims is very reasonable, these skeptical attitudes are often deemed "conspiracy theories", especially when they lack substantial evidence. Ironically, conspiracy theories (not the alleged conspiracies themselves) actually benefit certain groups of elites, albeit in limited ways. For example, consider so-called "9/11 truthers": people who believe that the terror attacks of September 11, 2001, were an "inside job" of US elites, involving on-site detonation of the World Trade Center towers. Truthers' views indirectly benefit elites, since their belief in a "deep state" conspiracy to destroy the Twin Towers (as a false-flag operation against radical Islamists) downplays the very real global animosity that US foreign policy has generated for decades, and how the towers were a predictable target for those opposed to US-style capitalism and empire—such as radical Islamists. And despite the substantial damage done to elite financial corporations (in terms of property, highly skilled personnel, and short-term stock market value), truthers still think that elites let the attacks happen. In other words, so-called conspiracy theories often get things wrong; arriving at correct conclusions requires trust in empirical evidence, information exchange, and peers. Elites are reluctant to offer such resources, especially when conspiracy theories distract from systemic critiques of empire and capitalism.

Often the general and reasonable critique of elites is slandered as "conspiracy theory", thus discouraging a systemic analysis of power. For example, by referring to anti-World Trade Organization arguments as "conspiracy theories", pro-elite forces are able to use the label as a linguistic weapon to attack dissidents who are simply critically analyzing powerful actors, thereby undermining the trust that dissidents share with the general public. Some people, through lack of trust in common people's analytical skills, may side against their peers—all under the manipulative influence of elites. A common antisemitic trope inspired by the fabricated Protocols of the Elders of Zion argues that Jews control world affairs. This has led the right to claim that wealthy Jewish banker George Soros manipulates US politics by paying leftist protesters to attend rallies against police, fascists, and—stunningly—capitalism. The wealthy do indeed dominate the world, but it's not a single Jewish person doing it in private; instead, it's a few thousand wealthy people—most of whom are *not* Jewish—doing it via the stock market, completely out in the open.[57]

According to political scientists Russell Muirhead and Nancy Rosenblum, contemporary conspira*cism* is classic conspiracy theory devoid of the theory—conspiracism lacks any useful argument of *why* or *how* something is happening, in addition to a lack of compelling data. They describe the quite crazy claim that Hillary Clinton was running a sex-trafficking ring out of a Washington, DC-area pizzeria (called "Pizzagate"), which lacks any orienting theory of *why* she would be doing this. Such conspiracism can easily spread, despite its illogical arguments.

Distrust can be generated by powerful groups seeking to destabilize their competitors. Muirhead and Rosenblum point to political parties as early "conspiracies" in colonial American history—out-of-power forces critiquing the dominant order.[58] Parties of the past were real conspiracies (as was the elite-led Business Plot in the 1930s[59]), serving real purposes, for which there is much data demonstrating them to be real. Thus, conspiracies can be real things; but appending the word "theory" to "conspiracy" implies the conspiracy doesn't really exist. For example, the Twin Towers really *did* collapse on September 11, 2001; but there is scant evidence of a plot by the US government (let alone American Jews) actively or passively participating in this destruction. Noam Chomsky and others have challenged truthers, arguing that the correct way to convincingly demonstrate that the towers were detonated by explosives (and not two jet planes flown at a high velocity) would be for engineers making such claims to present their "evidence" to peers and open it up for debate. No engineer has managed to publish such evidence in a peer-reviewed venue.

All this is relevant for trusting elites, since actual conspiracies require trust among conspirators and a distrust of the wider world. Conspiratorial people distrust elites who run some dimension of society. Additionally, conspiracy theories are propagated by people who have some reason to distrust elites but do not have an appropriate framework to place their critique and distrust within. Consequently, conspiracy theories—by offering ludicrous "strawmen" for elites to point to and discredit—actually empower elites in their efforts to dissuade people from engaging in any critical analysis of elite power. "Rich people don't run the world—that's just a crazy conspiracy theory! We are a democracy!" This ultimately undercuts the ability of everyday people to trust their own power and each other, and stymies efforts to engage in struggle against elites. Empirical evidence is important in countering these dismissals, as sociologist G. William Domhoff has done in his careful, multi-decade analyses of the American power elite—which he locates within the corporate elite nationally, and large property owners and developers locally—who are able to strongly influence policy outcomes in their favor.[60]

Importantly, conspiracy theories have the latent consequence of introducing chaos, paranoia, and distrust into society. Philosopher Jason Stanley argues this is why fascists are particularly fond of conspiracy theories: Such ideas can destabilize the existing order and disorient the mass population, thus permitting a strongman to assert dominance and deliver the society from its purported evils by way of a simple (and reductionist) Truth that will wipe the slate clean.[61] To the extent that conspiracy theories (or conspiracies) make us lose our trust in each other, they serve the ultimate ends of empowering the already powerful.

TRUST IN THE RIGHT CONTEXT

Even though social trust is generally a good thing, its expression still remains conditional for many people, and rightfully so. Trust is extended under some circumstances and not others, even toward the same people. It's only the most special people—usually those we are close to, intimate with, or related to—that we have unconditional trust in.

But most people we encounter are not friends and family, and while they may be trustworthy in some regards, we reserve judgment for future settings. People may alter their assessments of trustworthiness due to how a person acts or responds in certain situations. Someone acting drunk, lecherous, or mischievous is likely to be treated differently than if (or when) they are sober, polite, or orderly. Thus, under temporary conditions, someone who may generally be trustworthy will be held at arm's length due to heavy drinking, displays of toxic masculinity, rambunctiousness, and the like.

Some people may be trustworthy for some tasks but not others. For example, someone may be a loyal friend and kindhearted but not show up on time for their agreed-upon obligations. Usually, we come to learn the extent to which someone can be trusted and for what purposes, thus trusting them "just so far". In times of intense conflict or change, people may show up more often and become more trustworthy, but when the pressure is off, become flaky and unreliable again. This variability may have to do with whom that person is accountable to: They may show up on time for meals with their stern grandmother but be less punctual with an activist meeting where they are afforded great leeway. Predictably, people can be trusted to help out their close friends more than strangers, and thus someone's flakiness has more to do with whether the flake trusts those to whom they are accountable.

Since everyone is different, there is no reason to expect uniform behavior from others. After tentatively "feeling out" a relationship, though, we usually develop a clearer sense of how much someone can be trusted and in what ways. Thus, with time, tentative caution can hopefully transform into social trust in most situations. For relationships established with untrustworthy individuals (who otherwise lack power), this tentative-trust trial period will eventually reveal such an individual's bad judgment, bad intentions, or general untrustworthiness—even brief contact can be helpful for improving trust decisions.[62] Of course, immediate radical trust is unlikely and overly ambitious, but we should be open to the latent potential of our fellows and willing to expand our trust circles. Since trust is established in relationships, they must somehow be created in the first place—this requires initiative.

Trust thrives in special climates, under the right conditions. It's easier to expect generosity, kindness, accountability, and reliability when there is less social inequality. Without such ideal conditions, trust tends to become more strained. Try as we might, efforts to build trust in a severely unequal and violent society will be difficult to say the least.

Even though trust in others is often a wise decision, it's important to not "over trust". While it'd be wonderful to live in a world where every single person could be trusted, there is just too much variability in people's personalities, psyches, and interests for such a uniform approach. More importantly, by automatically trusting the judgment of others in the group, we may be facilitating a course of action detrimental to the group and ourselves (especially in terms of the powerful). Thus, it's important for people to "trust" others at the same time they critically consider other peoples' ideas. Allowing people to not go along with the entire group shouldn't be viewed as distrust. Just because a friend doesn't share the same interests or value the same goals as most of their other friends doesn't make them untrustworthy. Another example of this problem may be an activist group that functions on the basis of consensus decision-making. If the group members are overly committed to eliminating all conflict or disagreement, individual members may try to find only the safest road to travel, not challenge group assumptions, and may even acquiesce to charismatic leaders.

Ideally, when everyone decides to respect collectively agreed upon rules, trust can flourish. Acknowledging and tolerating dissent is especially important. This is analogous to how certain games are played, where players all have influence over the game's play parameters and consent to the game's rules. For example, poker or sports like boxing require people to be fair and not cheat, but do not imply consensus or uncomplicated cooperation. Trust of a sort can exist when the playing field is conflicted, yet fair. But if one person always deals the cards or if boxers' physical sizes are mismatched, the game is unfair and privileges one over another.

Some people are trustworthy in some regards but not in others. We can be sure they will do certain things but still not trust in their cooperation with us. For many people in the US, especially working-class people of color, the police may be trusted to be hostile toward them, but it is risky to extend trust toward them, as police may try to entrap, arrest, or attack them based on implicit biases. If we are in a dangerous situation or having a medical emergency, the presence of hierarchical authorities doesn't always equate to greater risks. Sometimes, a single police officer or work supervisor can do incredibly helpful things for us, maybe even save our lives. Humans of all varieties can rise to the occasion, despite privileges, inequalities, and socialization. Thus, it is the context and status that matters most. This reflects anarchists' appraisal of the state: The state can be trusted to be generally oppressive, bureaucratic, and indifferent to non-elite human needs. This suggests that we "trust" some hierarchies to be predictable but distrust their intentions toward us.

TRUSTING AND TRUSTWORTHINESS

Social scientists typically use survey questions that ask respondents if they have confidence in various institutions. Problematically, this conflates trust with trustworthiness—or, rather, confidence with confidence-worthiness. I may "distrust" the police (be wary around them, expect belligerence, etc.) but have full trust or "confidence" that they will act to enforce racial hierarchies. But what is most important is that I do not find them trustworthy, that is, find value in trusting them. While we should be trusting those who are trustworthy and distrusting those who are untrustworthy, reality is not always so simple. So, I explore below the complications and disjunctures between trust and trustworthiness in a series of comparisons.

To trust the trustworthy makes good sense. For example, friendships are evidence of how we regularly trust those who are well intentioned toward us. We can build relationships and other things with trustworthy people. This is the ideal nature of a well-functioning society. An equally good idea is to distrust untrustworthy people. There are lots of institutions that warrant our skepticism, if not outright rejection. Due to their inherent nature and power over us, it's reasonable to be skeptical of police, employers, and fascists. Thus, our efforts at cop-watching, militant unionism, and antifascism also make good sense—this orientation is practical self-defense and involves necessary actions to prevent delusion. Both trusting the trustworthy and distrusting the untrustworthy are logical, easy decisions to make.

However, people don't always follow a rational or reasonable course of action, even when assessing someone's trustworthiness. (And sometimes an assessment of trustworthiness is impractical or impossible.) These divergent patterns round out this typology. First, trusting untrustworthy people is a bad idea. For example, believing confidence-men, treacherous politicians (is there another kind?), or a "friendly" boss, will lead us to be taken advantage of, "getting burned", and exploited. Ideally, instances in which we trust those who do not deserve it are rare and hopefully accidental. Unfortunately, many dynamics can obscure our vision and logic; for example, abusive or philandering romantic partners often have sophisticated strategies for deception, apologizing, and reverse-psychology that makes a victim believe it was their fault. The same is true for experienced, well-funded, and agile actors who desperately rely on our tacit trust, and profit immensely when they can secure it.

Also, distrusting trustworthy people is a bad idea. Lots of people "deserve" our trust, but don't readily get it. For example, we regularly fear strangers and expect the worst from them. Many tend to be suspicious of "others" regularly demonized by US society. As noted at the beginning of this chapter, if we don't know much about—let alone personally know any—immigrants, Muslims, atheists, LGBTQ+ folks, and so on, then we may be hesitant to trust them. Even though both parties would benefit from trust, we lose the opportunity. Ideally, this mistake is also a temporary occurrence that will cease once a rapport can be built between people, transitioning from ignorant distrust into informed trust. The problem is that all the reasons that lead to distrust initially will likely stay in place unless they are formally challenged. Many people are unwilling or uninterested in challenging their preconceptions of others, and there are powerful institutions invested in maintaining social distrust and othering.

Thus, the challenge is knowing how to correctly assess a potential trust target and then prudently act on that assessment. At the heart of this analysis is the reality that both beneficial trust and harmful trust exist (just as there is beneficial distrust and harmful distrust). Beneficial trust extends positive benefits to both parties—social trust is a good example of this. Having thick trust—deep and varied—with many people creates a more vibrant, strong, creative, and adaptable community. But sometimes trust is harmful, as it extends a positive benefit to only one party, while the other loses out. Political trust is often (although not exclusively) an example of this: Politicians, political parties, the state, and all its various agencies and apparatuses gain far more advantage from citizens' political trust than those same citizens do. The consequences are even more extreme for non-citizen residents (i.e., immigrants). When an undocumented immigrant trusts the political system enough to call the police, they may not only endanger their community but very likely themselves.

To determine trust and trustworthiness for a given population, surveys are often used. Survey questions about "confidence" imply at least three rather different things. First, confidence may simply be a proxy for *likability*—for example, a positive appraisal of the police. This characteristic is somewhat intangible and probably emotionally based. Mere reforms (e.g., the change in a police chief) could easily flip the public's perception of likability. People may "like" someone or something with little cause or justification, perhaps basing their feelings on appearance or second-hand reputation. Second, confidence could really be about *predictability*—whether an institution or its actors will act as expected. In this regard, many on the left assess police as predictable—they are apt to side with fascists over antifascists during a street demonstration, for example. Thus, predictability is less about how positively the public views the police, and more about whether the public believes the police will perform in sync with popular expectations (which may be positive or negative, depending on the individual). All things being equal, can we be confident that police will do what we expect them to do? And, third, confidence could honestly be about *trustability*—how deeply does someone trust an institution. This is most relevant for assessing pro- or anti-authoritarianism, as trustability pertains to the structural purpose, practice, execution, and outcomes of the police in general. In other words, do people find themselves in sympathy with the mission of policing? And, since trust implies a willingness to take risks, are people willing to take a risk and rely on the police (i.e., hope the police respond when requested and deploy their capacity for force only when necessary)? But political trustability is a fickle measurement that's contingent on how well institutions are performing.

These three interpretations of "confidence" all speak to relevant issues but are clearly not the same. We may like someone but not trust them. Others may act predictably but are neither likeable or trustworthy. Regardless, most scholars have chosen to interpret survey questions about confidence as trustability. This is also the position this book adopts, not uncritically. But it's only fair to acknowledge that likability and predictability are also characteristics of confidence too.

SPECIFYING RISK

If trust is essentially the willingness to take a risk with someone or on something, then it's crucial to understand what that potential risk *is* or *could be*. The risk of trusting long-term friends is usually pretty low; they are unlikely to let us down. We can therefore take greater risks with friends. If they do let us down, it may cause a serious re-evaluation of the friendship. Trusting strangers is more complicated, because the risk is mostly unknown. It is possible that a stranger could be cruel, a thief, or violent. They may have opposing interests or values—for example, prioritizing that women be seen and not heard, or that men ought to be braggadocios. These risks appear to be more extreme than risks with friends: facing potential violence versus simply being let down. Since "strangers" are such a large group of people in society—they dwarf our friends in number—it means we're always having to reassess such risks for every new person we meet.

How about the risks involved in trusting hierarchical systems like major religions, the state, or capitalism? The individual representatives we meet from any of these (a priest from the Catholic Church, a cop from the local police force, a principal from the school district, etc.) could easily embody most of the above characteristics too. They may be cruel, sociopathic, criminally inclined, and violent, or they may be pleasant, their words honest, and their intentions plain. But since they are agents within hierarchical systems, they operate in a structural context that forces them to act on a whole other set of interests too. Large bureaucratic systems generate incredible risk, more efficiently, and on a wider scale. Additionally, the nature of these systems can make that harm or exploitation more impersonal, catastrophic, fatal, or far-reaching. The risk a soldier faces within the ranks of the US military is arithmetically more serious than the risks they face from friends, given the penchant for the military to involve itself in war-making, officers to harass and assault the rank and file, and the macho milieu to amplify the potential for interpersonal violence.[63]

If we place trust in these systems, we delay taking steps to more directly solve problems. Since hierarchies are unlikely—and probably *incapable*—of truly delivering freedom and justice, we risk "putting all our eggs in one basket". Placing trust in these systems means presuming it's less risky to trust the state to deliver on some of its lukewarm promises at poverty reduction, thus distracting our attention from investing time and effort in more fruitful possibilities. Much of these promises are lies or at best false goals. For example, the patriarchal, single-generation, nuclear-family is not only unsustainable in the long run, but undesirable for goals like justice and freedom.

If we don't know whether we should trust something or someone—and if the risk in trusting them is potentially too great—we ought to consider conducting an intellectual "threat assessment". What potential risks do we face for trusting a manager's promises versus the potential pay-off of such trust? Or, are the risks lower for trusting our fellow workers, forming a union, and engaging in collective struggle at the workplace, and thus is the pay-off higher for *this* trust? Risk is a complicated thing to assess, but assessment is worth the effort for the hazards we can avoid.

TRUST TO DO WHAT (IN PRACTICAL TERMS)?

The above is all well and good, but *what does it mean* to trust, to risk? What does social or political trust actually imply on a day-by-day basis? Unfortunately, these questions raise further questions. Let's consider social trust first. Someone who possesses social trust is able to presume that others will not attempt to kill them, nor rob from them. We may also expect to solicit help under any circumstance—extreme or routine. But what about generating an expectation that others will go to great lengths, and perhaps endure incredible risks and harm for us? Is someone with generalizable social trust able to expect others to "take a bullet" for them? Or does social trust translate more abstractly as "the Golden Rule" put into action; that we can expect others to treat us as we would like to be treated (generally)? Survey questions that ask whether "most people" can be trusted seem to imply that there are untrustworthy folks roaming around—what about them? How do we live our lives when we may surely encounter a few sociopathic and dangerous people?

The practical expectations around political trust are also nebulous. In regard to the state, does a political truster actually behave as the state wants them to? Are individuals able to assume the state will behave as *they* wish it to, in return? Presumably, a political truster thinks the state will act upon its stated values. Will an individual political truster be able to clearly understand—and accept—the state's behaviors as an expression of elites' will? In other words, how do people with political trust manage the cognitive dissonance that emerges in trusting the state, despite its repugnant behaviors that diverge from its purported values? In practice, is a political distruster better able to understand that the US state's claim of defending "life, liberty, and the pursuit of happiness" diverges from certain important realities, including: racist and classist injustices of the death penalty and the prison-industrial complex; the ravages of supporting corporate capitalism; and a century's worth of foreign coups, assassinations, invasions, wars, murder, and mass destruction?

In practical terms, social trust and political trust may manifest in some, all, or none of these forms. It's important to understand that trust is not straightforward, nor expressed uniformly by everyone, nor consistent over time. In the next chapter, I explore how social trust can be negatively impacted by social hierarchies, leading to not only the above confusions but often terrible outcomes.

3

The Cancer of Hierarchy: How Social Trust Gets Fucked Up

THE INTRUSION OF HIERARCHY IN TRUSTING RELATIONSHIPS

Everyday interpersonal relationships require and manifest trust. Yet, transgressions of that trust can quickly eliminate trust not only between the trusters, but between all other parties too. Transgressions commonly flow via hierarchical domination. In other words, hierarchy can damage trust in a way that rapidly infects all other trust relations. Indeed, as one group of scientists concluded after a vast series of experiments, "unequal-power relationships inherent in hierarchies may come at the costs of perceived conflicts of interest and low interpersonal trust".[1]

To use a personal example—although I have changed the actual names—my friend Jack had a close female friend (Kim) who was assaulted by his former roommate. Jack had not chosen the assaulter (Everett) as a roommate but lived with him nonetheless. Kim trusted Everett, due to her reasonable perception that Jack also trusted him, which led her to accept his invitation for a date (during which she was assaulted).

Many months after the incident, Kim told Jack what had happened. In addition to an array of emotions (shock, sadness, anger), Jack felt shame and a sense of failed responsibility. He had been uncritical of his former roommate's beliefs and intentions. Jack did not consider Everett's macho posturing and braggadocios sexual boasting important enough to disclose to Kim when she initially inquired about Everett. Clearly, misogynistic attitudes and uneven power relations led to Kim's assault. Even though Jack did not share his former roommate's repulsive attitudes, he did not force-fully challenge them, nor did he publicly or politically oppose them. Unfortunately, like many males with anti-sexist personal beliefs, Jack ignored warning signs of this former roommate's violent capabilities and history.[2]

Kim, and their other common friends (whom she *had* told about the assault), waited before telling Jack about the incident. Presumably, they questioned his intentions and loyalties. Her misplaced trust in Jack's well-intended friendship (and the expected disclosure of Everett's untrustworthiness that it ought to imply) rightfully ended up reducing her trust in Jack.

While Everett is an individual—who made his own terrible decisions—he was conditioned by terrible hierarchies, leading to predictable consequences. Thus, a macro-level institution like patriarchy (i.e., elder male dominance, especially of women) can easily manifest at the micro-level in our personal lives—in this case causing massive disruption in Jack and Kim's mutual trust, to say nothing of safety and health. Kim's subsequent loss of trust in Everett is a good thing; he, and his misogynist attitudes and behaviors, are not trust-worthy. And her surely reduced trust in Jack was also a reasonable precaution. Patriarchy found its way into these trust relationships and damaged them all.

The trust Jack and Kim shared took a while to heal. His trust in her was undiminished and he wanted his trust reciprocated but understood why hers might have decreased. After Jack learned of his former roommate's behavior, he was livid, thus destroying any functioning trust he may have had in Everett. Finally, the tentative, brief, expectant trust that existed between Kim and Everett was shattered by the assault, never to be repaired—for the best. This chapter explores in greater detail how hierarchy's presence—as in the lives of Jack, Kim, and Everett—can quickly eliminate egalitarian trust. Passive acceptance of hierarchies—as with Jack's passive acceptance of misogyny—is poison to trust. Trust underlies most social exchanges, which are greatly affected by hierarchy and status inequality.[3] This chapter explores just how this can happen.

HOW INEQUALITY/DOMINATION MAKES US DISTRUST

There's a lot to distrust in our modern world. You probably already have a long list of such things. Scammers trying to get money from people through deception online or over the phone. Companies spending billions of advertising dollars trying to manipulate people's emotions and sell products consumers don't want. Malevolent individuals employed within non-benevolent bureaucracies—like abusive cops, soldiers, social workers—whose everyday job requirements place them in situations that evoke distrust from others. And so on. It's totally reasonable to be skeptical of someone encouraging *more* trust in people. It's sensible to be a bit paranoid when someone says "hey, trust me!" In fact, it's probably safe to assume that those who *need* to say "trust me" deserve very little trust, just like anyone who promises anti-racism by saying "I'm not a racist, but …". There're reasons why we balk at trusting others—and hierarchy is at the heart of these reasons.

Corporate-owned mass media perpetually reinforces the lingering, suspicious distrust we hold. Its "if it bleeds, it leads" philosophy presents the very worst of human behavior front-and-center and makes malevolence seem the norm. This creates an expectation of *everyone else* as criminal and deviant, hyping the risks we face. While US crime itself decreased during the 1990s, the number of media stories covering crime continued to increase.[4] Is it any wonder that a few hours of TV viewing is linked to a dramatic decrease in someone's social distrust?[5] Consider what people see constantly on TV shows: assholes on reality shows; greedy game show contestants; crime dramas; comedy dramas about manipulative and unethical people; and local news programs that almost exclusively cover accidents, violence, and corruption. TV is a unidirectional medium, hyper-focused upon selling products to its viewers. As media critics Edward S. Herman and Noam Chomsky have pointed out, the primary customers of mass media are not viewers or readers but elite corporations who pay for advertising time or space.[6] TV's tendencies toward authoritarianism, ultra-corporatism, and nationalist pride are part of its design, and its execution is more than a little fascistic in nature. TV lures its viewers via unflattering representations of humanity, all for the purposes of manipulating those viewers' emotions, to make corporations richer.

Hierarchy has a crippling effect on people who are subject to widespread, societal domination. People with the lowest social trust are more likely to be those with less education, women, and persons of color. Occupying an unsure and unsafe social position—and knowing for certain that you're at the bottom of a social hierarchy—makes people lack confidence, be on their guard, live stressed-out lives, and so on. Consequently, a disadvantaged social position is detrimental to us personally and our relationships with others. It's *reasonable* for those who face the most discrimination, injustices, and hardships to distrust many of the people they encounter, due to their routinely negative experiences with cops, abusive intimate partners, indifferent employers, opportunistic criminal elements, and landlords. Being disempowered socializes us to trust less. This is as unsurprising as it is infuriating.

Since trust is reciprocal, disadvantaged people may trust less because they're receiving very little trust from others. Negative stereotypes about the poor, underclass, and working classes tend to be internalized. These stereotypes—that the poor are lazy, unethical, reactionary, stupid, foolish—affect how society treats the economically disadvantaged but also how the poor view themselves. Low self-esteem inhibits our ability to trust others, since we first must be able to trust ourselves. Innumerable field audit studies show that employers actively discriminate against poor people, women (especially mothers), LGBTQ+ folk, and people of color. Most notably, one study found that American employers would rather hire (and thus implicitly trust) white criminal felons than Black *non*-felons.[7] People of color, women, mothers, and queer people are less likely to be called back for job interviews or offered favorable housing compared to whites, men, fathers, and straight people.[8] If someone spends a lifetime being turned-down, disrespected, and mistreated—while seeing others around them succeed—they are more likely to conclude these experiences indicate an innate inferiority, which is what capitalist, patriarchal, and white supremacist ideology preaches.[9] Bitterness at hierarchy-generated failures generate distrustful dispositions.

American history is replete with examples of social distrust generated from hierarchical conditions. Consider anti-miscegenation policies. Some of the earliest European laws in the American colonies in the late seventeenth century were designed to prevent African–European coalitions.[10] This elite obsession wasn't just focused on fraternal, intimate, or sexual coalitions but political ones. If whites and Blacks were able to come together in love and create complex, blended families then white supremacy would have far less strategic power and ideological traction in the American colonies. Early slave rebellions in the colonies often involved white indentured servants, and the maroon communities, where runaway slaves would retreat to (often anchored in the territories of indigenous nations), included white runaways too.[11]

Later, during America's industrialization, race was strategically used as a wedge to heighten tensions between workers and prevent broader coalitions against capitalists. This split labor market paid white workers slightly more than Black workers, thus making the former fear the competitive labor potential of the latter, and making Blacks begrudge their better paid white counterparts. This served as the basis for attempts by racist elements in the US labor movement to ban non-white members and keep workplaces racially segregated. This logic also pitted each new immigrant or migrant labor force (e.g., Irish, Germans, Italians, Poles, Russians, etc.) against established, native-born white groups, under threat of lowered pay.[12] Black codes in the US South also stymied multi-racial coalitions among the working-class, encouraging a sense of superiority and inferiority among poor whites and Blacks, respectively. By preventing races from fraternizing, different groups remained ignorant of their shared class interests and lacked the temporal opportunity to build solidarity and plan their shared resistance.

Multi-racial resistance movements obviously require trust across racial groups. For example, if Blacks and anti-racist whites distrust each other, how can those whites collaborate in pursuit of justice for Black Americans? If Black people think that all whites must be distrusted, then why would they advocate for a multi-racial society, since there's no point trying to share power? In order for people from different backgrounds to work together, they must first figure out how they can trust each other. In particular, how can people of color trust the motivations of whites, who may have ulterior motives for joining the struggle? The abolitionist and civil rights movements included some white participants who primarily had *white interests* at heart, wanted to create a singularly white American society, and believed all sorts of negative, racist stereotypes about Black people. On the other hand, there have been attempts to create true trust and joint struggle. These possibilities range from being allies and comrades to whites "taking the lead" from people of color. Others have advocated whites being "accomplices" and experiencing "danger together" with people of color, facing the same risks from hierarchical forces for their shared resistance.[13] Trust is key in all of this, but white supremacy and white privilege make it difficult (but not impossible) to establish cross-racial trust.[14]

While not a structure per se, the hierarchical personality type of right-wing authoritarianism (RWA) indisputably diminishes social trust. According to Theodor Adorno and his colleagues, an authoritarian personality is linked to conventionalism, submissiveness, aggression, anti-intellectualism, superstition, stereotyping, power, toughness, destructiveness, cynicism, and exaggerated concerns with sex—all features at odds with greater social trust.[15] Trust in powerful people typically comes at the cost of trust in your fellow equals. For example, confidence in hierarchical institutions like the police is, predictably, linked with RWA. Police also possess higher levels of RWA than the general population, and the longer someone is a cop, the higher their RWA.[16] Unsurprisingly, police usually distrust the communities they patrol, especially when those neighborhoods are filled with poor people and people of color.[17] According to social psychologist Bob Altemeyer, the confluence of RWA with a social dominance orientation (SDO) results in individuals who tend to be power hungry, unsupportive of equality, manipulative, amoral, religiously ethnocentric, and dogmatic.[18]

The state's hierarchy is also a source of distrust. In addition to the state's need to tax its population and conscript it into armies for the purpose of war-making, social control and repression of the population are the primary means for a state to maintain its dominance. Of course, not all of this is directly violent control, but the state implicitly wields the threat of violence, as the state is the only actor that affords itself the ability to legitimately threaten and use violence. Trust suppression is a key consequence of the state's power and social control efforts, especially in social movements (which require trust to succeed).[19] States have employed innumerable strategies to control movements by fostering distrust—both among movement participants, and between movements and the general population.

Inside movements, US state agents have engaged in snitch-jacketing, in which undercover state agents try to provoke conflict among movement participants by accusing *others* of being undercover state agents. This was a successful component of the FBI's secretive Counter Intelligence Program (COINTELPRO)—and was widely used to disrupt various movements of the 1960s. Predictably, if a movement is aware of the possibility of infiltrators, let alone their actual presence, interpersonal trust will likely diminish. Even more extreme are agent provocateurs who push movements in directions that will sabotage their efforts. This often involves encouraging people to engage in illegal activities that the state can then entrap people in, ultimately suppressing the movement. COINTELPRO most vigorously targeted left-wing movements, including the Communist Party, the civil rights movement, the New Left, and various Black and Red power movements.[20] In contrast, while the FBI did try to demobilize—but not suppress—the right-wing violence of the Ku Klux Klan, this was only because the Klan's violence was considered the *wrong expression* of racism in the US.[21] States prefer organized inequality, led by capitalist exploitation, rather than the disorganizing violence of vigilantes.

Such actions have of course been pursued by many other states seeking to provoke distrust among their respective subject populations. Totalitarian states (e.g., state socialist countries like the Soviet Union, the People's Republic of China, and Cuba) have been at the vanguard of such practices. For example, the East German state employed hundreds of thousands of police informants in its unequal society during the Cold War. People were so afraid of who (possibly friends, neighbors, or family) was going to inform on them that few people dared to oppose the state.[22] More recently, the internet and social media have enhanced the capacity and cheapened the cost of states monitoring their populations. When people know the state monitors communications in online social networks (e.g., Facebook), this intimidates dissidents and makes many fearful of communicating through those mediums, publicly or even privately. For example, Egyptians during and following the Arab Spring knew their online communications were monitored by the Egyptian state, which used public Facebook posts to arrest protest organizers.[23] The paranoia generated by an intrusive state will even work in the absence of any actual intrusion. This panopticon-esque threat makes activists suspicious of new people who show up, expressing interest in taking radical direct action. Knowing that you *could* be watched may make you act as if you are *always* being watched.[24] How can people nurture deep, long-term trust with their comrades under such conditions?

The effects of state domination can be considerable, especially in dictatorships. The ability to control information, movement, public behaviors, and innumerable other aspects of daily life tends to result in dramatic *public* expressions of political trust, accompanied by substantial, simmering *private* political distrust. Once these dictatorships collapse—as they all tend to eventually—what happens to trust? The South American dictatorships from the 1960s through 1980s in Argentina, Brazil, Chile, and Uruguay not only provoked massive diasporas but appear to have soured these populations on statist solutions, thus fueling anti-authoritarian movements from below.[25] The pitch toward despotism also brings scapegoating of minority populations, as the state encourages social distrust in official or unofficial enemies to secure its dominance. The treatment of Muslims in India by the ultra-nationalist Hinduist Bharatiya Janata Party (BJP) and prime minister Narendra Modi illustrates just how dangerous state-led scapegoating can be. Relatively low levels of interreligious conflict blossomed dramatically into fratricidal violence with the BJP's electoral success and passage of discriminatory laws in the 2010 and 2020s.[26]

As already indicated, police, whether local law enforcement or spy agencies, exist to collect information for the purpose of social control. Even though they are the "long arm of the law" in the US and distribute "street justice", courts are the ones who "legally punish". The mission and presence of police discourages trust among dissidents, while enhancing trust among the pro-status quo and patriotic, since police are allegedly the bulwark against chaos, communists/anarchists, revolution, criminals, terrorists, and other "threats" to authoritarian patriotism.[27] The police's power to control is dependent on the quality of information they collect, which facilitates their capacity to manipulate and intervene. Average people residing in a society with a panopticon-empowered state are categorically weakened, forcing people to conceal their true opinions, avoid committing "thought-crimes", worry about how their actions are perceived, and so on.[28] To gather information, states employ a vast network of formal and informal monitoring. The formal network includes state employees, private contractors, physical infrastructure, and surveillance technology, while the informal networks include informants who provide the state with detailed information about the lives of people residing in their communities. The estimated number of police informants in the US is high.[29] The casual awareness that so many informants exist contributes to low social trust, especially among those over-policed or operating in the underground economy on society's margins. Most police "work" is not crime prevention but mundane information-collection—and informants are the best sources of such information. Their "snitching" does much to undermine community solidarity and trust, especially that which could otherwise resist the police. Here, a paraphrased version of Friedrich Nietzsche's (in)famous quote bears repeating: We should distrust those for whom the desire to punish is strong.

What may appear to be simple differentiation is often, upon closer inspection, social inequality. For example, segregation (by social class, race, ethnicity, religion, nationality) may appear to be merely "choice". However, segregation usually stems from powerful groups distancing themselves from disadvantaged groups and forcibly depriving them of access to resources. Class and race segregation are widespread in the US, and housing inequality throughout the twentieth century has involved formal policies like underfunding and redlining and informal practices like blockbusting, white flight, and realtor racial steering. Unsurprisingly, the hierarchies propelling segregation result in distrust. People further segregate as a result of fear, dislike, or because they believe they cannot rely on others.

Social scientists have quantified segregation's extent, using numerical measurements such as the dissimilarity index (DI). The DI measures what percentage of each group living in an area would have to relocate elsewhere to have a proportionate distribution of poor and rich (or whites, Blacks, and other people of color) living together.[30] According to data from the 2000 census, cities like Buffalo, NY; Flint, MI; Newark, NJ; Chicago, IL; New York, NY; Milwaukee, WI; Detroit, MI; and Gary, IN were so racially segregated that at least 80 percent of their populations would have to relocate to other neighborhoods in order to evenly distribute the city's white and Black populations.[31] The high segregation rates across US cities show how privileged people can successfully hide away from others, isolating themselves from those races or classes that they distrust. Segregation is the culprit causing social distrust, not merely diversity.[32] The fewer egalitarian interactions people have with different people, the more inaccurate the perceptions they have of each other. To flip these patterns illustrates new potential: The more contact you have with people different from you, the more likely it is you will be able to identify common humanity. This supposition forms the basis of the "contact hypothesis": Having contact with different groups will decrease stereotypical views and prejudices, encourage more interaction, and raise social trust.[33] Pre-existing attitudes and values are apt to intervene, conditioning people to treat their encounters with others in accordance to those orientations.[34]

Many have argued that if only progressive movements can acquire political power and re-tool the state's mechanisms into machinery for social justice then all will be well. But what has historically happened when social movements achieve power? Consider the Bolsheviks in Russia or various movement leaders in South America's "pink wave" during the 2000s. Predictably, having control of the state encourages even former radicals to think differently about themselves and their goals, and ultimately lead most to compromise their values. Journalist Ben Dangl describes how movements have to stay eternally vigilant—and even remain at odds with their former movement allies when they assume high office—or risk being subsumed by the tidal wave of those leaders' new state power.[35] Thus, simply having hierarchical power even divides people who share similar political values and ideologies, ultimately fostering distrust. The leaders who acquire power come to distrust the very movements that swept them to power, as those movements may no longer be under their influence. More crucially, the movements themselves become divided by those who want to give their former comrades in power a chance to fix problems (repeatedly cutting them slack when they fall short of their promises) and those who see no reason to suddenly compromise their demands on the state. Movements therefore become torn between trusters and distrusters.

It's not surprising that states have an interest in controlling their populations. The best way for states to exert their domination over a populace is to establish surveillance. James C. Scott referred to these state-led efforts as rendering a population "legible", that is, mapping its patterns purportedly to facilitate easy, efficient, and rationalist state intervention.[36] Surveillance is more necessary in societies with greater inequality. In order for states to predict the intentions of "the rabble", they must know what those subjects are doing. To keep the powerful and wealthy from being overrun by the less powerful and poorer classes, states seek current, analyzable information. In particular, states have—at their core—a concern with controlling and suppressing radical movements that challenge their authority. This necessitates efforts to crush the liberatory potential of movements (and the social trust they are built upon). Generating snitching networks within disadvantaged and subversive communities (as described above), government-run spying and surveillance, propaganda, and outright counterintelligence (a sanitized phrase that refers to trying to destroy movements, not just gather data about them) are fundamental state strategies.

Why would a state record or spy upon its population if it had complete trust in it? This is something of a rhetorical question, as all states are coalitions of powerful elites who seek to reinforce unequal social arrangements, and thus by definition lack complete trust in "their" populace. Additionally, knowledge of this surveillance encourages a population's active distrust of the state. When people know they are being watched for potentially malevolent reasons, they become agitated and begrudging. People who know they are being watched for the purpose of domination will often seek to circumvent this surveillance.[37] For example, a plethora of digital encryption technologies have been developed with these very concerns in mind: Pretty Good Privacy (PGP) and GPG, Tor, Signal, and so on. Given the state has the greatest capacity for surveillance (particularly organizations like the US's National Security Administration), encryption is a potentially leveling solution to the mutual distrust between states and a populace.

When encryption technologies are wielded by the state (especially when the only available crypto is riddled by backdoor entry points for the state's access), the populace suffers underneath crypto's power.[38] However, when a populace has access to powerful encryption that is mathematically challenging for the state to break on a case-by-case basis—and whose algorithms have been publicly developed and are transparently auditable—then the populace is able to survive its distrust in the state and avoid state surveillance. Encryption is premised upon the presumed—and typically real—overreach of the state into people's lives, meaning a reasonable political distrust is rife among encryption users. Human rights organizations such as Amnesty International and Human Rights Watch, mainstream UN agencies like UNESCO, and activists around the world strongly support the right to use encryption in the interest of curtailing state surveillance, dating back to support in the 1990s for using PGP.[39]

International domination also perpetuates distrust—witness the consequences of US empire upon people's perceptions. Imperialism destroys trust in ways that don't easily dissipate. The US maintains over 800 military bases in 160 countries—this has not endeared the rest of the world to the US, especially in the many countries where these bases are controversial among the local populace.[40] Although many Americans may consider the US to be the "world's policeman", non-Americans don't believe this is a good thing. The US's poor image is surely due in part to the incessant intervention, invasion, harassment, and war-making it has engaged in for most of its existence.[41] According to a Worldwide Independent Network/Gallup poll conducted in 2013 of residents from 63 countries, the US was perceived as the greatest threat to world peace.[42]

Of course, there is a difference between the opinions of distrust offered by the people of other countries and the strategic geopolitical support offered by the heads of state of some of these countries. For example, the US's neighbor Mexico has historically considered the US an important trading partner and military ally, but Mexicans on average are not so kind in their assessment of the state that rules to their north. When an entire society is assessed as a "threat", very little trust remains. The US not only deports thousands of law-abiding Central Americans back south and fuels the incredible violence inside Mexico stemming from the US's War on Drugs[43] but has also destabilized the agrarian economy of Mexico through its infliction of neoliberal policies (most notably the North American Free Trade Agreement). The military power the US wields across the planet returns in the form of spent karma and grumbling resignation at the US's hegemony. In its most violent manifestation, anger at US dominance can be witnessed in "blowback" terror attacks like those of September 11, 2001. The association of white Americans with US foreign policy is enough to decrease much of the world's trust in US citizens too.

Some of the most enthusiastic supporters of military adventures and ultra-nationalism are fascist and other right-wing movements, which thrive on hierarchical forms of trust. Here, trust resides in strong leaders (or even just a singular leader) on top. There is little reason to place trust in particular "others", especially if they be immigrants, leftists, or members of disadvantaged racial, sexual, or religious groups. Hierarchy is a fundamental part of these movements' DNA: Strict obedience to leaders' commands is typically followed by swift attacks on perceived enemies, who are afforded no mercy. Fascists and right-wingers prefer to trust in the supremacy of their leader over any argument, humanity, or generosity offered by their opposition. By wiping out diversity (as pursued in Nazi Germany), fascists in North America and Europe aim to create a society filled with the kind of people they wish to trust: white Christians of their national background. For fascists, possession of those narrow traits creates trustworthiness. Not coincidentally, fascist leaders are the ultimate embodiment of such features. Suffice to say, fascist organizing is a threat to society itself—and especially its most vulnerable members—because it instills fear and distrust in everyone.

Conservatives in particular have significantly increased their distrust of apparently non-ideological institutions like science. Especially insofar as they are religious, these conservatives' distrust of science has important consequences, particularly their rejection of climate science.[44] Relatedly, RWA is linked to a rejection of democracy, equality, and interpersonal trust. Right-wing ideology actually discourages social trust by emphasizing the "evils" of other people in the abstract, or even human nature itself. Instead, it advocates trust only in "yourself", family, "the nation", and powerful authority figures (e.g., heads of state CEOs, generals, and religious leaders). In practice, these ideological mandates are selective, as right-wing support for such authority figures dissipates if a leader's perceived ideology conflicts with their own—for example, Barack Obama, whom right-wing conspiracies identified as a socialist, "secret Muslim", or, shockingly, a community organizer.

When political scientist Ivan Krastev asked, somewhat rhetorically, "Can democracy survive when we don't trust our leaders?", he proposed a series of strawmen. But his question deserves serious critique. First, do we actually have meaningful democracy now? Are they really "our leaders"? And fundamentally, we may be merely trusting leaders who are thoroughly untrustworthy. Convincing people to trust political leaders doesn't make for a strong democracy; it just makes people more easily ruled.[45]

The harmful effects of hierarchical leaders have also led to the diminished stature of progressive social movements. People have been sold out by leaders in the past: for example, business-friendly union leaders or movement spokesmen who join the government when a good offer is made.[46] Diminished trust in movements also stems from leaders who have moved on, died, or moderated their demands, thus causing their flocks to become jaded by the deflating possibilities that movements seem to promise. An alternative framework decenters "leadership" within movements away from charismatic individuals (often articulate middle-class white men) and their high media visibility. In this alternative framework (often called "leaderful" or "anti-followership"), more participants have influence within movements and can thus take greater credit for movement successes. Movements would likely enjoy more support if this anti-authoritarianism were more widely understood by the general populace that movements seek to attract. Still, inner-movement problems provoke internal distrust and a leeching of committed members. Notably, occurrences of sexual assault within movement communities, long-term failures, organizational competitiveness, and a lack of cooperation have blunted the capacity for unified resistance. Some of these problems stem from hierarchical socialization, or the continued influence of patriarchy and other forms of privilege within movements.

Generating conflict by imposing hierarchies on different groups is a classic divide-and-conquer technique that suppresses interpersonal social trust. For example, American prisoners share common interests against their jailers yet typically remain divided by racialized prison gangs, sexual assault, and grudges implicitly tolerated or even endorsed by prison authorities. The effort required to suppress prisoners is greatly lessened when prisoners spend their time fighting with and focusing their animosity on each other.[47] It's no coincidence that most modern-day prison revolts and strikes have involved strong cross-racial alliances. Resistance within such a draconian and manipulated environment as an American prison requires incredible trust in fellow prisoners; they must not back down, flip, or snitch, and instead support each other regardless of circumstances or background.

The inequality generated by hierarchical systems is a breeding ground for many kinds of crime. In fact, this is a near truism in the social sciences and is regularly factored into analyses: Class inequality leads to property crime.[48] Unsurprisingly, crime has numerous negative effects on society, a principal one being social distrust. If people are afraid of being mugged, assaulted, murdered, or having their home burglarized, they will retreat into their shelters and not trust those beyond its walls.[49] Even people with law-abiding neighbors trust less if they perceive potential for crime victimization. In this distrusting environment, people may turn to authority figures for "solutions". For example, poor people often paradoxically demand that police patrol their neighborhoods more heavily to "get crime under control", despite how this often backfires against their own interests. (Police are just as likely, if not more likely, to use force against the law-abiding than those apprehended in the act of law-breaking.[50]) Crime thus suppresses social trust, even while enhancing political trust. William Julius Wilson's "truly disadvantaged" theory of inner cities reflects this logic: As jobs are eliminated (through deindustrialization, neoliberalization, or off-shoring), tax-bases shrink, and schools decline in quality. Thus, desperate people turn to alternative options for making ends meet: namely crime. A neighborhood with increasing crime is quick to become a distrustful neighborhood, which further compounds growing social disorganization. Those who have the resources to leave the neighborhood take their chances elsewhere, which further diminishes the neighborhood's economic resource base, housing values, and social stability.[51]

Ultimately, poor people fight other poor people on behalf of wealthier classes—tycoon Jay Gould once remarked that he could "hire one-half of the working class to kill the other half". Even working-class and poor Americans tend to believe classist stereotypes about their own class. Inequality breeds jealousy. People suspect each other of scamming the system, and of being lazy and undeserving.[52] This jealousy reduces class solidarity, empathy, and positive community. Despite middle-class anxieties about a criminal working class preying on their slightly greater wealth, people tend to victimize those closest and most convenient to them. When private property reigns and people are discouraged from sharing, the opportunities to build trust are squandered.

That people often feel they must look to authority figures and rely on them for necessities is a tragic consequence of how inequality generates distrust among social equals. This upward-oriented assistance-seeking creates a cult of personality, wherein people are encouraged to trust leaders or authorities that often had a role in creating the problem in the first place. Looking outward to elites, officials, and outsiders to solve problems further reduces the potential for trust in your own neighborhood. City council members, police, and land developers often initially speak in a very sympathetic and generous manner, promising to fix problems.

However, it is to the advantage of the state and other authorities to propagate ideas that reduce our trust in each other—for example, broadcast news stories about crime, terrorism, corruption, selfishness, accidents, and so on—in other words, promoting fear can empower those who benefit from that fear. City councillors can get re-elected because an electorate fears crime or homelessness, police can protect us from lurking dangers, and developers will inject cash into neighborhoods, thus raising property values. In the boldest formulation, trust in and obedience toward authority figures may constitute blind worship of the powerful, even authoritarianism. By affording trust and respect to those who have power and give orders, people willingly acquiesce to powerlessness.

When considering how hierarchy encourages distrust, it's helpful to rethink the usual formulation. What looks like "distrust" in some contexts is actually trust of a particular kind, albeit in hierarchical systems and relations, as opposed to people. Consider patriarchy and its toxic reinforcement of gender segregation. People who "distrust" members of the "opposite sex" actually have a great deal of "trust" in the rigid system of gender roles derived from patriarchy. Men who "distrust women" because those women "only want to marry a high-wage earning man" or "want to control a man's life" are swayed by the patriarchal practice of paying women less, under-valuing their contributions, and making them dependent on men. Women who "distrust men" do so because patriarchal domination makes some men unworthy of trust, as they may try to manipulate or sexually assault women. Belief that "all" members of a group (like the opposite sex) are one way (i.e., gender stereotypes) indicates a strong adherence to, or trust in, inflexible gender norms. Can egalitarian gender relations exist, let alone thrive, in the context of patriarchal beliefs in the submission of women? It is very unlikely.[53] Thus, patriarchy has protected long-standing traditions that lead to broad trust in its harmful status quo, in lieu of trust for others.[54]

Patriarchy also enforces trust in the gender binary by demanding that everyone fully embody their "properly" cis-designated attributes. Transgender folks who can't effectively "pass" are targets for distrust because their critics are themselves so trusting of gender's socially constructed binary. Transphobia negatively impacts not only trans people but general social trust by recruiting people to be "gender police", wherein someone's current gender identity—to be compared against gender expression and practice—is relentlessly questioned. In particular, American transphobes are paranoid about which public bathrooms ("men's" or "women's" bathrooms) trans people use, instead of simply trusting that people will use whatever bathroom is the most appropriate for them. Transphobes often even oppose gender-neutral bathrooms (which would solve this "problem") because they view it as an acceptance of trans peoples' rights, which undermines their trust in the rigid gender binary.

Even with some "good [cis-gendered] men" under a patriarchal system, is it possible for true "trust" to function? In a context where some people maintain power over others, can women be expected (or asked) to seek out those good men to trust? The *average* power difference is what makes or breaks this potential. Thus, can (or should) women trust men in patriarchal relationships? Can citizens (to say nothing of non-citizens) trust police during traffic stops? Can employees trust employers? Due to their greater power, these authority figures can easily take advantage of their average greater size, legal right to use violent force, or ability to fire their subor-dinates. Thus, any "trust" that subordinate individuals have in authority figures under these conditions can only emerge as *partial* trust. In the era of chattel slavery, could enslaved Africans *really, truly* trust white people, especially their enslavers? If the individuals in power want to be trusted completely, they could relinquish their power over such subordinates. Police could disarm themselves and quit their jobs. Employers could transition their workplaces into cooperative enterprises, sharing both ownership and decision-mak-ing. Slave owners could—but rarely did—manumit their slaves from bondage. Of course, those in power do not generally want this. They care more about their power than enjoying the full trust of others.

Inequality also creates varied levels of access to information and knowledge. The gap between a powerful actor's and a less powerful person's knowledge leads to demands for blind trust. Those who have more information, wisdom, and experience (e.g., the highly educated, teachers, or elders) typically ask others to trust them—their expertise is valuable and is often shared. But knowledge can also be exploited for use against others. Merely possessing such resources is enough to demand trust, even when there is no other reason to do so. The powerful, who already possess information, rarely need to trust those lacking such information. In this sense, information is weaponized. While people lacking information can fight back in a variety of ways—passive resistance, creation of counter-knowledge, sabotage[55]—this only becomes necessary due to hierarchy's presence in the first place.

Ultimately, just a little bit of power tends to fuck things up. Consider lower-middle-class professionals (e.g., social workers, elementary school teachers) who have power over subordinates. Even though their power is circumscribed, it can still be wielded arbitrarily and capriciously. Historically, such professionals have exhibited moralizing, conservative, and disciplinarian personalities. And even when professionals have good intentions of aiding their charges, they still get to choose what happens to them. A foster child or a poor person's "trust" in a social worker is necessary because that person often has no other options in the bewildering state-bureaucracy. A student (or even their parents) are at the whim of their teacher and thus their "trust" often rests on an edifice of ignorance. Thankfully, these forms of authority are usually time limited. Moreover, students can narrow the gap between their knowledge and that of their teacher, thus undermining the nature of the teacher's claimed authority.[56] Thus, when inequality dissipates, the nature of trust is transformed.

HOW SOCIAL DISTRUST DISABLES US

Social distrust makes it difficult or impossible to do things we would otherwise be able to do. This disabling can be physical, social, or psychological, ultimately depriving us of a fuller life.

For example, scapegoating positions disadvantaged groups to receive blame and is cancerous to the social body. This "othering" deprives us of empathy: We don't, can't, or won't feel each other's pain, and recuse ourselves from important social tasks, like care work, charity, and general concern. At risk of overdramatizing this argument: Scapegoating and othering are the handmaidens of genocide and ethnic cleansing. When dominant majorities publicly distrust minority populations, the perceived humanity of that minority shrinks. Taken to extremes, othering makes people expendable, and even an impediment to safety or "progress". "Good Germans", who ignored the evidence of ethnic cleansing around them in the 1930s and 1940s, were desensitized to the plight of others. This desensitized orientation fed upon mainstream distrust in minority populations (i.e., Jews, Roma, homosexuals, communists).[57] In Chico, California, elected officials and prominent business owners continuously complained about the city's homeless population. Instead of extending compassion toward those down on their luck, demagogues victim-blamed the least fortunate in the community. Then, tragically but unsurprisingly, four teenage boys (who had homes) walked into a homeless encampment and shot someone dead (for which charges were later dismissed).[58] Now, regular evictions of camps occur, despite the fact not enough shelter space or affordable house is available.

When we distrust each other, we can't form social movements—because, obviously, social movements are social. They require dynamic collaboration, which becomes impossible in the absence of a minimal level of social trust. Movement participants need each other's support and back-up. Despite the noble image of the lone activist struggling against injustice, real movements require lots of people whose names, relationships, and acts of solidarity are typically lost to history but whose trust in each other was crucial.

Unsafe communities with low levels of social capital languish. When we fear each other's intentions, we're less likely to show up and provide support. Unsafe neighborhoods are filled with people who cower behind closed doors. The chaos that reigns under these conditions damages the usually supportive social fabric. This enables the most powerful and brutal among us to take advantage of this disorder and profit financially, achieving boss status in a dog-eat-dog environment. Trump is a stunning example of this on a national level.

If we distrust those in our own social class, what route out of poverty or our other problems do we have? Life becomes a solitary struggle and economic mobility an individualistic challenge. We assume other workers are getting a "better deal" than us, as jealousy blinds us to shared conditions and interests. Meritocratic assumptions aside, the falsely conscious worker believes they are working hard and that others are somehow being lazy or taking advantage of the system. The social trust implicit in class consciousness is surely a smarter route—viewing ourselves as jointly under attack by an unjust system that does *not* reward effort and sacrifice equally.

Distrust makes us afraid. Granted, there is much to be legitimately scared of in the world, but social distrust amplifies fear of the unknown, strangers, dark places at night, and other unpredictable circumstances.[59] Distrust of others is linked to fear of doing certain things and not doing others. If entire groups of people are distrusted, fear can easily cascade into larger and larger groups, including our loved ones and even ourselves. Of course, this benefits corporations that sell, among other things, security systems, weapons, insurance, and pharmaceuticals. As with NSA spying, which raises suspicions that all our movements are being tracked (which they mostly are), distrust can paralyze. Social fear is a precursor to social disintegration.

For those who have experienced past abuse or assault, trust is often difficult to extend to others in the future. Even under the best of circumstances, memories of past traumatic experiences are easily triggered. Consequently, people with experiences of abuse may avoid long-term friendships or seeking out deep intimate relationships. Existing relationships may be viewed with suspicion and people who have good intentions toward us may be second-guessed.[60]

Even less serious transgressions—ruined friendships, disappointments, and "back-stabbings"—make it harder to trust again. Even when most associations are "positive", a small number of (or even just one) soured associations can raise concerns about all others.[61] How many good activists and organizers have been "burned" by manipulative "leaders" or "comrades", politicians promising the stars, or a close confidant who double-crossed or had promised but failed to be discreet? Taking advantage of people's good intentions and goodwill isn't just foul—it's actively disabling.

Distrusting impairs and can even prevent empathy. The otherwise common and very *human* impulse to empathize with others is marred by distrust. When drug users are criminalized by the state and demonized in the media, people predictably struggle to see drug users as similar to us, or even fully human. If people are afraid of those who consume drugs, they will misunderstand why such people consume drugs. A user's pain—which drugs help them to cope with—is ignored or discredited.[62] Instead, non-users may sanctimoniously react to users, offering disgust and condemnation rather than empathy. For example, not-in-my-backyard (NIMBY) opposition to harm reduction efforts like clean needle exchanges further punishes people who are often suffering from traumatic experiences. This non-empathetic orientation prevents active and proactive assistance and solidarity. We lose sight of each other's humanity—and thus our *shared* interests are lost. How can drug addiction and poverty—let alone their sinister root causes—be meaningfully addressed without empathy?

A distrustful orientation can lead one to become pessimistic about the future: If we can't figure out how to improve things for ourselves, then lack of trust in others can make us truly fatalistic. For example, the paralyzing discourse around climate disaster, when combined with distrust in other people's ability and desire to mitigate such outcomes, has been called catastrophism.[63] This means we don't perceive a solution to our troubling situation or collective potential to reverse current trends. Consequently, and devastatingly, many might just give up.[64]

Distrust is also reflected in problematic social advocacy, such as the decades-long child-welfare campaign of "Don't talk to strangers". The risks faced by children were exaggerated by the media in the 1980s, creating a moral panic rooted in hearsay, exceptional events, and politically motivated manipulation.[65] This don't-talk-to-strangers advice created an entire generation (or more!) of people unwilling to trust anyone they did not already know. To be clear: It's foolish advice, if a child gets lost, they *should* ask strangers for help. If they avoid people they may avoid all contact with other people, becoming *more* lost. If children (or anyone really) distrusts strangers, they will find no lack of people to be wary of. When lost, kids should in fact stay in safer public spaces where co-surveillance is more likely. It's when there are fewer people observing someone's behavior that potential predators feel empowered to act questionably. Of course, less than half of all child abductions are committed by strangers, with the vast majority of abductions committed by family members.[66] Moreover, this anti-stranger orientation placed citizens at the mercy of police for assistance and a sense of safety. Instead of talking to others when danger occurs (e.g., calling a friend over to help diffuse a potentially violent situation), such policies encourage placing our trust in (and a "911" telephone call to) the police.

All of this socially accumulated distrust of strangers and others has long-term, negative side-effects for adults too. A childhood fear of strangers is significantly related to fear of intimacy in adolescents. Additionally, females taught to fear strangers express greater loneliness.[67] And the random and not-so-random acts of discrimination that people of color and women face every day in the US heighten the stress our bodies endure, triggering immune responses that can contribute to countless diseases and medical problems, from heart disease to premature births. In other words, being on high alert for discrimination and micro-aggressions from others literally kills people.[68] If a society executes a widespread campaign to promote distrust then the reasonable things people do for and toward each other become less and less possible.

THE DISTRUST INDUSTRY

The central antagonists opposing solidarity are not just random, disinterested hierarchical institutions, organizations, and groups. It shouldn't surprise us that distrust is encouraged whenever possible by those seeking to acquire wealth, regardless of the cost. Some of this distrust is shoved down our throats, at other times it is subtler.

To begin with an obvious example, private household security companies send employees to knock on the doors of people whose next-door neighbors have experienced burglaries in order to sell electronic security systems. They can use the publicly available data reported to police to target these solicitation efforts. The Electronic Security Association claims to represent a half-million "industry professionals" who service "more than 34 million residential and commercial clients" with services that "monitor intrusion" and "conduct video surveillance".[69] An estimated 20 percent of American households have video doorbells, like Ring.[70] Of course, such security companies provide more of an illusion of safety than real protection. If an alarm is tripped, the company must rely on local police to do the work. Additionally, private security forces—hired at offices, public buildings, and other locations—are themselves a big industry. Security guards are typically off-duty cops who patrol buildings under suspicion of some unspoken threat. After the 9/11 attacks, such security increased dramatically. Amazingly, the US has more private security employees than publicly employed police officers.[71]

Unsurprisingly, gun manufacturers tap into the same distrust as security companies. Such manufacturers thrive on perceptions of danger—whether from criminals or terrorists, or just about anybody the 45 percent of American households who have guns see on TV. American gun owners are more apt to be older, wealthier married males who are politically conservative and distrust the federal government.[72] These opinions did not emerge from nowhere. The National Rifle Association radicalized in 1977, aligning itself with reactionary segments of the population.[73] Now, gun manufacturers benefit—and exploit opportunities—from spikes in crime, moral panics, and even the election of Black presidents, just as the emancipation of Black slaves following the US Civil War fueled an earlier rush by whites to acquire weapons. Indeed, the US Constitution's Second Amendment originates in an early expectation (rather than just a privilege) for white males to own guns for the purposes of settler colonialism and slave control.[74] Another profitable strategy has been to scare gun users into believing (usually with little evidence) that government is seeking to curtail their gun ownership, and thus, implicitly, make them less safe. This NRA-led fear-mongering during the Obama administration—which initiated no substantial efforts to limit gun ownership—resulted in an amazing growth in gun sales[75] and state-based firearm deregulation in conservative state legislatures.[76] It wasn't just the first Black president that inspired a surge in sales; when the COVID-19 pandemic hit the US in early 2020, there was not only a run on essential commodities, like toilet paper, flour, and beans, but also guns.[77]

On a global scale, the military-industrial complex (MIC) profits handsomely from worldwide distrust. The MIC is a huge network of corporations (and their patrons and allies in government and the US military) that provide services to and produce weapons, tools, and other products for the military. It benefits from not only a consistent (and possibly increasing) level of warfare but also greater distrust. These companies actively demonize people throughout the world and the "threat" they pose to Americans, to US "interests", and the US "way of life". Additionally, the MIC benefits from the distrust other states have in each other, since military corporations sell weapons to them too, sometimes funding various sides of the same conflicts. For example, numerous countries sold weapons to both Iran and Iraq during the 1980s.[78] Today, a widespread fear of brown people from other countries—Muslims in general and Arabs in particular—saturates US culture. This attitude benefits the MIC's bottom line *as well as* the geopolitical goals of US corporate interests throughout the world.

Highly funded right-wing think tanks such as the Manhattan Institute, Heritage Foundation, and Cato Institute have grown in number and size since the 1960s, directing millions of dollars at perceived "problems" like labor unions, untrustworthy and "lazy" poor people, and social welfare "moochers", all for the purpose of undercutting social solidarity. These institutes' wealthy donors, like Charles Koch, benefit directly from the policies they advocate. While these think tanks (as "non-profits") do not benefit directly from their policy successes, their chief architects and beneficiaries do, as they are part of a nexus of interests that seek to encourage distrust and ultimately advocate cutting people off from social assistance and solidarity. By cutting taxes and welfare benefits, not only do the wealthy (and their corporations) save billions of dollars but they also secure a more precarious labor force, willing to work for lower pay.

Corporate mass media not only delivers the messages of right-wing think tanks but has its own vested interests in fostering distrust. All corporate media—whether daily newspapers, radio stations, TV channels, or even movies—have participated in propagating the idea that some people (maybe most people!) are out to take advantage of others. More specifically, media fosters the notion that human nature is untrustworthy—a message that helps sell subscriptions as well as hike-up advertising prices. When media consumers become afraid of terrorist "threats", immigrants, criminals, or "violent" leftists, they must find ways to cope with their provoked anxieties. Anxious people are apt to consume products, while satisfied people are, well, satisfied. Thus, generating consumer anxiety makes media space and airtime more valuable when media conglomerates sell that space to their real customers—the corporations that produce products.

On the surface, social media appears to be about facilitating horizontal social trust, but the corporate platforms that much of the world uses (e.g., Facebook, Tik-Tok, YouTube, etc.) are integrally premised upon distrust and mistrust. Not only do they actively generate conflict and distrust through their algorithms by bringing people into direct contact with extreme and combative voices but they have also done research to understand how this conflict is addictive. The more people use social media platforms—which means freely giving a corporation their preferences, ideas, opinions, and behaviors—the more power and influence those platforms have. Platforms create detailed user profiles that can accurately predict our preferences and even future behaviors, which are then sold to companies for the purpose of advertising and other manipulation.[79]

The institution responsible for manufacturing desires among a distrusting consumer public is the advertising industry. The advertising corporation's bottom line is dependent on reducing our satisfaction with our material status quo. For advertisers, it's ideal if people with problems seek help from their clients' products, rather than free solutions from their family, friends, and neighbors. Thus, it is profitable to curate various emotions and trigger consumers' reactions: insecurity, desire, and aspiration. Advertisers have done their jobs well when we begin to distrust our sense of self, thereby disliking or worrying about our bodies and social standing. This "guidance" involves a framed analysis of the world and ultimately requires us to place trust in their advice through financially investing in their clients' products.

No other industry begs for people's investment more than the insurance industry. The entire industry is premised on the comforting lie that insurance companies will support people after an accident or tragedy befalls them—which surely will, in our scary world. Needless to say, insurance companies have little incentive to provide full benefits or repayment and must often be legally fought in order for them to meet the fullest extent on their contractual promises. Insurance companies try to keep people worried about the future, so they will "hedge their bets" by buying as much insurance as possible. This often presumes the malice posed by others. For example, home insurance is bought due to a distrust in neighbors—they may be thieves, careless arsonists, and so on. Renter's insurance, car insurance, and even life insurance follows a similar pattern.

One final example: An entire sub-industry of specialized law firms in the US works in "labor relations", employed by corporations as "union busters". When workers are frustrated with their employer—as many often are—they may discuss collective strategies to resolve their grievances. The formation of a union that can legally represent workers in collective bargaining is seen as a major threat to employer profits and power. Thus, employers hire union-busting law firms to engage in surveillance, disruption, propaganda, and other quasi-legal efforts. In the past, so-called detective agencies like the infamous Pinkertons did similar work, often using brutal violence and even assassination to accomplish their ends. The core to all these anti-union efforts is to sow distrust and prevent strong bonds of solidarity forming among workers. Ideally, if a boss can inspire some workers to distrust the union organizers, inter-worker conflicts will stymie union efforts.[80] The American law firm Jackson Lewis—employed by blue-chip companies like Exxon Mobil, Hilton Hotels, IBM, Pfizer, and Target—is a world-famous union-buster enterprise; they employed nearly a thousand lawyers and did business of around a half-billion dollars in 2020.[81]

This partial list of distrust's beneficiaries—mainly profit-seeking corporations—reveals something sinister about societal distrust. The wealthy's sophisticated efforts to generate individual distrust is completely self-serving, and they appear indifferent to the hardships they create. Thus, people should instead distrust those same corporations who are benefiting and profiting from the generation of social distrust.

IDEOLOGIES OF DISTRUST

While industries and corporations aspire to—and successfully do—profit off distrust, there are other, deeper forces that propel distrust. Various systems of thought promote and encourage social distrust, not always for the purpose of profit. The people committed to these ideas are those systems' ideologues. The following three ideologies advocate wide distrust for most everyone, except for trust placed in, respectively, a single leader, one's own self, or one's own group.

Totalitarian ideologies emphasize that the leader is always right. Trusting the leader is of paramount importance, while anyone who challenges that leader is wrong. Since there are simply too many potential relationships in society, totalitarianism attempts to simplify these dynamics, reducing everything to the relationship between masses of individuals and the leader. Totalitarianism denigrates relations between individual everyday people, seeking to place all into a homogeneous mass where everyone is indistinguishable. Totalitarianism requires absolute trust be placed in the leader above all others.[82] Only when the leader tells you to trust your comrades should you do so—and only because *he* says so.[83] Systems of control lurk behind the leader, which are propagandistic, cultural, and coercive. The standard message transmitted: The leader (just as with Orwell's Big Brother character) is here for you to trust, love, and follow—and they know best too. Certain varieties of totalitarianism start off as populism and charismatic movements (like cults, and often Marxist-Leninism) but ultimately produce totalitarian styles. Fascism and monarchism are the purest forms of totalitarianism, as formal legal authority is held only by the leader.

Individualism of various stripes—especially libertarianism and free-marketism—argue that there is no relevant "society". Not only is the common good irrelevant but even mediocre (and possibly even hierarchical) attempts to regulate excesses, like the state, are illegitimate. In fact, the only collectively agreed upon (and state-enforced) norm is the right of people to own property, even to other's detriment.[84] The state's only role is to serve as security forces to enforce private property rights against those who lack sufficient property. As such, the state should be trusted that far, and no further. These Libertarians believe the fantasy of a "free market", where everyone is able to equally and fairly compete with each other, with this pure individualism creating good, universal outcomes. Built into this ideology is the assumption that individuals are inherently selfish, egotistical, and untrustworthy.

Ayn Rand is a prototypical example of this ideology—and a key reference point for today's Libertarians. For her "egoism", selfishness is a virtue, while collectivism is both "false" and impossible. Rand's devotees (like those of the Tea Party or the billionaire Koch brothers), have attempted systematically and strategically for decades to convince people to divest from "the public", which is untrustworthy. Consequently, right-wing Libertarians have relentlessly attacked schools, Social Security, health care, and anti-poverty benefits. Since most people reject ultra-individualism (believing that some, maybe many, others can be trusted), these goals are usually wrapped in a privatization guise: Allow private individuals (and especially private, for-profit companies) to do these same social tasks for a profit. The mythological notion of free will and free choice are also core arguments made in these privatization efforts.[85] Attacks on Social Security are ideologically driven but also aim to maximize profit for the wealthy. Chomsky has argued that such attacks aim to convince us that we should not care about other people, and instead look out for ourselves.[86] Thus, individualism advocates distrust in other people's intentions because they are acting just as selfishly as you.

Finally, nationalism encourages trust in your nation, tribe, church/religion, or race over all others. Only your own kind can be trusted; all others are only looking out for the interests of *their* kind (just like you!). This logic expands the notion of individualism to a group you are a member of, but blocks trust from groups we do not belong to. If there are "truths" to believe, they come from your side, while all other ideas, facts, versions, stories, and truths are rejected out of hand, because they originate in the untrustworthy "other". Implicitly, nationalism encourages people to Balkanize their relationships and communities into in-groups and out-groups. Anyone who criticizes this logic or acts in solidarity with those not in our tribe is not just a deluded "multiculturalist" but a traitor. Since most of these groups have leaders—tribes have chiefs, nations have presidents, churches have priests, and races have charismatic authority figures—your group will be run by someone you should trust above all others. The ruling institutions on your side should be blindly trusted: Trust your pope, your generals, your national myths. In the US, a petulant and boorish reductionism resurfaces regularly, claiming "America, right or wrong!", with advocates distrusting anything not "American" (even if that thing is objectively *right* or even *better*). Importantly, German Nazism was called *national* socialism, meaning primary importance and assistance was to be given to the German nation.[87] Unsurprisingly, internationalists—leftists like communists, social democrats, and anarchists—were some of the first targets of Nazism, because they supported all, regardless of nationality. Nationalism seems related to fundamentalism too. While religious fundamentalisms (whether Christian, Hindu, Jewish, or Muslim) pretend to be traditional, they are modern in source and orientation.[88] Fundamentalisms all feature a strong rebuke of any and all who do not share the "true faith". Non-believers are heretics, infidels, evil, fools, and so forth. Most fundamentalisms cannot even empathize with those "evil" others, so advocate strident distrust. The British "Brexit" movement and national vote was most likely to be opposed by UK residents with cosmopolitan politics, while supporters were more likely anti-immigrant and felt more politically disempowered by the global powerhouse United Kingdom.[89]

It's helpful to understand how ideologies that undergird hierarchical systems create and spread distrust. While different ideologies have varied values, emphases, modes of transmission, and end goals, they all involve generating skepticism toward others. While the following are economic, political, and social systems, they are premised on a set of historically noxious ideas, most of which rely on unquestioning, one-sided, blind trust.

Fascism, perhaps the most distrustful of all the following ideologies, discourages people from trusting anyone unlike them. Redemptive, punitive violence is, disturbingly, the only true acceptable relationship toward "the other", especially people who don't share your ethnicity or nationality. Trust in a powerful authority figure is encouraged, as is patriotism toward the fatherland. Expressions of violence and patriotism are how people prove their commitment to the leader. This leader-trust is blind trust and derived from mythical stories about the fatherland and its traditional values systems.[90] Consequently, while some fascist versions are labeled "national socialism", fascist ideology is vehemently conservative, hierarchical, and anti-socialist.

Even state communism, against which fascism has historically battled (e.g., World War II), deploys social distrust. Workers are not trusted to manage their own jobs; thus, the state "must" do such coordination *for* workers. Horizontal solidarity is presumably too low that people aren't trusted to willingly share what they have with those in need; therefore, the state manages the "redistribution" of things it seizes by force.[91] State communism demands blind trust from its subjects by claiming that the state and intellectual revolutionaries who steer it have the common person's interests at heart. Whenever necessary, the coercive capacities of the state are used to force "trust" on errant workers or peasants who distrust (and disobey) the state's leadership.[92] By scaring the populace and creating dependence on the state, party apparatchiks can divide the population, stoking fears of saboteurs seeking to "subvert the revolution by sowing distrust".

Capitalism is state communism's formal economic nemesis— despite the surprising similarities between the two systems. Under capitalism, people are only trusted insofar as they are committed to market exchange relationships with others. Of course, since people (whether as workers or consumers) are pursuing their own self-interested stratagems, they must outwit all others, who are presumed to be playing similar games. Workers aren't trusted to run their own jobs; thus, owners and managers must rule the workplace. Consumers are not trusted to pay enough to capitalists—they'd prefer to just cover the raw material and labor costs of goods and services, not support a profit margin. Consequently, advertiser propaganda encourages other consumptive values and behaviors for consumers. Capitalist ideology seeks to foster blind trust in the market's "invisible hand", a Frankenstein-esque elaboration of Adam Smith's passing reference in *The Wealth of Nations*. In this ideology, individuals must overlook the copious evidence of how capitalism emaciates us and others, while encouraging rabid competition between everyone, especially workers.

Patriarchy is a specific ideological system that not only organizes how people of different sexes, genders, and sexual orientations interact but also who should trust who.[93] Under patriarchal systems, men (primarily elder males) are entrusted to be "in charge" of major decisions and societal dynamics—family care is excluded from this calculus, as males aren't trusted to care for others. Women, meanwhile, aren't trusted to do masculine things (be independent, capable, or responsible). Since male- and female-identified people are expected to do different tasks—in fact, to be wholly responsible for these separate domains—they also should distrust each other's competencies within their own exclusive spheres. Thus, men discount female participation in the economy, leadership, and the public sphere, while women lower their expectations for male involvement in the domestic sphere (especially child-rearing, except for discipline). Patriarchy requires a blind trust in the wisdom of male father figures, the supremacy of male leadership, and the righteousness of (male) violence. By contrast, feminine values (cooperation, sensitivity, vulnerability) are distrusted by society (especially by patriarchal leadership), and ought to only pertain to rearing young children and supporting men in the home. Men are expected to be the wage-earners and protectors, while women are expected to rear children and manage the home.

Beyond these tightly delimited realms, men tend to be suspicious of female encroachment on "male" terrain, and libel individual female participants as "ball-busters", "tom-boys", "man haters", and so forth. Women (and other men, incidentally) are suspicious of males who wish to care for children or manage the home, viewing them as irresponsible, lazy, "effeminate", pansies, or potential molesters. Transgender individuals are a particular threat to patriarchal ideology—in ways comparable to those who seek to abolish gender[94]—as they call into question the "naturalness" and permanence of sex and gender, thus queering expectations and roles, and the capacity for others to adopt risks simply based on gender categories.

Another distrustful social system is organized around racial domination. White supremacy and whiteness ideology actively discourage social trust across group boundaries. People of color have historically been distrusted by white majorities, as well as by other minority groups. Despite official proclamations, people of color (especially African Americans) continue to be popularly viewed as inferior, violent, unreliable, and unintelligent. Even so-called "positive stereotypes", like the "model minority" stereotype of Asian Americans, implicitly raise the *difference* of Asians vis-à-vis whites, while praising their assimilation toward whiteness.[95] Whites are encouraged to have blind trust (implicitly, if not explicitly) in their own superiority—as such, their decision-making expertise, philosophical and intellectual contributions, work ethic, and inherent goodness are simply taken for granted, despite numerous contradictions. People of color often not only distrust whites, who socially, economically, and politically dominate them, but each other.[96] Prejudices against other disadvantaged racial and ethnic groups, and even accepted stereotypes about one's own group members, are widespread. Such biases and self-hate further amplify the general distrust people of color have for others. Proclamations of color-blindness merely conceal underlying racial logics and ideologies in racially unequal societies.[97]

White supremacy has emerged in many countries in the context of colonialism. Of the many varieties that have existed, settler colonialism is one of the more nefarious and impacts the Anglo-world the most: Australia, Canada, and the United States. There is no encapsulated trust between European conquerors and the indigenous they subjugated and then worked to exterminate. The theft of land and population displacement, a multitude of harms targeting colonized groups, and the imposition of new systems of domination—all central features of colonialism—do not engender trust. Settler colonialism moves people from the colonizer homeland to the newly conquered territory as settlers, seeking to possess land, appropriate resources, and enslave or convert the indigenous. The only "trust" that sometimes emerges from settler colonialism comes when the indigenous population is completely subjugated, broken, and assimilated, and so are coerced into accepting the settler's society mission, even to their own detriment. Any such trust in settlers is one that works at cross-interests, as the colonized internalize their own domination and identify more with the settler society than indigenous resistance to it.

Colonialism's long-term effects on trust can reverberate decades later. Distrust in a former colonizer's culture can lead to reactionary, fundamentalist positions within a former colony. For example, anti-gay laws in Uganda were passed in reaction to perceptions of promiscuous British liberalism (combined with fanatical American missionaries stoking homophobia).[98] Colonialism's hierarchy establishes mutual distrust and facilitates violence. The British mistreatment of Ireland didn't merely make the Irish distrust the Crown and Parliament—it led them to actively fight Britain, distrusting claims that Britain sought "peace". The Irish Republican Army (IRA) is an obvious expression of this distrust. The group's bombing campaign in Britain resulted in the establishment of a huge closed-circuit television (CCTV) surveillance system throughout London.[99] The system expressed the widespread social distrust felt by part of the UK elite, beyond just the IRA's revolutionary nationalism and armed struggle. While the IRA has faded away, the CCTV system remains mostly in place.

Finally, religious ideologies—especially fundamentalism—tend to exaggerate social distrust. While some religions encourage general trust in humanity, these are rather marginal orientations in the US (or co-exist alongside other contradictory ideas). Thus, many fundamentalist religions advocate a hierarchical transfer of respect, obedience, and resources to those at the top (of the religion and society). Particularly, many conservative Protestant religions (e.g., Baptists, Evangelicals, Mormons) actively encourage distrust for multiple reasons. First, humanity is not to be trusted, because humans are born into sin and thus are unworthy of trust. Second, followers of other faiths aren't trustworthy, as they are heathens or infidels who have an inaccurate, even blasphemous, interpretation of God. And third, trust in other people and social change is not worthwhile, as the only true salvation individuals can expect comes from divine intervention, and typically via an afterlife (which results from an individual's adherence to God's "word"). The blind trust that religious orders and leaders receive from followers favors the retention of their power.

Leaders can administer people's lives and regulate their behaviors, keep people dependent upon their "guidance" for a sense of self-worth and hope, and distract from practical actions in the present that would not only help them but others too. Thus, even though most major religions arguably derived from radical, counter-hegemonic social movements, their institutionalization across the world provided them with cultural and ideological power. Despite many religions possessing potentially revolutionary belief systems seeking a common humanity, hierarchical and fundamentalist religion is instead a counterrevolutionary force.

Rising religious fundamentalism is not merely a call to return to an earlier era—in fact, fundamentalism is quintessentially modern.[100] It propagates anti-"other" attitudes to the detriment of all except those in power. Often, fundamentalism is curated within a colonized country, which witnesses discrimination up close. Islamic fundamentalism has emerged for many reasons, but the Israel–Palestine issue serves as a telling case study. Average Palestinians and Israelis distrust each other, even though both would presumably prefer to live in peace than constant conflict. Antisemitism and anti-Judaism facilitate the Palestinian distrust of Israelis and Jews, while Islamophobia and anti-Palestinian beliefs (e.g., stereotypes of Palestinians as suicide bombers) facilitate Israeli distrust of Palestinians. Palestinian distrust in the Israeli state is surely rational given its warfare against the general Palestinian population. But this distrust should also extend to the ability of Hamas to adequately represent Palestinian interests in an independent Palestinian state. Thus, states are worthy of distrust by citizens and residents, regardless of which person or side they support.

The Israeli settler state has generated considerable distrust (mistrust) on the part of its citizenry against the Palestinian population and leadership—distrust in everything Palestinian and mistrust in an omnipotent Israeli state to defy logic and colonize another people in the twenty-first century. Crucially, there are many examples of Jewish and Palestinian collaboration, such as in the early kibbutzim[101] and the later joint struggle against the Separation Wall in Bil'in,[102] where common humanity becomes obvious. But hierarchal ideologies have imposed themselves between the two groups—often masquerading as religious conflict—in the form of the Israeli state and private property rights (or settlers' legal ability to flout such rights), thus generating distrust between people who could be allies or future fellow citizens. Under such conditions, it would be foolhardy to ask Palestinians to trust Israelis committed to settler colonialism and apartheid in the Occupied Territories, just as asking a battered spouse to trust her abuser would be an unjust request. True interpersonal trust will emerge should Israelis attack the hierarchy in their midst and dismantle their privileges vis-à-vis their Palestinian neighbors. Until this happens, Palestinian distrust is founded, although its justification via religious fundamentalism and antisemitism is a smokescreen.

A CULTURE OF DISTRUST

Culture is reproduced over time, providing continuity across generations. Consequently, in a distrustful society, we should expect a culture of distrust to permeate across time too. For example, Hollywood movies—a major source (or reflection, depending) of social ideas, values, and common history—is replete with distrusting narratives. In fact, the emphasis on contention and competition is central to most major movies. While some might argue that viewers' interest is primarily engaged through competitive entertainment, this overlooks alternative interpretations. First, the presumption that competing groups or individuals provide the main entertainment-worthy narrative discounts personal and collective struggles in which there are no "enemies". Second, common ground in Hollywood films is often found between characters as a result of competition—they conveniently discover their commonality through oppositional struggle—something rarely achieved in real life (e.g., co-workers who are at odds with each other are apt to remain that way until one leaves their job). Hollywood narratives also typically cast antagonists as uniformly bad and protagonists as good, despite the reality that we are all rather "complicated" and that goodness/badness is in the eyes of the beholder. Finally, Hollywood movies typically pit the main characters against individual-based caricatures and consequently lack any institutional analysis. Therefore, a movie may present a rich person as selfish and malevolent but lack any overarching message that it is the rich *as a class* or capitalism in general that is at fault.[103] There is a studious avoidance of film themes focused on collective empowerment or social movements, things that would provide (as well as require) greater social trust.

Music—especially popular music—is often (though not uniformly, of course) pitched at the lowest common denominator, with controversy avoided. For decades, American pop music has centered around simplistic themes of "love", wherein such love is just emotionality or lust.[104] The true complexities of "love" are almost completely absent from pop music's characterization, and not simply because lyrics about such topics don't rhyme. Additionally, commercial music emphasizes vapid individualism and selfishness. The singer/lyricist is the center of attention, controlling the narrative—presenting their uniform worldview in an unquestioned, instrumental fashion. Collectivity is ignored/absent, as are the values of "we-ness". Since pop music is a commodity, it studiously avoids any political contention or other complications that dissuade purchase. The necessary trust that binds us together rarely serves as a rallying cry in pop music, especially when such solidarity necessitates challenging deep-seated hierarchical domination (e.g., white supremacist capitalist patriarchy) instead of tepid calls for color-blind, liberal "unity" to transcend difference.

All of this is important because the stories we tell ourselves, from day-to-day and year-to-year, influence how we see the future and how future generations will see their present. If the stories we emphasize in movies, music, and other forms of media are not centered around themes of cooperation in pursuit of justice and freedom, is it any wonder that people struggle when they find themselves faced with challenges? When people are in cooperative settings—with friends, neighbors, co-workers—will they be able to figure out how to collectively struggle against hierarchy for shared power? Individuals may want another way forward but can only imagine taking their own individualistic, reformist actions.

THE MANIPULATION OF TRUST

Great effort is often invested by elites to generate trust. At the same time, distrust can be just as valuable to elites, so this is also prioritized. Such goals are accomplished through institutional manipulation. First, discouraging social trust involves generating suspicions of social equals. Under most circumstances, social trust is reasonable, so there may be an inclination toward eventual trust in the absence of elite interference. Powerful actors thus have a material interest in discouraging trust, as it forms the basis of collective counterpower. Second, encouraging political trust (actually mistrust) involves tricking or fooling people into trusting hierarchies, authority figures, and domination generally. Since elites usually propel these efforts to manipulate trust, we should ask what they gain from enhanced political trust in society. Clearly, elites seek state power—to craft favorable, profits-oriented legislation—which could be undermined by political distrust.

The many mechanisms for these manipulations do not fit into one simplified category. The easiest approach is to propagate fear. Scaring people is an incredibly cheap and effective technique to motivate distrust in others and trust in elites (who are to act as protectors of economic stability and physical safety). Fear-mongering often rests on a variety of sub-features. For example, hype and exaggeration work to amplify the expected threat posed by others, distorting the actual risks. Lying via contrived stories, exaggerating the quantity of alleged threats, or adding innuendo about the intentions of "untrustworthy" people are all efficient motivators of fear.

Another sub-feature is deliberate obfuscation: attempting to confuse someone or trick them into their fear. By conflating one group—regardless of how sloppy or inconsistent the logic—with some established threat, a manipulated target may equate one with the other. For example, conflating Muslims with political terrorism is common in Islamophobic societies—despite the mathematical improbability of millions of American Muslims being collectively responsible for a small number of terror attacks.[105]

Yet another mechanism of manipulation is distracting or blinding a target. Encouraging people to think about the *potential* threats posed by trusting one's neighbors, as opposed to considering the *likely* benefits of trusting them, compels the target to ruminate on what the manipulator wishes them to. By blinding a target to contrary examples or common sense, manipulators can encourage political trust in lieu of social trust. Hyping up the threat from blue-collar criminals, perhaps engaged in burglaries or robberies, is a way of distracting from far more common thefts, such as wage theft. Over 15 percent of low-wage workers are cheated out of their due pay each year—estimated in 2017 at $8 billion annually.[106]

As described above, there are established (and profitable) industries and potent ideologies that drive these mechanisms forward. Those with great economic resources will predictably invest in such propaganda. Lots of manipulation tools exist for these tasks, which corporations, states, and other powerful actors readily deploy. The mass media is an incredibly powerful cultural agent, along with the educational system. Applied psychological analysis, pursued by both scholars and the millions of college graduates hired by Corporate America for these tasks, has formidable statistical power enmeshed in its increasingly precise models.[107] Of course, in the absence of the carrot, the stick can be called upon—pressure techniques that hit people in their vulnerabilities (i.e., their economic precarity, psychological or emotional insecurities, or susceptibility to threats and blackmail).

I've dedicated a lot of this chapter to describing the ways in which distrust—particularly social distrust—can be cancerous, infecting the social body and disrupting society's liberatory and justice-seeking pathways. Unsurprisingly, it turns out there's many vested interests seeking to keep people distrustful of each other and a lot of money to be made in the process. But, in response, is trust always a good thing to seek? The next chapter explores reasons for being cautious—or at least more nuanced—about how and who we trust. Mistrust is an equally dangerous trap to fall into.

4

Misplaced Trust: Being Smart about Trust

SAY NO TO BULLSHIT "TRUST"

From 2001 through 2003, I was active in the American anti-war movement. Following the 9/11 terrorist attacks and up through the first years of the Iraq War, I helped organize and attended protest rallies and marches, participated in conferences and campaigns, and attended likely over one hundred "peace vigils". During that time, despite nearly half the American population opposing the US's military action against Iraq,[1] there was a sense inside the movement that we were a small, vocal minority, mostly on our own. Occasionally, some movement participants wanted to reach out to authorities for support.

For example, at a weekly peace vigil—standing on a sidewalk with signs—an angry man approached, arguing with vigilers. The man then hit one vigiler. Even though most in the movement assumed the police would do nothing, some thought it important to legally document the growing list of episodes of anti-movement violence (such as this), so a police report was filled and mechanically processed. There was no resulting follow-up from the police department. When another peace vigil was planned in a nearby suburb in front of a shopping mall, the organizing group was concerned that someone might attack the group of mostly elderly vigilers. Therefore, a phone call was placed to the police to let them know about the vigil and the perceived threats. The officer who answered the phone was cold and disinterested in safety concerns. His only question: "do *you* plan on breaking the law?" One last example on this theme: At the peak of pro-war fervor, a local peace group got approval to participate in a St. Patrick's Day Parade (mid-March 2003) and authorization from the local university to hold a pre-parade rally in a nearby building. Once the newspaper reported that an anti-war contingent would be in the parade, the parade-coordinating organization revoked their previous permission to be in the parade. Then, in response, and without cause, the university reversed the rally room reservation too. The group decided to "participate" anyway in the parade, by walking on the sidewalk alongside the parade route (a completely legal act). Some participants had constructed a large puppet to hold during the parade, which wouldn't fit on sidewalk, so when the group began marching down the sidewalk (prior to the parade's official start), a few walked on the side of the road. A police car immediately approached and two cops stopped the group of 50 marchers, charging us *all* with arrest. One officer roughly manhandled people holding the puppet, while the other made numerous false claims about what we were doing and what the law actually was.[2]

Even with this small handful of examples, it's clear that any desire to place trust in the police (and other authorities) was misplaced. Even when police do act reasonably, respectfully, or in the public interest, the end results depend on the context. But, given police officers' pro-authority, pro-patriotic, and pro-war sentiments, it didn't matter to them what rights should've been enjoyed by movement participants—police *chose* to not act in a supportive way. Police ignored, did not sympathize with, and distrusted anti-war activists. Thus, movement "trust" in the police was not reciprocal and was misplaced. To trust police in these instances wasn't just a waste of time, it was actively harmful and put vulnerable people at additional risk of police violence.

Trust—or at least that which is presented as "trust"—can easily reveal itself to be bullshit on closer examination. Simply being aware of others' poor intentions implies "I trust you—or, rather, expect you—to behave like a jerk". For example, impoverished inner-city residents often "trust" cops to behave with the hostile impunity of an occupying army. Using the word "trust" in these instances doesn't really achieve the standards we expect of it. Some anti-war activists "trusted" the police to not uphold our civil liberties, while others mistrusted the police.

Trust is not just knowing where others stand or mutual disdain—it's the joint willingness to risk. True trust needs to be reciprocal; unidirectional "trust" is just one-sided deference without respect-in-return (which looks a lot like hero-worship or slumming—depending on its nature). Thus, trust should not be given unilaterally without any evidence or mutual exchange. When workers trust a boss, they can easily be taken advantage of in the likelihood that the boss does not return their trust. Or, voters who trust in a candidate can easily be let down. Especially when offered from a position of disadvantage, trust is more of an aspiration than an actual willingness to risk.

Importantly, "hope" is not trust, but rather unfounded dreaming. The legions of young Americans who "trusted" Obama in 2008 to deliver the US to a post-racial utopia, bought his promises of "hope".[3] Voters' trust in him—or more accurately, their "hope without accountability"—led disillusioned liberals and some optimistic pro-Obama leftists to ultimately support Occupy Wall Street in 2011 once they witnessed the Obama White House's hands-off approach (stacked as it was with former Goldman Sachs executives) with banks and other financial companies. This betrayed trust was also evident in the 2016 bid of Bernie Sanders—a New Deal-style senator—as the Democratic presidential candidate, whose failed "Sandernista Revolution" convinced some liberals and progressives disillusioned by the pro-Wall Street presidential candidate Hillary Clinton to place their hope in the hawkish but tough-talk-about-banks Sanders.[4]

Hypocrisy is a powerful engine for generating distrust. For example, UK Prime Minister Boris Johnson's administration held parties in 2020, in the midst of a nationwide lockdown during the early days of the Covid-19 pandemic. While not widely known at the time, this hypocrisy ("Partygate") indicates that he and his fellow rulers believed themselves to be above the law. It's perfectly reasonable to distrust such a prime minister, indeed, to distrust prime ministers in general. Johnson's excesses just reinforce why they cannot be trusted: Great power always corrupts and reveals the hypocritical basis for rulers' power over others. Yet, many UK voters trusted Johnson, despite hypocrisies.

Having hope in those who ultimately let us down—misplaced, bullshit trust—can "burn" people. Such an experience can make people hesitate to trust again in the future. It may take many years for Democrats to lure left-of-center people back into the voting booth, given the party's realpolitik values. Being burned obviously hurts. More intimately, is it surprising that many women feel unable to trust men, whether romantically or otherwise? Of course, most men do not sexually assault women, but men's gendered privileges give them advantages that women who have survived traumatic experiences will be angry about.[5] It is asking a lot of those whose disadvantages have set them up for repeated disappointment to place trust in powerful institutions or those with great social privileges. It's a gamble for poor people and people of color to entrust a call to the police, to hope that more good than bad will result from such a call. The goodwill and hope placed in leaders has been taken advantage of repeatedly. Encouragement to "trust us" under such conditions—as Democrats repeatedly urge each election cycle—is condescending, harassing, and simply unfair. Trust ought to be placed when warranted and surely not when the offending party refuses to apologize for its past transgressions. Why should women trust unapologetic, macho men who have victimized them in the past? Why should leftists trust a Democratic Party that refuses to break with its Wall Street patrons, pro-Pentagon support and imperialist actions, and blame-the-poor ideology?

Trust in the US's two-party system has continuously rendered—for centuries now—two lukewarm, milquetoast white male candidates.[6] Structural features of the US polity both necessitate a certain degree of popular trust to be viewed as legitimate, while still endlessly disappointing wide swaths of the populace. This is not a fertile bed for growing trust. Despite claims by political scientists that political parties are perfected, essential organizations for managing unavoidable and necessary social conflict,[7] parties are also an infuriating monsoon for spreading mass distrust in a political system that refuses to address underling inequalities and injustices. In the case of the 2024 presidential election, the political system created nearly the exact same contest as the prior one—a run-off between Donald Trump and Joe Biden. With the exception of those two candidates and their fragile egos, who actually wanted such a repeat? Yet, until July 2024, that's what Americans were told to accept. The political system loses trust when it turns political questions of democracy, liberation, and justice into sideshows, subjugated to a *game* played between two individual personas.

Putting one's trust in voting and elections causes problems because it's premised on the assumption that this kind of trust will result in positive outcomes and that the people who seek state power are trustworthy. However, as science fiction novelist Douglas Adams wrote in *The Restaurant at the End of the Universe*, people who *want* to become president shouldn't be allowed to be president.[8] People who seek to be president (or aspire to other positions of power) are either power drunk or delusional people with a savior complex. Some will beg others to trust them, a request that speaks volumes. "Trust me" those in power tend to say. Depending on their role, this translates into "Vote for me!", "Don't worry, I'll protect you!", "I won't sell you out!", or "You'll always have a job!" But do those powerful people deserve the trust they request? People who deserve trust do not need to ask for it; past behavior has either created a trusting relationship or it hasn't. Trust is built over time and cannot be rushed, let alone begged for. A request for trust is a red flag warning.[9]

There are lots of regular attempts to convince people to trust things that lack substance or ethical standards. For example, things like advertising, product safety, food healthiness, or technologies (like trusted certificates for computers) attempt to blow smoke around ethical consumers, tricking them into trust. Organizations are regularly created for the purpose of feigning quality, sincerity, or responsibility. The Fair Labor Alliance (FLA)—whose name *sounds* great—is actually a textile industry-created initiative, professing to inspect sweatshops throughout the world on behalf of concerned consumers. But it was created to calm and coopt legitimate consumer concerns about capitalist excesses in the textile industry, without having any fundamental effect upon its profitability. Unlike its competitor, the Workers' Rights Consortium (formed by the labor advocacy network United Students against Sweatshops), the FLA announced its factory inspections in advance, thus neutering the veracity of oversight.[10] Such half-assed regulatory mechanisms may superficially sound like they aim to do good things, thus attempt to incur social trust and legitimacy, but ultimately prioritize the profitability of their patron corporations.[11]

Often there are attempts to guilt, blackmail, or coerce people into trust. Consequently, people who don't trust those in power often reap lots of negative consequences: violence, firing, lawsuits, social exclusion, and so on. The medical profession now has an official label for this, presumably irrational, distrust. Those who distrust the powerful can be labeled as having "oppositional defiance disorder" (ODD, unironically).[12] Psychiatrists who diagnose individuals with ODD are essentially substituting a psychoanalytical identifier for a perfectly reasonable anti-authoritarianism.[13] People's dislike of authority figures *is* rational given personal experience, but, with an ODD diagnosis, it's pathologized and labeled deviant. The professionals who have created this construct work within the hierarchical psychological and medical professions; ironically, an ODD diagnosis often results when a patient dares to challenge the underlying logic that people should respect those in power, such as doctors, professionals, and other elites. The strong-arming of "trust" for political institutions relies upon a thinly veiled "get in line" discourse. Attempting to convince someone who doesn't, for example, like their boss, cops, or politicians that there is something psychologically wrong with them not only insults that individual's (quite wise) intelligence but also may send them on a cyclical or spiraling path of depression, low self-esteem, victimhood, intoxication, medication, institutionalization, or worse. The ODD discourse—like much in the socially constructed *Diagnostic and Statistical Manual of Mental Disorders (DSM)*—struggles to conceal its own nationalist, authoritarian, and patriarchal logics, in order to consolidate its own power and establish a wide-base of unquestioning support. The very notion that *every* problem that someone has can be categorized and diagnosed is hardcore positivist, wishful thinking. Conveniently for the *DSM*, society produces ODD in great quantities simply as a byproduct of its socially unequal and disempowering nature.[14]

Perhaps the best strategy to avoid the relentless drumbeat demanding unwarranted trust is to follow this thought experiment: Consider why someone in particular or an institution in general wants you to trust them? What do they gain if you place your trust in them? In other words, we ought to engage in a critical assessment of their actual *interests* and how they would themselves *profit* or *acquire greater advantage* by our placement of trust. If their motivations are suspect, if their values do not match our own, or if they gain far more from this extension of trust than we, then don't offer your trust. This exercise can help us to recognize bullshit trust for what it actually is.

MISPLACED TRUST

Not everyone deserves our trust. Some have consistently abused our faith in them. When we mistakenly place trust in the untrustworthy, this should be understood as *mistrust* (i.e., the inappropriate placement of trust in those who do not deserve it). There's a lot of reasons why mistrust occurs. The lure of hierarchies often seduces us into putting trust in them. Hierarchical structures possess characteristics that trick and mislead. For example, corporate hierarchies have a well-funded polish (albeit often only surface deep), practiced sales-pitches and perfected slogans, years of "experience", and a pervasive ubiquity throughout society that make them almost seem *natural*. Although it's deathly problematic to place trust in those who possess more power, it happens regularly. The powerful sacrifice less in relationships with weaker partners, because their power allows them to avoid making concessions. They call the shots and retain the ultimate decision-making power.[15] People may willingly relinquish their free will by mistrusting. The era of autonomous city states in medieval Europe came to an end, in part, due to citizen's mistrust of centralized government. Peter Kropotkin describes how the city of Florence lost its "old spirit" and became subsumed by the centralized Italian state: "By too much trusting to government, [city dwellers] had ceased to trust themselves; they were unable to open new issues. The State had only to step in and to crush down their last liberties".[16]

Let's consider how various institutions and other social forces can acquire trust from their subordinates—despite compelling evidence that those weaker actors benefit less from this trust than those who wield more power. This resulting mistrust benefits hierarchical systems and often hurts those who, with hopefulness, extend trust. We'll analyze a wide range of social institutions and actors, including religious institutions, authority figures, politicians, celebrities, police, armies, employers, bureaucracies, racial and sexual dominant groups, and others.

Religion is a human-created system to facilitate and mediate the relationship between supernatural deities and their believers. Religions are often managed by individuals who occupy hierarchical positions in these religions (even when their position is strictly "advisory" or spiritual). The faithful trust religious authorities' merits to speak on behalf of a God or belief system. Priests, ministers, deacons, reverends, cardinals, bishops, popes, imams, clerics, and rabbis are just a few of the religious authorities within the world's major Abrahamic monotheisms. However, the leader's claims are not universally verifiable—otherwise there likely would be only one *true* religion. Followers often perceive religious figures to be "altruistic" and thus trustworthy, but leaders thrive on their central role in the religious organization and the admiring praise and deference of others, particularly their followers.[17] The trust that religious authorities receive from their followers offers them advantages—economically, politically, and socially—that they may solely benefit from. Whether sexual abuse within the many layers of the Roman Catholic Church's bureaucracy, financial extortion from televangelists, or the claimed importance of ministers over the laity of innumerable faiths, religious bureaucrats benefit more from trust relationships than do those frequently mislead, manipulated, and blackmailed within those belief systems. Granted, not every religious organization actively aims to deceive and many religious leaders vociferously believe themselves to be authentic and acting in good faith (no pun intended). But, the intimate, existential, and deeply traditional nature of religion means that religious leaders have more opportunities to exploit the religious than perhaps any other institution.

Non-religious authority figures—especially those with influence over state power—claim to solve problems for citizens and everyday people. If most people believe in the validity and good efforts of authority figures, then the greater those authority figures' power and influence will be. However, political authorities create far more problems for society than they typically solve. Most politicians work more for themselves and their narrow demographic of core supporters (often their class, race, or immediate interests) than for the entire society. In the United States, this can be seen from decades of pro-corporate policy that directly contradicts consistently studied and well-known popular opinion.[18] Authority figures predictably care most about those they owe allegiance to: They believe they owe more to the financial donors than voters. These interests will trump obligation to the common good more often than not. They have far more personal traits in common with elites—business people, layers, and so on—than with a working-class and middle-class electorate. Politicians also seek to demobilize the citizenry and channel them into the semi-regular endorsement of their official actions through voting. The state does not really desire mass participation because participation makes a society incredibly difficult to govern (and dominate), as it reduces the ultimate power held by authorities. Thus, the perpetuation of the status quo is simply a guaranteed outcome of the trust extended to political authorities by a citizenry and other residents.

Unfortunately, outsider politicians (of a progressive or social democratic stripe) are different only in degree from reigning political authorities. Progressive politicians (e.g., Paul Wellstone, Cynthia McKinney, Dennis Kucinich, and Bernie Sanders in recent US memory) and "third parties" (e.g., Greens, Labor, Spain's Podemos, Bolivia's Movimiento al Socialismo, etc.) give rousing speeches to the masses, hoping to turn out a large electorate in their favor. Trusting that these few politicians—if only placed in power, or given enough law-making authority—will act in the general interest is an attractive premise to people critical of the status quo. Electing someone sharing your values and then trusting in their promises to use your mandate to fix all problems is highly appealing. However, these "outsider" politicians dangle carrots in front of people, only to pull it away when needed. For example, a young Greek politician with the anti-austerity party Syriza was elected in 2015 but then sold out his electorate by negotiating with European Union bankers.[19] This recent history of left-wing governments throughout Latin America's "pink wave" (e.g., Bolivia, Brazil, Ecuador, and Venezuela) is also fraught with partial follow-through, lies, and even repression.[20] Structurally, electoral efforts steal social movements' energy and inertia, convincing protesters to quiet down and accept the status quo (and the belief that representative democracy will finally work). On the cusp of Bill Clinton's election in 1992, a large national coalition of organizations prioritizing progressive causes fell apart because some participants thought Clinton would deliver their goals. Instead, the coalition's energy was sapped away from fighting for social change to get someone elected.[21] Nothing better illustrates this lure than Bernie Sanders's 2016 run for president, which used the language of "revolution" and "movement". However, the "revolution" Sanders spoke of was not revolutionary.[22] He spoke of a limited electoral "revolution", as he ran for the nomination of one of the two dominant business-led political parties (the Democrats), despite his own "independent" affiliation in Congress as a democratic socialist. If all the young people (and there were tens of thousands) who actively campaigned for him would have instead helped form labor unions, antifa crews, mutual aid societies, and other local campaigns, a real social revolution would be far more likely in the future.[23] Putting trust in other influential people (even leftists) to act how you want is unfortunately just more wishful thinking. Why not simply work to create that world yourself alongside your fellow social equals?

A rough, British equivalent to pro-Bernie Sanders advocates pushing for renewed trust in the Democratic Party is pro-Jeremy Corbyn advocates pushing for retaining support in the UK's

Labour Party. This pro-Labour advocacy occurs despite the party's acceptance of market economics and embrace of neoliberalism, especially under the leadership of Tony Blair. If there's serious interest in overcoming capitalist exploitation (as Labour has often professed interest in), can it really originate from established political parties? Joining the statist party system, even as critics of capitalism, is likely to eventually warp all moral compasses. Similarly, in Israel, pro-Labor Party support for early pro-Zionist leaders—including Golda Meir, Yitzhak Rabin, and Shimon Peres—did not result in Labor extending its vision of justice and liberation to Palestinians and the Occupied Territories. Perhaps the most provocative examples of leftist sell-outs are the parties and politicians of Greece's Syriza and Spain's Podemos, who rode a tidal wave of anti-austerity energy into power, only to quickly cave to global capital once they got elected.[24] Voters trusted them, shown by the time spent supporting their candidacies—and thereby redirected their energies from protesting and organizing in the streets. Such trust appears to be a mistake that undermined the anti-systemic momentum that could otherwise have been achieved. Voting for the lesser of two evils is a pragmatic choice but doesn't and shouldn't require trust.

Beyond politicians, other leaders on society's periphery hold sway over substantial groups of people. The trust demanded from both cult leaders and other cults of personality simultaneously discourages trust in everyday people. Whether religious, political, or otherwise, cults establish subservient relationships between followers and those in charge. Cults like the Peoples Temple or the Democratic Workers Party (New Left communists) had strong, persuasive leaders who dissuaded members from seeking solidarity or solace with outsiders. Obedient followership is expected, dissent is punished, and members are shamed so they do not leave the cult—a cult's argument is that the rest of society cannot be trusted, so stay here! The line between a "cult" and another authoritarian or messianic organization is a bit vague. The Revolutionary Community Party (RCP; Maoists) has innumerable cadre organizations whose political analysis and strategies revolve around RCP founder Bob Avakian. Later in life, United Farm Worker leader

Cesar Chavez aspired to create a cult around himself, complete with a compound.[25] While not as militant in imposing punishment for attempting to leave, a cult of personality exists around Comrade Bob that reproduces unquestioning support for him and distrust in any other leftist sect or analysis. Organized religions may only differ from cults in matters of degree; the Church of Scientology exemplifies that distinction, and it also condemns non-Scientologists and attacks any external criticism of the Church (especially its founders L. Ron Hubbard and David Miscavige) through aggressive litigation.[26] Members are unlikely to establish new, lasting trust relationships with those outside the cult, because there are external and internal mechanisms of control that govern members' behavior. Self-sealed social circles all but guarantee limited contact with others with whom members could eventually learn to trust.[27] Trust among cult members flow vertically through fallible leaders at the top as opposed to horizontally with others. Members are discouraged from trusting other data sources, including their own powers of observation. Many cults have formally combined religion and politics, including mainstream American political parties. The lifelong affiliations, groupthink, and antagonism-toward-outsiders fostered within political parties creates cultish distrust of all others and mistrust in party leaders. The US's Democratic Party can be cult-like (especially for the party faithful), but the Republican Party is *absolutely* cult-like, especially since Trump emerged on the scene. In practical terms, the Republican Party has de-emphasized much of its pro-corporate, evangelical ideological core and is now built around fealty to the personality (and ego) of Trump. The "MAGA" (Make American Great Again) faction in the Republican Party is no longer the small, noisy faction it was in 2016—it now constitutes the party's majority. MAGA's crass populism is jet fuel for Trump's narcissistic rule.

Although they may have no claim to organizational authority, charismatic people can also perpetuate social distrust. Celebrities and famous "saviors" are expected to swoop in and solve "problems" for us. Rich and famous people, but also notorious celebrities, occupy a prominent place in American culture. Of course, news coverage of celebrity behavior exaggerates the impact of their lives upon society. When a celebrity donates money to a "cause" or starts a charity in their own name, the rest of us lose a bit of our own self-efficacy. They provoke uncertainties, like: Why should we look to everyday, ordinary people to collaboratively solve our personal and collective problems, especially when it seems that only the famous are doing it? Even charity from well-meaning celebrities can relegate and resign us to the role of spectator. Unfortunately, becoming a passive observer of saviors makes us lose our important empathy for others and a passion for justice.[28] Charity ends up enhancing the moral legitimacy of donors, especially as they have so much more money at their disposal to "give"—for example, the praise for some extremely wealthy individuals like Bill Gates, who give their ill-gotten fortunes via their own charitable foundations, in support of philanthrocapitalism.[29] Philanthropy's benefits are self-limited by the rich, who also are often the very same people generating the harms that their benevolence is supposedly intended to address.[30] However, solidarity is far more important that charity, because it functions horizontally, according to Eduardo Galeano.[31] And, being willing to put ourselves at risk (with others, as accomplices)[32] requires trusting others in a way that faith in celebrity benevolence simply does not accomplish. Celebrities, by definition, have their own interests—otherwise, why else would most of them pursue celebrity? (Also, if their names and egos do not matter, then why not donate money anonymously?) Even the assumption that a famous name will attract more donations or attention to an important cause reduces the cause's importance to what the celebrity perceives. The only trustworthy celebrity is one who does not seek or encourage fame, and who actively seeks to subvert it. A culture that celebrates celebrity generosity but discourages progressive social movements seeking collective change is clearly opposed to horizontal trust in lieu of trust in charismatic "leaders".

State actors are many and desperate for mass trust. Police are an important element of state social control. To the extent that citizens (or non-citizens) believe law enforcement to be a neutral arbitrator of justice, that population will continue to trust the police more than they trust each other. As an institution, police benefit from populations that are incapable of handling deviance or their disagreements collectively, democratically, and peacefully. Indeed, it is difficult for many to understand the role police play in society—that of armed government bureaucrats. This difficulty stems from propaganda[33] and the violence that police wield over their subject populations. Not everyone equally trusts police though.[34] Those who are more privileged find it easier to trust police, since police essentially work *for them* (or at least serve to protect their interests). In contrast, police have historically suppressed immigrants, workers, and people of color. A privileged person's trust in the police exemplifies a relinquishing of control to those armed government bureaucrats, as they trust them to mediate between the disadvantaged masses (and thus may be coming to steal from their privileged lives). But a person of color is less likely to want to call the police, because doing so might actually get them killed. The great paradox of policing—operating under conditions of unchecked power and implicit bias—is that law-abiding citizens are more likely to get killed when police stop them, because such citizens are often indignant of police harassment. But people who know they broke a law are more likely to obey orders once they are caught and thus get better treatment. A law-abiding civilian's reasonable anger is apt to enrage a cop who, predictably, dislikes their authority and biases being challenged. This challenge to their authority seems to be a central cause in police-led escalation in their interactions with citizens; having a loaded weapon and "street-based justice" at their disposal isn't enough moral authority.[35] The institution of policing seeks to disadvantage people by invoking respect for its authority and thus discourages people from seeking assistance except through police officer's interventions. Unsurprisingly, law enforcement officers are more likely to be social reactionaries, with greater right-wing authoritarianism and support for social inequality.[36] The people who seek employment as police are more likely to have a personality predisposed to "law and order", authoritarianism, and the use of righteous violence.[37]

The modern army seeks to occupy and control designated enemy populations through non-lethal means, if possible—violent or lethal, if necessary. Bombs disrupt an occupied population's mistrust in the occupier. Thus, "non-lethal" means are cheaper, less dangerous, and politically safer. However, to do this requires generating trust with local populations, often indigenous leaders. While less death is surely more desirable than more death, this methodology makes it easier for the military to occupy and subjugate a population. Military personnel, such as the US's Human Terrain Systems employees (including social scientists), compromise their professional ethics to "do no harm" when studying local culture and social systems, to provide the army with efficient, actionable information for pursuing the military goals of empire.[38] The trust generated— often through manipulation and bribery—between occupier and occupied perpetuates major international crimes. Comparable local law enforcement campaigns to garner the trust of poor neighborhoods and people of color has a similar faux-benevolence to it, as it makes social control less difficult for police, rather than focusing upon expanding social justice for such communities.

Trusting capitalists is also a very dangerous idea. Influential business people are primarily interested in doing things that return great profit. If they can make cheaper products or overcharge, they likely will.[39] Thus, employers cannot be trusted to work for the common good, since they are exclusively motivated by self-interest. Any benefits employers create for employees are secondary to their own enrichment. Thus, even while capitalists claim to be "job creators", their furnishing of employment positions is not a selfless, charitable act. Employers discourage workers from forming unions, which would increase worker trust in each other, while decreasing trust in the boss. Employers even discourage sharing too much information with fellow workers, such as wage rates, as this not only raises class consciousness about worker exploitation but also allows workers to unify against the boss. Employers implicitly distrust employees—they distrust their motivations, commitment, work ethics, and so on—and thus employers manage them, propagandize against unions, discourage workers from sharing their incomes, and set up surveillance systems (e.g., CCTV cameras, key-logging software, requiring punching a time-clock for shifts). To place trust in employers is a unilateral act of faith, and is thus not only unhelpful but actively harmful.

Placing trust in a bureaucracy is a bit like throwing your support behind a hurricane—bureaucracies are complex, powerful, inflexible, and indifferent to an individual's behavior or choices. Bureaucracies supplant trust in individuals for trust in an abstracted and diffused system. Thus, people only need to trust the rules and roles within a bureaucracy, not the people who follow or fulfill them. More specifically, bureaucracies are fairly indifferent about whether people trust them or not; they care not if you trust in the rules, as long as you follow them. Hypothetically, bureaucracies do predictable things and render "fair" results, but they are thoroughly influenced by power; one's available time, resources, and interest; and are rarely designed to create justice or equality. In practice, bureaucracies tend to be notoriously unreliable and impersonal—thus, it's rather foolish to place trust in such a juggernaut. Unsurprisingly, people do not like to give their trust over to a faceless bureaucracy (or an organization that regularly changes the faces put forth), something that moves slowly and unpredictability, and does not have their interests at heart. Ultimately, bureaucracies serve themselves and their own inertia more than they serve their "constituencies", and a bureaucracy's survival and justifications are more important motivations for them than any other interest group's (with the exception of their economic and political architects and patrons).

Trusting white men, who are those predominantly in positions of authority as bureaucrats, landlords, managers, officials, intimate partners, and so on, may be asking a lot from people of color and women. The structural advantages created by white supremacy and patriarchy, for both white people and men, privilege them in ways that make trusting them a nebulous prospect. Should people of color be expected to automatically trust white people after being profiled, discriminated against, and mistreated—to say nothing of the intergenerational memory of lynchings, internment, deportation, and other crimes perpetuated against them—by whites with and without formal political power? Should women be expected to trust men (in general) after they've typically had numerous negative experiences with other men, like abusive fathers, partners or spouses, dates, bosses, or even strangers? To take the example of gender, the #MeToo phenomenon of 2017 involved hundreds of women (and some men) publicly naming powerful men who had sexually assaulted or mistreated them. The common thread linking all these men was their powerful positions and statuses. Their privileges had not only attracted followers and supporters but also resulted in these men receiving the benefit of the doubt when victims began sharing their stories and leveling accusations. The very existence of these leveraged, prominent positions provides an incredible *capacity* for abuse. Of course, not all powerful men engage in sexual misconduct, but the vast majority of those engaged in misconduct have some form of power over those they victimize.[40]

Even though they feign selflessness and thus attract general support from many people, non-profits and NGOs today have largely become corporatized by the slow creep of pro-capitalist ideology, business management practices and structures, and business deals, and even power-sharing coalitions with corporations.[41] Many movement actors are also implicated in these behaviors, especially when they abandon the grassroots and align with dominant, ruling interests. The organization INCITE! Women of Color against Violence calls this the "non-profit industrial complex" (NPIC). Organizations and movements in the NPIC acquire support because they *seem* to reflect many common peoples' values and goals yet in fact subvert, neuter, or distract from those progressive ends. Our trust in them as social change agents is misplaced and abused by NGOs and NPIC movement actors, as well as the corporations for whom NGOs run interference. Corporations like free publicity for "doing good". They stunt social change and channel it into reformist directions rather than toward radical and revolutionary ends. Business owners fear the spread of anti-capitalist sentiments. And ruling elites want to profit from the work that NGOs will do for them, in exchange for the price of a few grants, donations, or coordinator salaries. According to Dylan Rodríguez, the NPIC is accompanied by the prison-industrial complex (PIC); these complexes emerged in the post-1960s era to respond to social tumult—especially Black liberation movements—to suppress through outright physical domination and to ideologically control the actions of sectors of the liberal left that wanted to challenge the system.[42] The societal distrust in Black Americans expressed by these two institutions (the PIC and NPIC, respectively) is equaled by the mistrust that so many Americans—especially white Americans—place in the NPIC.

According to sociologist Émile Durkheim, modern societies tend to feature associational bonds between people. Since we are inter-dependent upon each other—to satisfy our daily requirements, to provide rare services, and so on—we all need each other.[43] The rich and powerful need the poor and disempowered, and vice versa. While there is some truth to parts of this, these are questionable relationships to place trust in. While there are obligations expected of elites—for example, *noblesse oblige* from the European medieval period, which thrust the aristocracy and peasantry into a symbi-otic relationship—it's usually those who possess the most political and economic power who are most apt to neglect their obligations. Yes, peasants harvested all the food and could riot if need be, but the gentry still had weapons and powerful allies on their side and could (and did) use the law to cast out the peasantry whenever they wanted. Peasants could thus trust aristocrats, but only so far.

In a more recent example, the 2008 great economic recession—brought about by Wall Street's greed—caused immeasurable harm in the US and throughout the world. To fix the presumed problem, the US Congress gave Wall Street a $700 billion infusion of cash from taxpayers. This was done on the logic (and promises) that bankers would start loaning money to average Americans who needed it, such as those at risk of house foreclosure. Banks could easily loan money, which average people could make good use of. But the banks were cheapskates with this free cash and paid off their own debts, acquired each other's assets, and rewarded their execu-tives with huge bonuses. Congress's "trust" in banks to do the right thing was foolish, a bit like trusting a known murderer to put their knife-wielding and stabbing skills to better, more socially produc-tive use by lending them billions of knives, only to be surprised when they continue killing. Such mistrust (and money) simply prolonged suffering and fattened the pockets of the already wealthy. If widespread distrust—apparent in the record number of phone calls politicians received from constituents for an earlier, failed version of the bailout bill—had succeeded in pressuring Congress to not extend the multi-billion-dollar loan, the results could have been different. Society could have let banks fail, forced them to pay off their poorer customers first, allowed homeowners and renters to remain in their homes, and worked to fend off sheriffs threatening eviction. In other words, our trust would have been better placed in doing mass eviction defense than sitting back, fingers crossed, waiting for Bank of America, Wells Fargo, and JP Morgan Chase to start lending home loans again.[44] Incidentally, citizen trust in banks was lower than Congress, as record numbers called and lobbied "their representatives" to not bail out failing financial institutions. Under such pressure, Congress failed to pass an earlier bill on September 29, 2008, only later approving the $700 billion bailout.

Not everyone who unknowingly tells a lie is a liar, but those who are liars (e.g., the aforementioned bank executives) know what they're doing. A psychologically engineered version of mistrust is called "gaslighting", referring to the 1944 film *Gaslight*. In the film, a deceptive husband strategically misleads (read: lies to) their spouse (played by Ingrid Bergman), convincing her that her perceptions are incorrect. The style of gaslighting is used whenever powerful institutions in general (or individuals in particular) lie, mislead, and deceive to acquire unquestioned psychological persuasion over a less powerful actor. The resulting self-doubt primes the target for mistrust in that powerful authority figure. Manipulation tricks someone into inappropriately trusting someone wholly untrustworthy. Through repetition, a gaslighter undermines their target's capacities to empirically observe and interpret their reality. In the end, the gaslighted person comes to rely upon their manipulator for an interpretation of "reality" and "truth". The manipulator is objectively untrustworthy, but the tricked person doesn't know any better, as they have been fooled by a malevolent psychological-operation campaign targeting their reasoned defenses.[45] Sadly, a gaslighted target cannot trust their own judgments or senses; worst, the manipulated target is unlikely to know they have misplaced their trust, thanks to the long-term deception. The "trust" that results from gaslighting is gained through an attack on the target's self-esteem, sanity, desire for affection, and dependency. The tactic is common among abusive spouses, particularly to avoid responsibility for sexual infidelity.

Beyond this long list of often untrustworthy institutions and other powerful actors, even some of our social equals are untrustworthy. In fact, it would be naive to argue otherwise. Unfortunately, we are all damaged by our hierarchical socializations, which influences those who intend ill, seeking to manipulate, dominate, or exploit others. Ironically, people tend to think that *other people* are the untrust-worthy, unethical ones, who are lazy or making mistakes, and so forth. But, this can't possibly be the case, since most everyone thinks this about most everyone else (including us, you, and me). In other words, we see ourselves as trustworthy while considering others not to be. Since so many people also consider themselves trustworthy, either we're all generally *wrong about ourselves* or we're wrong about each other. The simplest answer to this apparent paradox is that we're most likely all rather trustworthy—we just sometimes have poor perception skills and are easily manipulated by the above insti-tutions that seek to encourage our distrust of our peers! It's easy to distrust our peers and unfortunate when our trust is abused, but it's more important that we try to trust them.

While its problematic to impulsively, uncritically distrust our seemingly untrustworthy peers, it's also unwise to leap to trust those who seem the most trustworthy. Should we simply have trust in the intentions of the best among us? Should we idolize and promote the actions of "altruists" as the ideal? This generates a deceptive and unattainable standard for us to emulate—and to fail at. Further, altruists may not really be altruists. Those who seem like the most obvious fit for this label, often secretly seek the praise and grati-fication for their "selflessness". Look no further than the gigantic egos of religious leaders and politicians who (often unconvincingly) claim their actions are motivated by altruistic desire to do good for everyone else.[46] Watch any debate between political candidates—

each is convinced (and tries to convince us) that *they alone* are uniquely skilled at solving our particular problems. The sheer mathematical improbability that there exists such an ideally suited savior is made all the more tragic by their sincere arrogance that *they* are that savior.[47] Such "altruists" always seek credit for their contributions, even when minor in scale. Thus, altruists accumulate a status greater than they deserve. Celebrities are a good example of presumably emulation-worthy altruists. Media hold them up as exemplars of good behavior, charitable giving, and principled stands. But celebrities are only impressive because they can attract lots of attention and because they have accumulated so much money, of which some they can afford to give away. Thus, the lucky, elite few (like celebrities) are structurally more able to act "altruistically", as they have more spare time, expendable income, or charisma for self-promotion.

Thus, there are many reasons why mistrust occurs. Trickery, blindness, moral ambiguity, and domination all can lead people to invest trust in those who aren't deserving of it. To really understand how and why this happens requires a deeper assessment of hierarchy's ideological and economic interests.

THE MISTRUST INDUSTRY

Just as there is a distrust industry that profits from sowing distrust where we ought otherwise to trust, it's not surprising that some groups profit handsomely from encouraging trust when trust is not warranted. Indeed, lots of money can be made by generating and sustaining mistrust. I refer to these groups as part of a "mistrust industry" because they both create mistrust and profit from it.

To the extent that capitalism requires false consciousness among workers and consumers—class ignorance thwarts anti-capitalist resistance—then pro-capitalist ideologues can profit by guaranteeing widespread mistrust. The two wings of the mistrust industry propelling capitalist mistrust are nonprofit and for-profit based, respectively, education and advertising (presented as "information"). The former erects the intellectual scaffolding that permits the latter to flourish. While education appears to be more sophisticated and subtle propaganda, advertising is crass and presumably clear in its bias. Yet, many people remain ardent supporters of both, despite the mistrust that education and advertising nurture.

A central component of education is the "hidden curriculum"—what's *really* being taught, albeit often informally and without drawing too much attention to such lessons. For example, while American history or civics classes are presumably factual and objective, they actually emphasize a hidden curriculum driven by—and in pursuance of—blind patriotism, American exceptionalism, and an uncritical acceptance of the status quo. It's difficult for the average American high school student to acquire a strong critique of American democracy from such courses. Education has the ubiquity and moral force to convince people (such as citizens) to trust the state and other dominant institutions such as patriarchy and white supremacy, despite many students being at a structural disadvantage vis-à-vis those institutions.

The "profits" of educational mistrust accumulate indirectly. Since public education is funded by the state (i.e., via tax dollars), it nurtures a commitment in the state system. The state benefits from a patriotic populace that willingly enters public or military service. Taxpayers, who are inoculated with the belief in the moral rightness of the work ethic, buy into the rat race implicitly advocated by higher education. As Pierre Bourdieu indicated, education is generally a system of social reproduction, benefiting the already wealthy and privileged, disadvantaging those from less educated and less class-privileged backgrounds.[48] Capitalists—as employers and goods and services vendors—profit from the static assessment of the world that education conveys, with its emphasis upon the permanence of capitalism and the state. An ahistorical understanding of major institutions contributes to the continued dominance of those institutions. People who place trust in systems that replicate inequality—especially poor students who benefit the least from such education—are making strategic mistakes.

There are other, more reasonable, trustworthy benefits to education, but its "industrial" quality—motivated by the need to create trusting citizens and workers on behalf of systems of power[49]—

swamps basic educational benefits that sometimes are and should be the primary emphasis of education: skill-acquisition, critical thinking skills, scientific reasoning, and an opposition to illegitimate authority. The education system—primary and secondary, as well as post-secondary—is also being privatized, in order to more explicitly benefit wealthy investors of charter schools and for-profit universities.

The second wing of the mistrust industry is more directly linked to markets and profit-making: advertising. In fact, advertising is a robust industry that explicitly advocates misleading customers for the purposes of profit. Specifically, advertising exists to convince people to trust companies selling products and services and to overlook (and thus avoid distrusting) their actual motivations (i.e., profit-making) or malevolence.

Critical theorists of the Frankfurt School focused intensively on the rise of the advertising industry in the twentieth century, along with pop culture and mass media. According to Herbert Marcuse, mass culture pacified and stupefied, creating a "one-dimensional man".[50] Of course, the advertising industry assumes that feelings of need or desire must be deliberately created—otherwise, if we already knew exactly what we wanted and needed, an advertising industry wouldn't be needed. In the absence of advertising, people don't actually need or desire the things that advertising seeks to promote. Were it not for advertising, people would consume less and perhaps not feel as many "needs" or "desires". In other words, we would more likely feel authentic, self-derived needs and desires, rather than those instilled by profit-seeking corporations. A capitalist economy requires an advertising industry to provoke a sense of inadequacy and anxiety, to compel people to shop in pursuit of fulfillment. Thus, advertising lurks behind all capitalist enterprise.

The dimensions of this industry are impressive and clearly indicate the enormity of mistrust demanded of people. According to the Association of National Advertisers—which advocates for the expansion of marketing—nearly one-fifth of the US's jobs are "supported" by the advertising industry itself (20 million Americans in 2014 and 28.5 million in 2021), comprised 19 percent of total US economic output, and generated $7.1 *trillion* in sales.[51] The colossal centrality of the advertising industry raises a simple and crucial question: How could something that presumes to tell people what they *really* want be such a core part of an economy? Not only does one-fifth of the US's economic activity take place in advertising, but the other four-fifths of output appears to be, at least in part, the result of such advertising. Something is wrong when economic activity—producing and consuming—is contingent upon sophisticated psychological methods of manipulation. Advertising may be more ubiquitous than ever before—every owner of a smartphone now has an advertising and tracking tool in their pocket. It should be uncontroversial to suggest that we ought not to trust advertising to accurately reflect our true needs.

A fundamental question ought to be: In societies where elites, liberals, and prominent academics claim the important, central values of trust, why should an advertising industry even exist? In fact, it exists to launder the public image of unpopular corporations, to distract from corporate malfeasance (e.g., exploitation of workers, environmental pollution, unsafe products and working conditions), and to manufacture desires by instilling in us, and then constantly reminding us of, our inadequacies. The trust that people place in the ideas and messages derived from advertising efforts is misplaced, and thus is, in fact, mistrust. And there is a lot of money to be made in this business.

Highlighting people's identities as "consumers"—in lieu of individuals with rights, freedoms, and entitlements—serves to generate mistrust for capitalism itself. Propaganda that encourages people to primarily feel "empowered" in stores with their wallets undercuts other forms of solidarity we'd more naturally feel for each other. As it turns out, feelings of false empowerment can come from other sources too.

POLITICAL TRUST FOR THE WRONG REASONS

Powerful institutional actors tend to advocate participation in the system. "Just trust in it!", they encourage. Former US transportation secretary Pete Buttigieg writes in his treatise *Trust: America's Best Chance*: "The elegance of democratic legitimacy is that the people, in turn, should be able to trust their institutions … reciprocating on the trust placed in them by the Constitution".[52] In the US, this is an annual, or at least an every-four-years chorus. By voting, running for office, or appealing through the "proper" channels, *you* can make a difference. The system will work! Believers in justice, freedom, and peace just need a better election day turnout, more progressive candidates, more small donations that can pay for TV ads, and so on.

But by doing these actions, people validate the system's legitimacy, giving those who desire justice, freedom, and peace a false promise of hope, which ultimately prolongs the wait for real, transformative change. Notice that the most common form of participation—voting—does not represent a fundamental challenge to the status quo but tends to increase faith in it. Legitimacy means that people see the system as inherently okay or even just. Perhaps it is not functioning as it should, but it is fixable. So just be patient! Thus, despite the system's intergenerational, even multi-century, failure to deliver on its "promise" of democracy, freedom, and happiness, this political trust just results in another generation committed to myths and the mirage generated by doctrine, mythology, and smokescreens.

There are many sources encouraging greater political trust. As noted above, a prominent promoter of the notion of status quo change via elections is American education. Civics and American history classes focus on presenting the system as good. Students are taught an ideological message mischaracterized as non-ideological. This narrative claims that the American political system is uniquely virtuous, an amazing invention of the Founding Fathers that all should take pride in and that works just as theory suggests. American history is purportedly replete with well-intended, visionary settlers, who created a wonderful, prosperous society, with only a modicum of distasteful practices (which are relegated to footnotes or stricken from the record altogether). This is part of the infamous "hidden curriculum" that normalizes the US's system and presents it as "best".[53] The hidden curriculum is the core ideological message that mass education intends to convey, and it lurks behind the education system's virtuous claims. Thus, civics and history classes argue that the political system will self-correct through the wisdom of its stabilizing institutions. And these institutions have common people's interests at heart, of course. This simplistic interpretation of the US's origin story is strongly contested in the historical record.[54]

The US's origin story is wildly inaccurate. The country was not founded in pursuit of liberty—unless "liberty" only pertains to the lives and livelihoods of affluent white settlers. Surely, a fully realized liberty was an irrelevant concern of American slave owners and large landowners, who kept African slaves and European indentured servants under their thumbs. Defense of the institution of slavery—from impending abolition in England and African slave revolt—was a key factor in the American Revolution of 1776.[55] Thus, there was no such trust in "the American people" to be found within the ranks of the Founding Fathers—unless "people" are only white, male property owners. As an elite and *not*-popularly-elected group of wealthy white men, they displayed an incredible suspicion and fear for the insurrectionary potential of the common person living in the American colonies. Predictably, there was no trust for Africans, Native Americans, or women. But even their fellow whites—who might be better understood as a "rabble" or mob—were untrustworthy.[56] The Founders didn't construct a "true" democracy based on equal access to power, since they feared the numerical majority of poor people would simply vote away the privileges of the landed and slave-owning elite. Thus, various anti-democratic mechanisms were enshrined in the pro-private property Constitution that replaced the Articles of Confederation; Madison's Federalist Paper No. 10 can be viewed as a statement of class dominance.[57] Where the Articles constructed a weak central government in favor of decentralization, the Constitution prioritized a strong central government that could properly put down insurrections (e.g., Shay's Rebellion). An elite Senate was created (the equivalent of the British Parliament's House of Lords) for whom there were no direct elections; lifetime appointment of Supreme Court justices all but guaranteed a conservative judiciary that lagged behind popular sentiment; and an unelected Electoral College (today, the last of its kind in the world) that enabled small-population states and especially slave-owning Southern states disproportionate political influence. The words of Constitutional Convention delegate Alexander Hamilton clearly illustrate the distrust that he and his fellow elites had in the common people:

> All communities divide themselves into the few and the many. The first are the rich and well born, the other the mass of the people. The voice of the people has been said to be the voice of God; and however generally this maxim has been quoted and believed, it is not true in fact. The people are turbulent and changing; they seldom judge or determine right. Give therefore to the first class [the rich and well born] a distinct, permanent share in the government. They will check the unsteadiness of the second [the masses].[58]

The promise of "life, liberty, and pursuit of happiness" is regularly referenced as something that Americans should "trust in" (along with "In God We Trust"). The phrase serves as the motto for America's "promise" to all—the American Dream. But we know that people who experience poverty are not able to experience happiness at the same level as those who are economically stable. In fact, poverty depletes people's health and life. Racism destroys life—disadvantaged people of color have shorter life spans, greater chronic ailments, and so on—and curtails liberty by locking up Black and brown bodies at a mind-bending rate disproportionate to white bodies. Patriarchy ruins the chances for women to pursue their passions, by subjecting them to decades of paternalism, gendered tracking, occupational segregation, sexual harassment and violence, underpayment for their labor, and the all-consuming burdens of the second shift. Thus, in an unequal society, we cannot trust this "promise", since such dubious promises are far from a guarantee. Incidentally, Locke's original aspirational goal was for life, liberty, and *property*.[59] Apparently, elites realized that guaranteeing people property was *too much* and instead offered "opportunity". Instead of guaranteeing access to these things, they simply have a "right" to *possibly* possess them. Of course, all US citizens have the "right" to become president, a millionaire, or live a comfortable life—but how often is this going to happen to people who are on the wrong side of institutionalized privileges and hierarchies? Social scientists have long noted that social mobility is more the exception than the rule, and that societies with larger between-class inequality experience the least mobility.[60]

Democrats are perhaps the most adamant purveyors of trusting in working through the system. The Democratic Party continuously labors to convince the left to "trust" the system, to vote for their candidates, and not give up "the fight" (curtailed to an electoral struggle, not within social movements). This keeps Democrats "in the game" and bolstered with legitimacy. They are even willing to let outsiders like social democrat Bernie Sanders temporarily "join" the party in order to reinvigorate its "base". That the Democratic Party's leadership is so disconnected from its "base" that it requires a social-ist to rouse enthusiasm, is telling. The party swings far to the right of its voting constituency and those who regularly turn out to the polls to cast their lot in with the Democrats—or just as often—against the Republicans. The Democrats are the "lesser of two evils", and millions vote not so much *for* Democrats as *against* Republicans.

The system wants—even needs—people to trust in it because this makes it able to endure radical challenges. Such challenges often come from the left—organized in social movements or expressed in explosive uprisings. "Trust" resulting from bullshit promises that the system or the Democrats have absolutely no interest or ability to delivering on, cannot inadvertently manifest in real trust. Political trust in the state is by its very nature alienating, wasteful of energy, counterproductive, and a strategic dead-end. By convincing millions of Americans that they need to wait for the next election to push toward freedom and justice—and not go into the streets *now* to fight for it immediately—works to depress the momentum and power that progressive forces for social change would otherwise enjoy.

Political distrust can occur for the wrong reasons too. There is considerable distrust in government within the American right wing, but it's worth considering the reasons why. On one hand, the far right is attempting to coopt the anti-authoritarian impulses that have historically made the left wing so attractive (thus stealing the left's "thunder").[61] However, anti-government distrust is primarily generated by what government represents and its contradictions with right-wing values. The right opposes the minimal egalitarian efforts that states pursue to redistribute resources via social welfare and enforcement of equal civil rights, and the half-hearted attempts to regulate and curtail corporate excess. Social democratic egalitarianism can be rather popular, even among conservative people (insofar as it benefits them), so the right usually frames state policy as *unfairly* helping people of color or other *undeserving* people. The latter reason—curtailing plunder by the ultra-rich—is often downplayed by the corporate right, as it appeals to populists.

Of course, the radical trust critique can appreciate distrust in the state, but not for the same reasons as the far right. Radical trust prioritizes principles that are rejected by the right wing—freedom and justice. The far right's distrust in government stems from the state's proclaimed efforts to create a literal, stable society; the right rejects this outright based on their values of individualism, tribalism, and hierarchicalism. Instead, radical trusters distrust government because the state never truly dedicates itself to this egalitarian mission, it pursues it in inequitable and misleading ways (thus perpetuating inequality), and because horizontal mechanisms rooted in community, mutual aid, direct democracy, and voluntary association are better means to achieve this highly attractive end. The state's half-hearted bureaucratic efforts will never achieve its modest goals—and even if it gets close to achieving economic parity, as in the former Soviet Union, it's at incredible cost to freedom, creativity, choice, and joy.

The far right also distrusts experts (concerns sometimes shared by the left)—including those within government (e.g., public health experts). This distrust undermines the ability of otherwise reasonable people to fair-mindedly interpret reality. Sociologist C. Wright Mills saw the importance of this, in his advocacy for a society that is both reasonable and free.[62] The constant attack from the far right on reality, knowledge, and science undermines the possibilities of Mills's freedom. Yet, this concern is sometimes shared by the left, which sees corporate greed and political deception in some expressions of expertise. Radical trusters' key concern is how some experts take advantage of their specialized authority for selfish gain. The right tends to be conspiratorial, while radical trusters point out how capitalism and the state systematically drive untrustworthiness among experts. But expertise itself is not inherently problematic (although experts can be)—knowing and understanding things is not the key issue—so long as knowledge is not monopolized or withheld from all, and as long as the expertise isn't used to facilitate power over (e.g., using scientific and technological know-how to develop landmines, online monitoring algorithms, and artificial intelligence tools, which can be directed to murder and dominate others).

Antonio Gramsci described the cultural systems of control that lead people to reflexively accept the status quo's various institutions (legal, carceral, policy) without critical thought, as hegemonic.[63] Thus, all tend to participate in our own oppression—and uncritically offering trust to political elites makes us complicit in the harm that is eventually meted out against us. Of course, some people "get something" from this political trust: They may "get ahead" or just survive a little bit longer in unequal societies. Since hegemony leads people to assume this is the only reality possible, political trust may be impulsive. But, if we somehow *know* that hegemonic rule can be challenged—and this can be witnessed in various historical moments (like the ones described in Chapter 5)—then we have a *choice* about whether to politically trust or distrust. It is dangerous to reject the responsibility to challenge hierarchical institutions or simply play victim when things inevitably don't work out the way we'd prefer. Such self-fulfilling prophecies raise a pair of crucial questions: Do most people currently want to be free? And could they even know what an expansive, counter-hegemonic view of freedom would really be? If not, then political distrust is not enough—resocialization is necessary to help people to act and live differently, not just reject political elites.

SOCIAL TRUST FOR THE WRONG REASONS

Sometimes the right things happen for the wrong reasons. These may be accidents of historical circumstance or the convergence of interests that happen to be, in retrospect, beneficial. Perhaps unsurprisingly, some have made pro-social trust arguments for rather shoddy reasons. A perfect example of this problem comes from the world-renowned intellectual—and popularizer of the "end of history" phrase following the Soviet Union's demise—Francis Fukuyama, who argued that "high trust" facilitates economic prosperity and makes businesses successful.[64] Surely this is the case; just as members of a sports team must trust each other in order to coordinate for their success against an opposing team, capitalist enterprises must also find ways to foster social trust among their diverse and *unequal* employees in order to defeat other enterprises in the marketplace. Anthropologist David Graeber makes this same (tongue-in-cheek) observation of "communism" *within* ostensibly capitalist firms,[65] just as sociologists point to cooperation happening within deadly conflict.[66] But, corporate profitability is a weak argument to make for trusting other people. There are higher-order reasons to trust than selfishness, and elite capitalist ascendancy.

Yes, relationships of trust are good, but should the primary purpose of trust be to enhance the wealth of already wealthy people? This is Fukuyama's argument. Regardless of claims that "all boats" are buoyed by greater economic prosperity, the rich will continue to get richer under capitalism. Is trust principally important for the formation of large, privately owned corporations? This is a myopic narrowing of "society" to a marketplace for consumers and employees—the presumed purpose of all human interactions—which assumes that the further enrichment of the wealthy is the main engine of social life.

Fukuyama's premise is also askew, as prosperous countries have not always been "trusting" ones. For example, the great wealth accumulated in the US from the Civil War until World War I—which made the US the richest country on the planet—was *not* because all the poor immigrants, "freed" Blacks, displaced indigenous, and native-born whites all trusted each other (because they *didn't*). Instead, this wealth derived from massive dispossession of indigenous land and the ability of US corporations to profit despite labor unrest, including state and corporate violence against those laborers. The US had a very violent labor history and violent racism during this period, suggesting massive distrust between workers and capitalists, as well as inter-ethnic and inter-racial distrust among the working classes who competed for jobs.[67] This violence was often organized, between groups that had little trust for each other: worker organizations, unions, and poor working-class communities on one side, with employers, police, strike breakers, and right-wing vigilantes on the other. The struggles of the labor movement imply incredible distrust. However, much of this resistance is also reflected in Kevin Van Meter's argument that workers (as with slaves and peasants in earlier periods) have engaged in constant, everyday acts of resistance, which don't appear to manifest as social movements but still indicate an enormous amount of system distrust and self-activity. In other words, whether the claim that trust brings prosperity is true depends on *between whom* such trust exists and *who receives* that prosperity.[68] Workers rarely trusted their exploitative bosses and didn't receive the majority of the benefits from that time period's economic prosperity—nor in the present period. Social distrust between different racial and ethnic groups was also relatively low during this period—were Fukuyama correct, greater trust may have led to a unified trust among the working class against their bosses, further threatening capitalism.

Fukuyama's views mirror the neoliberal assumption that capitalism will bring world peace. Yes, "peace" is a good goal, but for its own reasons. Capitalism brings unacceptable consequences. The lack of overt violence in "peaceful" capitalism ignores the incredible suffering, hardship, and inequality that accompanies it, which are simply different versions of "violence". Neoliberals still praise capitalism's "peace" even when premature death results due to malnutrition, homelessness, or lack of health care. The Roman politician Tacitus observed that, during the expansion of empire, human communities are turned into a "desert", thus creating "peace". In other words, "peace" without justice and freedom is really just a muted, less dramatic form of violence.

The means are often more important to consider than the ends, especially when the means are themselves of such great importance—this is true with trust. Prevailing trust in a boss or capitalism—that simply enables some to profit from the working class—is not a means worth defending. Exploitative working conditions are a precondition of business success under capitalism. Thus, trust is a terrible means for the goal of business prosperity. In any humane society, the wealth and profitability of corporations should be second (if not third, fourth, or last) priority, not the first. Violence and war also facilitate economic prosperity for warring countries, but this is a shitty means. Capitalists typically don't have to pay the ultimate costs of such violence (with their lives or resources, as war is subsidized by tax-funded militaries and poor soldiers), although capitalists benefit from violence's use. Trust between soldiers and workers simply for the purposes of supporting imperialism and capitalism are not worthy aims.

Trust for the purpose of business success is especially troubling when many bad outcomes accompany such "success". US news media often considers Wall Street's success (read: looting of the planet and immiseration of human life) to translate directly to the livelihood of American workers. This faulty logic is rarely interrogated, as the closing value of blue-chip stocks on the market is used as a proxy for how "the economy" is doing. The phrase "the economy" is an abstraction of the things that should really matter most. Not only are working people generally absent from news media stories but their organized interests (as workers or unions) are overwhelmed by a preoccupation with corporate, monied interests, whose hegemonic status greedily absorbs all the attention. Capitalism is not only a poor justification for trust—capitalism has itself very little justification for existence given its catastrophic effects. In sum, trust has many better reasons for existing than capitalism.

States also directly and indirectly try to build trust to benefit their own interests. Soft power is a form of cultural trust that societies and their ruling states attempt to foster throughout the world. Soft power consists of the non-physically violent ways to exert power and influence, to wield power against otherwise non-cooperative peoples. This is often done through cultural promotion of ideas, values, and mass media. For example, Hollywood movies, and educational and sporting exchanges help to spread the US's influence. Getting another country to "develop" like Western countries helps to not only create a society that is "advanced" enough to desire and afford Western-made products but also precludes violent inter-state conflict to engage in trade. Creating "trust" in US-driven ideas and values is not done for the higher benefits that such things offer (presuming they can be achieved), but rather to extend influence over others. For example, the promotion of "democracy" abroad during the Cold War was often more about battling encroaching "communist" influence (read: Soviet aid or pan-nationalism), than a legitimate concern for the well-being of another country's citizens. In other words, the US state is not engaged in an altruistic mission when it deploys its soft power or diplomacy but is pursuing the same self-interested advantages that all other states do.

Other times, soft power is achieved—and thus mistrust engineered—by organizations that seem entirely altruistic (be they government-funded or not). Consider the Peace Corps: Its volunteers work internationally to help communities to accomplish a variety of practical goals and projects.[69] The Peace Corps attracts idealistic young people who seek to "make a difference" and to "help others". A macro-level analysis of the Peace Corps' results shows that it serves as pro-American propaganda, spreading the idea of a "helpful America", particularly in countries that have good reason to be skeptical of US foreign policy.[70] Local economic development efforts sponsored by the Peace Corps also help to "modernize" infrastructure in poorer countries (build roads, bridges, schools, an electricity grid), thus raising its level of development to then sustain US corporate investment. "Opening up" poor countries to outside development benefits wealthy American interests far more than it benefits individual poor people.[71] In certain ways, aid recipients may be comfortable making such a deal with "the devil". But, by seeking greater trust for its beneficial consequences, people may ignore the many harms that accompany it. For example, placing trust in seemingly benign American volunteers can legitimize inequality, justify economic exploitation, or continue the ravage of the Global South. The CIA-styled National Endowment for Democracy is even more nefarious in intent—it funded and sometimes organized (without official connection to the CIA) pro-US organizations in countries with governments hostile to the US, for the purposes of undermining regime legitimacy.[72]

Even more seriously, we often trust others simply because they are close to us. For example, people are usually more likely to trust their family, friends, and neighbors. This makes sense in most cases, but it's not universally wise if we risk people taking advantage of us. Proximity is not always a good justification for trust. The lion's share of violence that people experience happens at the hands of people they know, often long-term acquaintances or family members. Sexual assault, abuse, and other forms of predation in particular occur between acquaintances and even close, "trusted" friends and family. That people who are closest to us may be quicker to violate our trust than strangers is surprising to most people, especially when it happens to them. Sociologists and criminologists have long been familiar with these patterns; people we personally or intimately know (and are emotionally invested in) or see regularly simply have more opportunity to abuse our trust than strangers we meet upon rare occasion.[73] So, contrast this mistrust of close acquaintances with the stereotypical and rampant distrust and fear of strangers that most people have. Strangers have less reason to abuse, cross, or take advantage of us—thus, they usually pose a low risk of harm to us. Strangers have a much lower probability of harming us than those we know. In a US Department of Justice analysis of violent crime from 1993 to 2010, victimization was higher for *every year* by known offenders than by strangers. Stranger-committed homicides never rose above 16 percent, and 62 percent of violent victimizations by strangers were committed in public places (only 9 percent in victim's homes).[74] This doesn't mean we should trust strangers more than friends, but it does suggest that strangers could and should be trusted more than they usually are. It also indicates that those whose lives are intertwined with ours are perfectly capable of harming us, despite how often they say they "love" us. Professing trust in those closest to us, even if they have harmed us, is disingenuous, unwarranted, and is an important example of mistrust.

TEMPORARY DISTRUST AND FUTURE OPTIMISM IN THE SYSTEM

Many people express distrust in the political system or current political actors. Given the reigning arrangements and politicians' actions, this is reasonable. However, some of these cynical distrusters also want to trust *future* political actors, or a slightly improved or reformed political system. In other words, they temporarily distrust but seek to trust leaders who will do *a better job*, albeit within the same hierarchical system.

This orientation is likely more common among liberal (or conservative) people than radicals. Radicals are skeptical about reform, specifically distrustful of reform's promised transformative power. The belief that "the right people" in power will restore the trustability of a failing system implies a *desire* to believe in a just system and the myths widely held about it—all evidence to the contrary. For example, liberals were outraged whenever Donald Trump expressed a variety of racist sentiments via dog whistle. Many of those same liberals longed for a return to the presidency of Barack Obama, who on numerous occasions recused himself from exercising any responsibility for anti-racist leadership—whether curtailing violent police power or supporting refugee rights.[75] Many liberals also regularly express a desire for fixing society's culture. Wanting to somehow tweak American culture, to make it a bit less racist, is a good start. But a few tweaks will not do the job: There hasn't been a single moment in the US's history when it has not been a white supremacist society.[76]

Support for the US political system regularly oscillates based on one's political affiliations; for example, Democratic voters express greater political trust when a Democrat is in the White House, while Republican voters express political trust when one of theirs holds the presidency. Many Democrat-leaning people who were critical of the US state while George W. Bush was in office became patriotic fans of the US once Obama was elected—despite him increasing the frequency of drone strikes and the rate of immigrant deportations. Thus, in the middle of Bush's last term (2006), only 22 percent of Republicans distrusted the federal government compared to 55 percent of Democrats. By the middle of Obama's first term (2010), those figures had reversed: Only 23 percent of Democrats distrusted the federal government, compared to 52 percent of Republicans.[77] Obama expressed liberal anti-war and pro-immigration positions, playing the role of a progressive to get elected, then spoke the words of a liberal while in office but performed similarly as other recent presidents when it came to empire and Central American immigration.[78] Conservatives and other reactionaries had strong antipathy toward "the federal government" while Obama was in office but celebrated the election of Trump. Surely the anti-system expressions of liberals and conservatives is sensitive to their "team" having power. Thus, being an "outsider" and cynic involves criticizing your nemesis in office but then becoming an enthusiastic booster of the political system once your side reclaims the presidential trophy for four or eight years. Democratic Party glee at the election of Joe Biden as president in 2020 ushered in euphoric proclamations of being able to trust government again—all the while stocking his administration with pro-corporate bureaucrats who promised to return things to business as usual. Ironically, low trust in the 2020 election from Republican voters was generated by outgoing president Trump, who spread fanciful tales of election subversion. Then, when Trump won the majority of votes for the first time in 2024, Trump declared the election to be fair, thereby reinstating Republican trust.

This pathos prevails elsewhere too. At my current employer, an unpopular university president (and provost and vice president for "business and finance") provoked such disgust and frustration from employees that the faculty senate passed a strongly worded motion expressing a "lack of confidence" in those administrators. This is the academic equivalent of employees declaring a desire to fire their boss—with zero enforcement powers, of course. However, once each of those three administrators left (all in less than a year's time), faculty approval of administrators improved markedly, since "better" administrators were now in place. Nothing fundamental had changed in the way that the state budget provisioned monies to higher education, the administration did not slash their own salaries or create a direct democracy among employees. The university continued to shrink its base of full-time tenure-track faculty and staff counselors, create additional layers of non-faculty middle management, and raise student tuition and fees. But the veneer of leadership's trustworthiness was polished up enough to temporarily quiet the dissenting majority.

The true lesson to learn about expectant trust in future leaders is that new figureheads, cosmetic reforms, and other tangential changes don't solve systematic problems. Remember the adage: It's not enough to slap a Band-Aid on a gunshot wound. We should instead keep our eyes on the key target. Our targets should *not* be the individuals temporarily occupying the offices of power; rather, we should target the offices themselves for transformation.[79] Unless drastic changes take place to the role and power of those offices and institutions themselves, it doesn't matter much who sits in the physical chairs. Sure, there's a wide variation of degrees of potential ineptitude and malevolence. But power tends to corrupt regardless of how principled an individual is.

The lure of change in the near future is strong. Psychologically and emotionally, it's very important to be able to have hope in a better future. Without this optimism, most of us would collapse into depression. But, expecting the future to just magically be better without a fundamental change in the status quo arrangements is delusional. Change usually happens because average, everyday people make it occur. Thus, we need to be optimistic about—and even *trust* in—the possibility of a better future, while not relinquishing our responsibilities to bring it forth, ourselves. Passively stepping aside and crossing one's fingers, hoping for the best, is to actively obstruct the potential birth of that ideal future.

5

Trust, Disaster, and Changing Circumstances: Trust's Volatility

TRUST IN TIMES OF (NATURAL) DISASTER: WHEN PUSH COMES TO SHOVE

Although it may sound strange, we can see the best in people during the worst of times. I'll also append this bold claim with a disclaimer that'll make it sound more reasonable: "... but also the worst in people too". During the "worst of times", such as during disaster and crisis, lots of things change, as society's quotidian arrangements are shaken to the core. When push comes to shove, people can deviate from their typical socialization—which often encourages them to look the other way, tolerate injustice, and remain focused on their own issues—and instead widen their perception of possibility, necessity, and egalitarianism.

In spring 1997, I spent long days sandbagging neighborhoods in Grand Forks, North Dakota, where I was a college student. We were sandbagging because the north-flowing waters of the Red River that traveled through the city had risen to historically high levels and were threatening to flood the entire city. Eventually the city was evacuated when the river crested past the 500-year flood level, saturating three-quarters of the city. During this disaster, I visited neighborhoods I had never seen and worked alongside strangers. It was a thoroughly paradigm-shifting experience. I've never again felt quite the same as I did then. While there was a loose coalition of centralized decision-making bodies functioning in the background, replete with authority figures (elected and not) who were guiding the flood response, everyday people worked together in their neighborhoods to solve problems as they (quite literally) arose. People made decisions among themselves, figuring out how to strategically address weaknesses in the makeshift system of sandbagged walls people collectively built to protect homes. The available labor was a mix of residents, bused-in college and high school students, random volunteers, and an assortment of Air Force personnel from the local military base. I never saw anyone who wore badges, declared themselves leader, or made demands of each other. It was during these days that I made fast friends with strangers. I hitchhiked for the first time in my life—an experience that felt completely normal, authentic, and surprisingly un-scary.[1]

In the immediate aftermath of the flood, I spent time trying to process my experiences. Why did I feel so good helping others, with no selfish reward waiting for me? Where did the comradery come from, among my fellow unskilled laborers? The generosity of people astounded me—strangers made meals for people, they offered them nearly everything they had, and spent nearly 24 hours a day doing manual labor to help people they didn't know just one day earlier.

The way I felt was so strange and unusual. When I talked to other people about it, I got two responses. Those with whom I had spent time on the dikes, passing-along sandbags, understood what I meant, although few of us had the vocabulary to accurately describe and conceptualize these feelings. There was a bond we felt, as joint survivors. We shared purpose and we had experienced feelings— quite wonderful feelings—in the midst of tragedy we have never felt before. But, for people who weren't there, they didn't seem to understand what I described—I got weird, quizzical looks of confusion, as if I was delusional or suffering from some kind of post-traumatic stress disorder (which, in all honesty, I wasn't). They hadn't *felt* what I did—they didn't get it. So, I reached out for answers. On a whim, I wrote a letter to Noam Chomsky—a seemingly all-knowing philosopher, linguist, and social critic whom I had begun intensively reading during the previous two years. I described what I had participated in, what I saw, and how I felt. I was astonished when he wrote back. He respectfully acknowledged what I had written (stating that what I had "reported" to him was "interesting"). He recommended I read Peter Kropotkin's *Mutual Aid*, which he claimed was the unacknowledged foundation of socio-biology, too controversial for the official canon of the field, given its ultimate conclusions and implications.

For Kropotkin, mutual aid is a type of future-oriented trust that doesn't require pre-existing connection. Societies do well when they encourage people to cooperate with and trust each other. In fact, the survival of those who band together against outside threats—whether natural threats, bad weather, or military invaders—is best achieved by cooperation, not competition. The adversity and challenges people face are too much for us to handle alone. We presume that others will "pay it forward" (a phrase constructed long after Kropotkin) for us, just as we do for them. In other words, we do what is necessary for the collective, when it is needed. Kropotkin argued that the modern state and capitalism prevent us from recognizing and engaging in this everyday solidarity. These hierarchies bureaucratize our natural, compassionate impulses using impersonal social welfare policies and markets to haphazardly attempt to fulfill our human needs. Thus, our modern daily lived experiences often appear devoid of mutual aid.

Disaster and other emergencies disrupt the typical and the reliable. These make it so we cannot rely upon things to happen or proceed as before; the previous social scripts are scrapped and the future is uncertain. The usual social norms, inequalities, and institutional practices fall away as people scramble to develop new ways of interacting to deal with new circumstances. Predictably, the old norms, inequalities, and institutions often get in the way of this adaptation!

Natural disasters like 2005's Hurricane Katrina and 2012's Hurricane Sandy provoked radically different behavior than those occurring with the normal social scripts. Common Ground in New Orleans and Occupy Sandy in New York City emerged in the aftermath of the failures of national government and city authorities.[2] States tend to be lumbering and slow to respond to disasters. Individuals, on the other hand, can be quick and usually serve as the first responders, especially when they are well networked. Being prepared was essential in Mexico City, where residents who survived the September 19, 1985, earthquake educated themselves about the best way to respond to earthquakes and then mobilized themselves 32 years later for the September 19, 2017, earthquake that struck throughout central Mexico. Crews used sophisticated techniques for signaling, searching through rubble, and coordinating labor.[3] A deadly wildfire in Paradise, California, in 2018 required massive mutual aid as tens of thousands became refugees.[4]

Official disaster sociology has given scant attention to these emergent dynamics. The field is typically more interested in state and NGO response to disorder, and how the pre-disaster order is re-established. It would be wonderful if the sociology of disaster instead focused on how a collective purpose often emerges in the middle of tragedies. Rebecca Solnit describes in her masterful book *A Paradise Built in Hell* that, in such circumstances, people easily identify their common humanity and reach out to those in need. Previous divisions around class, race, or nationality can disappear. Spontaneity and mutual aid are not only predictable responses to disaster but end up being necessary, effective responses. Disaster compels people to reach out, become charitable, and connect with others. But without pressing need—perhaps, without disaster— many might never take the step of reaching out to those in need. That is the conundrum for us to solve: Why does it take such severe catastrophe and tragedy for our better natures to reveal themselves?

Trusting during disaster benefits from some kind of pre-existing social trust, an expectation that our actions will not be in vain, that others will appreciate and reciprocate, and that people will not take advantage of our charity. Disaster can also create new trust too. We can begin to see that people are usually trustworthy, even though we may previously have presumed otherwise.[5] For the sociologist Émile Durkheim, these kinds of expectations are necessary preconditions for society. Such "pre-contractual solidarity" implies that we are willing to extend solidarity to others, even before we meet them.[6] Viewed for the first time, this may seem reckless: Why trust others we have no reason to trust? From Durkheim's perspective, this trust makes all past, current, and future sociality possible. Otherwise, why don't we just hide in private, personal caves all by ourselves?

We are a social, cooperative species—a conclusion shared by Kropotkin too.

Calamity can easily push things in the "right" direction, building greater social trust, and even push toward a more cooperative society. But, in addition to the very real danger of disaster itself, it is also possible that disaster can spur things to go very wrong, even propel society in a fascist direction (the German experience with post-World War I economic depression and Nazism is a key example). So, what makes the difference? There is very little research on the factors that endanger social cohesion in extreme ways, and for quite obvious reasons: It's not possible (or ethical) to conduct controlled experiments on entire populations to figure out the answer to this question. But it is undeniable that context matters immensely. Humans clearly have the potential to be amazing, but we also have the capacity to be utterly terrible too. Phil Zimbardo's book *The Lucifer Effect* describes the US soldiers who tortured prisoners in the Iraqi prison Abu Ghraib as otherwise "normal" people trying to adapt to extreme circumstances. Prisoner torture was not the result of a few "bad apple" soldiers but a predictable consequence when the entire barrel is rotten.[7] This is less an indictment of individuals and "human nature" than of hierarchy and authoritarian social structures. Noam Chomsky is known for suggesting that "human nature" is immensely plastic and that any of us could be "saints" or "gas chamber attendants" given the ideal conditions[8]—these conclusions are reflected in a wide swath of mid-twentieth-century research, like the Milgram experiments, in which subjects were ordered to administer (fake) electrical shocks on fellow humans, at levels that—had they been real—would likely have killed them.[9]

The assumption that humans are rooted in original sin is a Judeo-Christian idea, central to Western civilization. It reflects a Hobbesian view of the world, wherein all humans are descendants of the world's first sinners—Adam and Eve—who "fell" from God's grace. Thus, the default "state of nature" is cutthroat, competitive, and violent. It's not just a few "bad apples" out to get you, the whole world is your enemy. Within this framework, trust is not only illogical but even *unnatural*. Given how many contemporary societies—throughout the world, not just in the West—have been influenced by these ideas, trust may be the exception rather than the rule. To trust even in "normal" conditions seems both unlikely and reckless, let alone in disaster conditions.

Some people are more at risk during disasters; they are also the same people most likely to face disadvantage, discrimination, and brutality in everyday life too. Poor people and women are particularly hit hard by disasters, and their lack of resources make it far more likely for them to die during such tragedies than the wealthy and men. And, given America's long history of racial inequality, it's not surprising the people of color find themselves on the losing end of disaster too. The co-founder of New Orleans's mutual aid organization Common Ground, scott crow, describes in *Black Flags and Windmills* conducting armed patrols to defend against racist white vigilantes who terrorized Black residents after Hurricane Katrina.[10] Clearly, disasters are not worth celebrating for their own reasons. Disasters may have some "silver linings" in how they tend to change our daily routines and provoke new forms of social organization, but they are also brutal and harmful to those already most predisposed to distrust.

Thus, the clear vision that disaster affords us—to be able to see that humanity is far more compassionate than we presume—does not mean that disasters should be sought. Seeking catastrophe simply to bring humanity closer together is not necessary or wise. In fact, powerful actors often *seek* disaster for very, very different reasons. Journalist Naomi Klein's *The Shock Doctrine: The Rise of Disaster Capitalism* compellingly argues that capitalists seek to exploit disaster for their own profit. Free-market absolutists regularly utilize catastrophe to redraw the map in their worldview, replete with privatization, authoritarianism, and selfish individualism. Thus, one additional concern about disaster is worth mentioning, further tainting their value for human liberation. Disasters—since they are usually unpredictable—shock people. Klein describes how the powerful take advantage of crises and the disorientation survivors feel. For the powerful right wing, disasters have been seen as "opportunities" to enact fiendishly unpopular policies, such as privatization. For example, Milton Friedman and his "free market" acolytes enthused about Hurricane Katrina's destruction providing the opportunity to privatize New Orleans's public education system.[11] These shocks throw off people's equilibrium and may negatively impact social trust (or enhance political trust in hierarchical states). People can become susceptible to suggestions whispered by those in power—that we ought to trust them and their recommendations to rewrite society's rules. The powerful can appear "even-keeled" in chaotic times and seem to provide just the right solution and well-funded plan to apparently "solve" a problem—but doing so on their terms and for their own economic benefit.

The remedy to the effects of the shock doctrine is to retain high trust in each other during crises and disasters. If people retain their social trust, they can remain immune from a disaster's disorienting aftershocks; then the powerful can less easily take advantage of the situation. We can remain grounded in our trust with others and resistant to political exploits. This "inoculation" can make all the difference, as we'll still "know the score" as opportunity-seizing elites swoop in. Thus, disaster may still provide opportunity for positive, progressive social transformation, if we unite to fend off serious challenges to the common good and the ruin that the shock doctrine brings.

SPONTANEITY AND EXPERTISE

Spontaneous order arises in various situations, particularly when the rules governing that situation are unclear or absent. This is certainly true in times of crisis, as people must self-manage and collectively administer their affairs, when outside authorities are slow, unable, or unwilling to impose their preferred version of "order" upon the situation. According to Colin Ward, spontaneous order is possible because alternative norms are like seeds lying dormant in the snow. New social relations and alternatives simply require more ideal conditions to germinate and flower, thus dramatically changing the social landscape.[12] If radically transformative social norms are seeds lying in snow, then social trust is the rich bed of soil awaiting the snow's thaw.

During natural disasters, people must respond to unpredictable circumstances, as the things usually presumed impossible occur at a moment's notice and thus surprise everyone when they suddenly occur. Since natural disasters and their impacts are technically unpredictable (although often foreseeable), our responses must be flexible. States are very poor at being flexible; their hierarchical and bureaucratic nature mandates clear, taut lines of command and obedience. Information flows up this chain of command, and orders demanding obedience flow down these chains once a decision at the top has been made. Despite massive state resources, state processes are difficult to navigate, time-consuming, and fraught with inaccuracies, inefficiencies, and injustice. Thus, states are slow to mobilize since bureaucratic red tape and hierarchical authority slows things down. Everyday people can respond and act more spontaneously to their circumstances, and will be quicker and more able to save lives during the crucial first moments of disasters.

Spontaneity may sound a lot like an impulsive embrace of chaos. Surely, in the middle of a natural disaster, chaos is simply unavoidable. If anything, everyday people's spontaneity is actually a reasonable reaction to that chaos and is an attempt to construct some kind of social order. Thus, while "spontaneous order" might seem like a contradictory pairing of words—spontaneous being unpredictable and order being predictable—that's not what the phrase means. Spontaneous implies an ability to improvise within an unstable moment, while order implies a deliberately created organization and set of assumptions. Spontaneous order requires a degree of social trust, and a willingness to listen to others' ideas and help them pursue alternative solutions. But having too much political trust in authorities during a crisis can be paralyzing—we just wait for a solution to be delivered to us from on high, wasting valuable time when we could be acting ourselves. Consequently, spontaneous order is intelligent self-defense, fueled by social trust, and seeking to empower individuals and their communities.

There are many examples beyond natural disasters that demonstrate the principles of spontaneous order. Some of the better examples focus on collectives that consciously avoid fixed leadership—exemplars can be found in music. For example, jazz may be most suited to spontaneous order, as it prioritizes improvisation. Musicians follow the lead of others, sharing control over the direction of a song. During a musician's "solo", other musicians play supportive harmonies and rhythms, allowing the soloist to shine and direct the song. Then, the soloist backs down and blends their performance into the group. It is essential to have trust in other musicians' abilities to play and to trust that they will share power and prominence in an egalitarian fashion. Improvisation presumes that a highly detailed plan is unnecessary, that competent musicians can manage their performance without a "leader", and that new and exciting things can be created by the group, which a single musical genius would be unlikely to on their own.[13] Another musical example is the deliberately conductor-less Orpheus Chamber Orchestra from New York City. The orchestra uses an agreed-upon method to start a performance and then they simply proceed, performing as musicians. They rotate leadership, which allows everyone to learn what it is like to facilitate the orchestra and develop trust in each other's abilities.[14] Performing very different music, the rock band Fugazi, from Washington, DC, never used a "set-list" ordering songs they would perform during concerts. The band members simply adapted to the lead-in music begun by their fellow band members and picked up the next song. In the documentary film *Instrument*, Fugazi describe this as a way of keeping things interesting for them and fluid, and to avoid staleness.[15] All of this musical spontaneity and improvisation requires inter-musician trust.

Spontaneity is also regularly part of everyday order. People possess many skills and capacities, and if a situation requiring their action arises, people can insert themselves. For example, when young children are in the presence of adults, many adults will often assume a minimal amount of responsibility for the safety of those children, even when not the primary parent or guardian. If a parent doesn't detect a potentially dangerous situation, other adults will jump in to help out, even if it is not their responsibility to do so. Adults also can help children or answer their questions without having to defer to the parent. By cutting out the "middleman", such situations become more interactive, complex, and social—all features that benefit a child's development, and demonstrate the value of trust.

Sometimes people try to establish guarantees to avoid potential problems. But, even when these efforts don't perfectly succeed, things tend to work out okay, as people are willing to adapt at the last minute to accommodate others and solve collective problems. For example, consider the popularity of "potluck" meals. Before the meal day, hosts may try to solicit information about what dish each of their guests plan to share. But such efforts are often unnecessary. People have diverse interests and will try to bring something they think others will not. Thus, top-down coordination is usually irrelevant. Guests may even communicate in a decentralized fashion with each other and prepare their dish based on the information they receive horizontally. By expecting others to make good-faith efforts to contribute helpful items at potlucks, the meal will usually turn out well.

Divisions of labor may emerge in roughly spontaneous settings—or such divisions may be designed from the beginning. But division still allows people to adapt to certain expectations and react to new developments. We don't need others to tell us how to do things, especially when we understand the role and its associated tasks (at a potluck meal, there may be a door-greeter or host directing prepared food to the kitchen, or people offering childcare, managing where coats are stored, and doing the dishes afterward). The person who regularly does that task knows better than an "expert" who has never done so and who simply coordinates many such tasks together. This is why worker cooperatives do not usually rely on experts for planning. If there is a problem to solve or an inefficiency to overcome, the individual(s) doing it will figure it out for themselves, will consult with those around them for alternatives, or will experiment to find a decent solution.

More abstractly, spontaneity occurs all the time, although often with an implicit order lurking in the background. People move through crowded streets and other busy circumstances without much need for traffic conductors. Norms like "walk on the right side" (or the left side) usually suffice to keep things working. While norms and other rules can guide our behaviors, we're still ultimately in charge of how we respond to problems. We "make do" and reach out for help problem-solving when needed. If we get injured or have a flat car tire, we acquire help and people find ways to help us—regardless of whether anything comparable has ever happened to the people involved before. While our daily routines are often partially predictable, this is never 100 percent the case, so we improvise whenever necessary, which tends to be often—using our best guesses when we can and making up the rest.

Economist Mancur Olson claimed, in his influential *The Logic of Collective Action*, "the anarchistic assumption that in the absence of the oppressive state a natural, spontaneous unity would spring up to take its place is now regarded as evidence of hopeless eccentricity".[16] Since there have been relatively few anarchistic uprisings for historians to study, this is probably an overzealous claim lacking proof.[17] But Olson also apparently had no knowledge or understanding of the Spanish Revolution, for example, which clearly negated his claim.[18] Additionally, he directly dismissed Kropotkin's claims out of hand, while never addressing Kropotkin's logical arguments regarding mutual aid, nor any contradictory evidence from emerging crises, like natural disasters.[19] This is the standard refrain by the powerful—and in Olson's case, academic would-be kingmakers—who have everything to gain by convincing people to relinquish their own expertise, efforts, and creativity. Olson—and other five-year planners, jargon-wielding specialists, and hero worshippers—claim *they* have the solution. Elites and experts who try to guide or suppress spontaneous order are unwilling to let others figure it out for themselves and possibly do it better, and thus allow us to gain self-efficacy, confidence, and collective power in the process.[20]

Decades after Olson hypothesized about free riding, it appears entire generations in wealthy countries are consumed by the hyper-individualism of self-branding. "Can truly social movements emerge in such self-obsessed societies?", Olson would surely ask. However, movements continue to pop-up, even among the presumably selfish youth—witness no better example than the spontaneous global uprising of May 2020 against police brutality and for Black lives (often referred to as the George Floyd Uprising, in honor of the Black man murdered in Minneapolis by city police officers). This uprising occurred in more cities and countries than any in all past human history. Youth, most with no political experience, ignored existing political organizations and entered the streets together. In the midst of the Covid-19 pandemic, they risked their own safety to send a resolute message. US cities with Black Lives Matter protests saw a measurable decrease in lethal force by police.[21] And in the process, they tore down dozens of racist statues, burned down the police precinct where Floyd's killers worked, and inspired a generation.

Perhaps the best argument against empowered experts comes from democratic theory. Electing trained and experienced bureaucrats (in the US this often means lawyers) to be the primary policy makers places power in the hands of people who seek power over others, via their expertise. Advocates of lottery-based decision-making systems like demarchy reference back to the original Greek version of democracy, wherein everyday people—or at least non-slave, citizen males—were entrusted to figure out what was needed and how to do it.[22] Decision makers selected via demarchy aren't driven by ego, selfishness, of profit-seeking. Olson is famous for his "free-rider problem", in which individuals make selfish decisions to not contribute to a public good, thus undermining that public good if too many do the same.[23] This trust-less and individualistic framing of social life is not only ideologically tainted but also ignorant of much of social reality (it relies heavily upon abstracted game theory).[24]

Although the two can occasionally overlap, there's a clear difference between experts and authority figures. Experts "know things", while authority figures command obedience through "legitimate" hierarchical institutions. Experts are workers who know something specific; authority figures are people who centralize power. Expertise can be helpful for learning and thus experts are important to those seeking to learn. Authority is mostly of use for organizing people to accomplish something—which likely benefits that authority figure's direction. Most experts have little authority over us, except that they may know more about certain things, thus privileging them in terms of status. But authority figures do not always have expertise; they may have expertise in the management of people, a skill that's fairly unnecessary, as most people can usually manage their own labor. What's often lacking from a group of people in a spontaneously emerging situation is not a manager but the need for labor coordination; this just requires enough expertise and a group of collectively empowered laborers.

How can people trust the unfolding insight offered by experts without falling prey to their authority too? We shouldn't just obey experts because of their knowledge—there should be more important reasons to place trust in them (e.g., their selflessness in using their knowledge, using their knowledge in line with values that we share, etc.). While it's surely problematic to just blindly trust experts, their insight can also be incredibly valuable, as it's often the result of informed experience and study.

There's a way out of this quandary that will help us know who to trust, how much to trust, and in what ways to trust. Consider experts like medical doctors, mechanics, electricians, or public health professionals—we shouldn't trust them because of their fancy degrees or certifications (which they often have) but because they have helpful insights that we often lack. It makes sense to trust them because our lives are enhanced by listening to them; they can advise medical treatments, fix our cars or bikes, help prevent us from being electrocuted, and stay safe during a disease pandemic. Trusting experts is reasonable if they appear to have our interests at heart, not just their own personal enrichment or empowerment.[25] Experts can thus be trusted (i.e., we can take a risk by following their suggestions) if they have proved themselves to be previously trustworthy—for example, if they have offered decent medical advice, have fixed vehicles reliably, have kept us safe from dangerous electrical wiring, and have offered sage prescriptions during past pandemics that kept the public safe from harmful diseases. Also, expertise is available to anyone to obtain—we can learn and read, experiment and practice, and get better—although this expertise may not be *professionally obtained* or credentialed. The democratic accessibility of such expertise differentiates it from authority, which is exclusionary and not available to most.

Experts have insight and judgment that we benefit from deferring to. Mikhail Bakunin offered a well-known example of this from his *God and the State*, regarding a bootmaker's expertise. In situations involving boots, he deferred to the bootmaker. Bakunin claimed that in matters "concerning houses, canals, or railroads, I consult that [authority] of the architect or engineer". He wrote: "I do not content myself with consulting a single authority in any special branch; I consult several; I compare their opinions, and choose that which seems to be the soundest. But I recognize no infallible authority".[26] Bakunin's description of "authority" made a distinction between a "natural authority" (often reflected in facts that appeared to be scientific law) that dictated our actual natures, and the superimposed authority of certain individuals. The former was fine and reasonable to respect, but the latter was unjust. He considered scientists (or "savants") as trustworthy due to their specific expertise. Science is a technique for discovering everything (thus "the absolute authority of science"), but it is incomplete and a never-finished endeavor. Since no savant can possibly know everything about everything, there is no reason to blindly follow an authority figure claiming to be infallible. Bakunin thus advocated for a form of decentralized trust in expertise (and its various experts) but argued against the centralization of trust in singular individuals.

There are multiple conclusions to draw from Bakunin's analysis. First, when considering "who to trust", he advises we seek out those who know a lot about a subject; experts are apt to have better answers for crucial questions, especially those which require technical knowledge and skill. Thus, it makes sense to trust an electrician's knowledge about electricity, a nurse's first aid expertise, a sociologist's understanding of social change, or a mechanic's skill at machine repair. This doesn't mean their knowledge is always correct, but barring some kind of malevolent intent, they're more likely to be correct than other people are. Second, however, we ought to reserve final judgment for ourselves, especially when the matter pertains to our own lives. The bootmaker is not an authority figure because they cannot and should not force you to wear certain kinds of footwear, although they are likely to make much better footwear than most of us could for ourselves. Thus, we ought to listen to experts, but their status as experts doesn't, by itself, compel us to act. And we may prefer a different construction or footwear style than the bootmaker would make for us. Since our feet are our own, we ought to be able to adorn and shod them how we wish.

We should use this advice to assess the views of the far right and conspiratorial, who appear more and more fascistic as every day passes. Why would we trust an Alex Jones or Jenny McCarthy about virology, since neither the blowhard anger-ball or 1990s TV star know much about the subject, and have conducted no research themselves? While non-experts may be able to understand technical subjects, and experts (such as virologists) may have flaws and make mistakes, experts still have a much better understanding of their subject matter. Far-right pundits often stake-out nonprofessional, lay claims to wide expertise, presented as a populist, "gut-level knowledge" of many things, characterizing their ideas as "obvious" to their embarrassingly large audiences. Their performative confidence pressures others into accepting their claims, even though it's a very bad idea to do so. But the far right doesn't reject science because they "know better" than the scientists. Rather, they make bad faith references to science, as they oppose certain scientific conclusions that threaten their place in the world (e.g., Big Oil's climate destruction). Additionally, the far right's modus operandi is to suppress critical thinking and anti-authoritarianism, two things central to science, at its best. It's no surprise that anti-intellectualism is a core fascist tenet, replacing rationality with emotions. Look no further than Hitler's *Mein Kampf* wherein he explicitly advocated getting power by rousing up emotions over reasoned argument.[27]

When seeking a more egalitarian society, Brian Martin advocates, we ought to distinguish "between beneficial and harmful forms of expertise" and to empower people with practice and support to become skilled at tasks that serve to create such a society.[28]

CASE STUDIES

In the next subsections, I present a few specific case studies of how spontaneity tends to work, particularly in moments of crisis, such as during urban revolt, wartime, and pandemics, and how these create fertile—but complicated—territories for trust.

Case Study: Urban Revolt

A helpful example to consider for the spontaneous energy and potential of disaster-like situations is urban revolt. Here, the explosive, destructive energy is driven by city dwellers and social forces, as opposed to by nature. I'm mostly interested in examples where disadvantaged groups—racial, ethnic, or religious minorities—rise-up against injustices, discrimination, inequality, and acts of violence against them. In the modern era, most rebellions begin in urban areas, amid shifting circumstances and unbalanced power relations.[29] Predictably, riot participants tend to possess very high political distrust.[30] The scales can tip quickly and violently against "the system" in these instances, upending years or generations of stratified stability and inertia (indeed, these tactics are more successful than purely "nonviolent" ones).[31] Or, the tide can quickly turn against an emergent, more equitable social order, too, if socially mistrustful instincts take hold among the rebels and general population. However, while it is not the focus of this example, other forms of revolt have occurred in the past, where dominant majorities—gentiles in Eastern Europe, whites in the US, Hindus in India—engaged in punishing, targeted violence against disadvantaged groups (e.g., Jews, Blacks, Muslims, respectively) to force them back into submission and suppress their aspirations of collective improvement in unjust societies.[32] Instead, I focus on the actions of the disadvantaged underclasses and people of color.

In situations of urban revolt, large numbers of people lose their previous inhibitions that discourage challenging the system, and they ignore the norms learned during a lifetime of pro-hierarchical socialization. Curiously, nothing really trains people perfectly for a revolt, but people often manage to adapt to new norms anyway, somehow. Building trust among small cadres of revolutionists prior to a revolt may help to nudge the rebellion, but this is never guaranteed.[33]

So, how do people work together in riots or insurrections? Such collaboration is complex, as not everyone is on the same team—struggle is waged by many against "the system", especially police. In the aftermath of urban revolts, individuals often describe feeling like they personally possessed great strength as they surged in crowds. Thus, people transcend their usual timidity, uniting in explosive energy.[34] In all this, trust is necessary to engage in physically active combat with the system's representatives or surrogates. Participants determine the "targets" of their rage (e.g., a police station) by simple proposal, reflection, consensus building, and individual initiative. The assumption that those who surround you in a crowd are similarly motivated reassures us and emboldens the crowd, generating temporary trust even among strangers. The longer a revolt unfolds, the quicker such stranger trust is established. This suggests that revolutionary conditions (ripe with freedom and justice) would easily facilitate quicker and more reliable trust among strangers.

An impressive historical study of the barricade in France and Belgium illustrates the multigenerational solidarity and consensus-building capacity of urban dwellers. Neighbors throughout modern French history collaborated to prevent outsiders—especially national armies—from invading their space. In fact, some French neighborhoods were so used to this revolt tactic that they had helpful engineering features constructed into buildings to use when necessary.[35] The ability of insurrectionary crowds to gather when crisis demanded it, articulate a collective analysis of a problem and solution, and then act together illustrates the capacity of everyday people to pursue their interests. Insurrectionary Parisians tended to trust those who built barricades and stood behind them together.[36]

The right-wing French social psychologist Gustave LeBon recoiled in fear of the French Revolution and these other insurrectionary moments in France's modern history. He wrote in 1895 *The Crowd: A Study of the Popular Mind* that crowds have a pathological group-mind in which emotions spread "contagiously", minimizing individual rationality and responsibility. Although contemporary sociologists are apt to dismiss his reactionary and condescending "analysis" of crowds, he seems to be right about group consciousness created in crowds—although he characterized it as purely reactive, emotional, and irrational.[37] Even though "mob mentality" can be real, there is also an incredible crowd *intelligence* that can emerge, as groups make smarter, better decisions than any one member would make on average—and they do so with collective strength to back up those decisions.[38] The "mob" was not only a tactical formation but also a demographic of radical urbanites in Revolutionary America, whose ungovernability periodically undermined British colonial rule.[39]

The aftermath of the Catalonian uprising of 1936 was witnessed by journalist George Orwell, later world renowned as the author of *1984* and *Animal Farm*. He described how it felt completely different in a revolutionary city, unlike anything he was used to. A rugged trust permeated Barcelona, and all manner of formality and deference to authority had disappeared.[40] People needed each other's solidarity due to risks posed by Franco's fascist army and other reactionary forces. The groundwork for antifascist resistance to the military's coup was laid by a network of defense committees established by the anarcho-syndicalist labor union, the Confederación Nacional del Trabajo (CNT). These CNT defense committees took advantage of opportunities (such as the raid upon the Barcelona's Drassanes barracks and the popular distribution of its arsenal among workers) and pre-existing solidarity among radical unionists, poured gasoline on the fire, and participated in street actions to stymie social control forces. Without strong and time-tested trust between these defense committee members and the trust they shared with other left-wing workers across the city, the events that kicked off the Spanish Revolution would have likely failed before they could truly begin.[41]

Later, however, trust dissipated, especially between different left factions; the Stalinist-dominated Popular Front and the Republican government suppressed other fighting forces (e.g., the Marxist, anti-Stalinist Partido Obrero de Unificación Marxista), before eventually undermining anarchist influence in Revolutionary Spain. All this rising distrust undermined the social revolution and led to its failure in 1939 and the subsequent reign of Franco's fascist government until 1975.

Urban revolts against racial injustice and police brutality involve people on society's periphery—who lack access to legitimate political action and power—often revolting against late capitalism. In doing so, oppressed classes in general and people of color in particular find solidarity in their resistance, wedging open civil society by their radical dissent and exposé of society hypocrisy. This solidarity finds people sharing in the middle of chaos, protecting each other, and squashing previous disagreements and conflicts, such as in the Tottenham, UK, uprising in 2011 following the police murder of Mark Duggan.[42] This revolt originated from considerable distrust in the police, and involved excitement, empowerment, and carnival.[43] Predictably, participants in such revolts usually remark later that such activities increased their trust in each other.

Case Study: Wartime Solidarity

Let's consider another example of spontaneous order and social trust in trying times: state-based wars and imperialist wars (the penultimate example of socially created disaster). People who share similar characteristics (e.g., residence, nationality)—and thus find common cause during wartime—benefit enormously from trust. The struggle to survive, let alone struggle against a military enemy, is formidable. When social trust is low in a besieged population, an enemy can easily acquire the upper hand. But, if there is high social trust, even an occupied population possesses substantial resources for resistance; they can coordinate sabotage and evasion, facilitate communication and resource provisioning, and keep people's spirits high and resilient. During unpopular imperialist wars, a dissident population may engage in collective resistance (draft dodging, blockading, and other subterfuge), which requires deep trust within an anti-imperialist movement.

In *A Paradise Built in Hell*, Rebecca Solnit describes the solidarity that emerged in London during the German "blitzkrieg" of 1940–1941: Generosity, good-spirits, and helpfulness were not exceptions to the rule but rather normal for citizens facing the onslaught of aerial bombardment.[44] The trust people share with each other during wartime will dictate how the population will survive war, let alone resist it. Trust may be important for communities to actively fight defensively against outside invaders, or against powerful dominators or occupiers who already control their space. Such defense requires a level of solidarity nearly unrivaled in any other circumstance.

This may seem rather strange to American readers, as we haven't had to worry about defensive wars for a very, very long time.[45] But, if we correctly view the US as a settler-colonial state, it's easier to see that defensive wars have been and continue to be fought within claimed US territory. Those who have waged "war" against oppressors in the US (specifically, the US state, corporate capitalism, the police, the US Army, etc.) include the American Indian Movement, Black Liberation Army, Fuerzas Armadas de Liberación Nacional Puertorriqueña, and other mid- to late twentieth-century liberation movements, and innumerable American Indian nations before that time period. These resistance movements thrived in environments of greater trust but languished with trust's evaporation.[46]

According to C. Wright Mills's thought experiment in *The Sociological Imagination*, most people have certain concerns during war—and we can understand much about the choices they make based on the times and places they live, and how social forces act upon individuals to generate personal troubles.[47] Specifically, individuals attempt to survive war. To do this requires working together to make the hardships and dangers bearable and survivable. This happens in families to be sure, but usually entire communities collaborate to survive war. If everyone is at risk, then the survival of others improves the chances that *you* will survive too. Another concern is to avoid or evade war. People who are targeted for conscription (through legal or extralegal means) may try to escape—simply not turn up when summoned, go "underground", or escape to an under-populated area or another country.[48] Monkey-wrenching the draft, perhaps by destroying draft records or counter-organizing targeted draftees, also makes general evasion more possible. These strategies require collaborators who trust each other, as hiding requires a security-oriented subculture that will not turn draft dodgers over to the government.[49]

The efforts to *end* war are more complicated still. When a soldier lays down their weapons and refuses to fight, they need to have support from fellow soldiers and the civilian population, so they can survive potential retaliatory violence or legal action. Clogging up an imperialist war machine and making it difficult to function requires lots of people, committed to long-term struggle. This is, in part, one of the factors that lead to the US's eventual withdrawal from Vietnam (along with the resistance of the Vietnamese people, of course).[50] Insurrection at home can burden law enforcement, requiring troops to be returned from international deployment. Working together across class and racial divides frustrates elites' efforts to pit one group against another. And, while Mills does not mention it, people may act to prevent war from beginning: street protest ahead of a war's build-up, and challenging jingoism, race-baiting, and warmongering before it leads to military conflict. Internationally coordinated efforts can apply pressure and slowly pick apart the capacity and willingness of a state to wage war (e.g., kicking foreign armies out of domestic military bases). All of this requires the presumption that people will have each other's backs, even in times of intense hardship and risk, even when no clear plan exists nor the possibility of success. People do some of their best work when they are inspired by each other's resistance, unifying around a common cause, and setting their sights on a nemesis that contradicts their deeply held values, as imperialist states often do.

For example, the Israeli siege of the Gaza Strip (within the Occupied Palestinian Territory), starting in 2023, leveled large parts of the Strip. But the population possessed incredible resilience—nurtured during decades of deprivation and hardship—born of social trust and collaboration in intense, hard conditions. Regardless of political affiliation (including to the reigning Hamas government), Palestinians in Gaza were able to respond to Israeli bombing attacks, coordinating medical services, distributing food and other essential resources, and channeling refugees to safer areas. Surviving such a war—especially within the 141-square-mile Strip, often referred to as the world's largest open-air prison camp—requires massive social trust. Individuals in such extreme circumstances cannot persevere without each other.

Civil wars are particularly unique "war" situations. It is less clear who enemies are, who is a combatant, and what the role of the state is vis-à-vis opposing forces. Radical trust can emerge in civil wars, allowing proponents of freedom and justice to successfully collaborate, beat back fascistic enemies, and create spaces for people to exist with greater control and less inequality. The Spanish Civil War (also known as the Spanish Revolution) is an excellent example of trust emergence. But, a more recent example can be found in the Syrian Civil War, in which various forces—especially the Kurds of Rojava—struggled to create a zone of autonomy, justice, ecology, feminism, and participatory democracy. The People's Council of West Kurdistan (MGRK) created a complex, federated council system that incorporated the region's many ethnic groups.[51] Being able to trust people with whom your own ethnic group historically quarreled or competed against is necessary, especially in the midst of violence, which tends to reduce trust in "the other".

Case Study: Disease Pandemic

Pandemics aren't "disasters" in the same way that earthquakes, floods, or hurricanes are—but they do have disastrous consequences upon human bodies and society. There are many diverse sources of modern pandemics, truly outside the control of any one given person: urbanization; climate change; inequality; and globalization.[52] During a disease pandemic, healthy people are not deliberately or directly harming the sick—that's the disease. But people can choose to either remain inactive, actively exacerbate problems, or help others. Staying alive in the chaos created by disease, which was sown by the chaos of these aforementioned forces, requires far more cooperation than during non-pandemic times.

How does trust matter in the midst of a disease pandemic? Two illustrative ongoing pandemics can illustrate the need for trust: HIV/AIDS and Covid-19. First, trust in the forces of authority is obviously misplaced. As already described, the state responds slowly to disaster, and pandemics are no different. For years, the Reagan administration refused to even utter the phrase "AIDS" in public, medical professionals and pharmaceutical companies balked at shifting their focus to addressing a "gay disease", and the general American population feared those with AIDS, even in situations posing no real threat. Trusting federal government sympathy, medicine's even-handed intervention, or solidarity from a homophobic society, was sorely misplaced trust. Expecting states to respond reasonably to Covid-19—to shut down their economies to stem the virus's spread, to encourage their citizens to stay safely at home and wear masks, increase the production of medical equipment and protective wear, enhance the availability of health professionals, and provide economic relief for the poor and suffering—proved equally elusive in the US in 2020. These necessary actions actually happened faster in centralized and authoritarian societies (e.g., China, Singapore). Laissez-faire societies, with image-obsessed heads of state (e.g., US, Brazil), hesitated to act and even recklessly referenced conspiracy theories instead of relying on medical science and established public health practices. Why should we expect large numbers of duped citizens to believe the threat posed by Covid-19 when they are distrustful of science, and simultaneously obedient to the shrugged indifference and bravado of wannabe-strongmen like Trump or Brazil's Jair Bolsonaro (both of whom scoffed at mask wearing and later tested positive for Covid-19)?[53]

Or, we could place trust in the common sense and competencies of "essential workers" who know best how to stay safe in their workplaces (if so empowered). With the knowledge of basic hygiene and sanitation skills, grocery workers can wash their hands, cover their faces with masks, and prevent the spread of Covid-19. But this requires trusting workers to do their jobs without interference from profit-hungry managers or the abstract dictates of capitalist competition—they will naturally seek to protect themselves better than their employers. Workers are more apt to share interests and trust customers than their employers.

Trust during a pandemic is most meaningful and practical in daily affairs. People who must practice social distancing due to their great risk need help. Being able to rely on others to provision food for the hungry, elderly or shut-ins, or the immuno-compromised, is key to survival. Providing mutual aid to parents, recently laid-off workers, and neighbors increases the likelihood that people will stem the spread of disease and stay alive. Trust is key to forms of resistance and alternative-building necessary to deal with the collapse of "normal" society (which was *absolutely unjust* beforehand), which was premised upon a competitive marketplace. Workers going on strike, neighbors defending each other from eviction, the homeless squatting abandoned buildings, campaigns to demand and obtain emergency funds (or debt or rent relief)—these are actions taken by millions during the Covid-19 pandemic. Mutual aid movements require higher-than-average trust to succeed, given the challenging times and increased stakes. People who are paranoid and distrustful will find they can only rely on themselves (and maybe close family) as a bulwark against a pandemic's spread—and the scary, but illusory threats they mistakenly believe are posed by their fellow neighbors. In the 1980s and 1990s, HIV-positive individuals joined together to form "buyer clubs" that could purchase the expensive drug cocktails for treating the disease. Gay activists formed networks like AIDS Coalition to Unleash Power (ACT-UP) to pressure policy makers, scientists, and the pharmaceutical industry. They protected each other, advocated for their disadvantaged group's interests, came out to their straight families and neighbors, and mourned the loss of their friends. Trust makes such resistance and resilience possible.

The Covid-19 pandemic also provoked the formation of mutual aid networks to collaborate, share resources, and help out neighbors. Mutual aid organizations sprung up around the world by the hundreds, if not thousands (especially if counting those not formally using the label "mutual aid") to address basic needs and complicated problems. In Rhiannon Firth's study of London-based mutual aid organizations, people bonded together in struggle, creating impressive potential that'd be seemingly inconceivable during "normal times". Spontaneity and everyday need fueled this explosion, and "mutual aid" was a helpful, if simply convenient, framework for participants to understand their actions. However, popularization introduced a lack of conceptual precision and eroded historical connections with mutual aid's radical tradition and values, which sometimes resulted in a watering down of core principles, as some efforts lost their egalitarian impulse.[54]

Trust was fundamental to these forms of resistance and survival. Pandemics force such trust out into the open, and to endure a pandemic requires trust. Mutual aid networks are created in the wake of pandemics, which results in the creation of trust. But, these mutual aid efforts also benefit from having pre-existing, resilient networks of individuals who already possess a pro-social trust orientation and can begin organizing immediately.

Urban revolts, war, and disease pandemics teach a valuable lesson—in each, we are shown a window into an alternative reality, another way of living. For example, the Covid-19 pandemic demonstrated that it's completely possible to interrupt the status quo—the economy, environmental devastation, and other forms of violence ground to a halt. People took time to reassess their lives and priorities, they stepped back from bullshit jobs and careers.[55] Animal populations rebounded as gasoline-powered transportation and its disruption dissipated. Many realized—perhaps for the first time—that they lived in a system that is socially *constructed*, with artificially defined rules, but that also had a big "STOP" button on them. And not only were most people okay when the craziness stopped but we caught a glimpse of other priorities and new human potentials of mutual aid. And even though the prospects of redirecting society or starting over likely seemed overwhelming—and there was still much destruction and death to be concerned with—the lesson remains important. It is possible to change; we know it is, because we saw it happen.

THE REASSERTION OF INEQUALITY
DURING AND AFTER DISASTER

Regardless of the good things generated from disaster's shake-up, the latent, hierarchical system is always lurking around the corner, awaiting the opportunity to reassert itself. Solnit argues that the elite panic following disaster can cause more harm than the disaster itself.[56] Disaster victims may be treated as criminals—this occurred in New Orleans following 2005's Hurricane Katrina. Black residents stranded by the torrential rain and flooding—and the crushing poverty that inhibited transportation out of the city—sometimes turned to illicit means of survival out of necessity. Their reasonable efforts to survive the disaster were punished; they were branded "looters" and condemned by the media and then targeted for extrajudicial killing by vigilantes and police. As a consequence, the normal ranking of priorities (save lives first, property second) was upended, placing the rule of law over individuals, protecting property over people's lives. Despite a new, just, and more creative world struggling to emerge from the wreckage of the old, hierarchy does its best to re-establish its supremacy.

Another way that spontaneous goodwill is thwarted comes from pre-existing inequalities between volunteers and the recipients of charity. The privileges that many volunteers bring to disaster zones cause innumerable problems. Even though they come to "help out", they also can import their class- and race-based biases. Such volunteers—despite how naive, ignorant, and unskilled they may actually be—can receive deference, louder platforms, and gratitude that they may not deserve. In fact, volunteers may implicitly demand such gratitude from affected community members. The "volunteer" work of privileged out-of-towners may be less altruistic than most presume and may be more about serving their own importance, sense of self, and raising their status vis-à-vis their peers. People with class and race privileges get extra credit, respect, and status enhancement. Ultimately, this can translate into greater influence than local residents. Privileged persons can inappropriately acquire a status as "experts"—even though they may not be experts and predictably know far less about the local area and its important issues. Their presumed neutrality and outsider status mean they are deferred to, despite their privileged backgrounds being anything but neutral.[57] Issues of privilege and inequality are particularly problematic within international solidarity activism, in which individuals from wealthier countries travel to poorer countries to volunteer their time and efforts but tend to acquire a disproportionate share of influence, despite their outsider status. These issues are central to the now mainstream critique of missionaries, whose "help" may not actually be help, and may reduce trust.[58]

Outsiders also import power that they don't deserve and that is highly destructive. For example, the Red Cross typically stumbles into disaster zones with its billion-dollar-deep pockets,[59] using a one-size-fits-all approach. Even though such an ill-tuned strategy usually flounders, the Red Cross gains immediate praise, due to its media and donor familiarity, thus further privileging its status. In fact, the Red Cross has so much face-legitimacy that it is typically the largest recipient of donations following disasters, despite often having no pre-existing presence in the affected areas. After the 9/11 terror attacks, the Red Cross was entrusted to relay over $1 billion in newly donated funds to those in need, including the families of victims. Instead, the Red Cross earmarked hundreds of millions of dollars for a "future attack", allowed local chapters to mismanage their accounting (the Red Cross internally called them the "Dirty Thirty" chapters), and the organization went on a construction spree, erecting Red Cross buildings across the United States in the ensuing years.[60] In 2024, Haitian Americans sued the Red Cross for profiting from "poverty and calamities" in Haiti to raise hundreds of millions of dollars that were allegedly mismanaged and appropriated to benefit individual employees and to pay off Red Cross deficits elsewhere.[61] The same unwarranted extension of trust to a charitable nonprofit occurred with Goodwill Industries, too, whose CEO in 2018 received an entire compensation package of $920,520, while concurrently paying portions of its mentally disabled labor force below the US federal minimum wage, due to a loophole permitting such practices.[62]

Also, even though amazing potential can be unlocked during disruptive moments, many people will be scared—those who already distrust each other are particularly susceptible to this fear. For everyone who engages in mutual aid to support their fellow community members, there's someone else who is selfishly hording resources or engaging in price gouging over those scarce resources. In a generally distrustful society, moments of crisis may be just as likely to further entrench distrust as it is to provoke greater mutuality, horizontalism, and social trust. As with the paradoxes described in Chapter 1 ("you need some to get more" and "most disadvantaged"), it can be incredibly challenging to break people out of their hierarchical and distrustful habits, even when the moments are ripe for trying something new. Given the pressures to "return to normality", the disruptive opportunities offered by disaster may be short-lived. It may be easy to miss the subtle changes that occur during such moments or there may be a variety of reasons why some may not seize the moment.

CHANGING CIRCUMSTANCES

When things change quickly—as they do in times of disaster—it's tough to know who to trust. Consequently, people are often forced to reconsider previous assessments of those who have been a constant and stable presence in their lives. Sometimes this is good, and the circle of humanity widens. However, sometimes this development is bad, as people's hearts contract and trust withers. Or desperation may cajole people to mistrust those promising quick fixes but who may have ulterior motives.

Émile Durkheim wrote about the rapidly changing and disruptive conditions of the modern, industrial era, calling the resulting fragmentation of social relations "anomie" (meaning: without norms). Such changes tend to under-integrate people into society. Those who would otherwise find a place to belong to, a community to participate in, and a role to play, instead end up isolated and, probably, distrustful. This surely describes the transitions from monarchies to nation states, and feudalism to industrial capitalism of Durkheim's Europe. But his description remains applicable to today's era of anchor-less and disaster-ridden global capitalism too. Air travel, all-weather roads and automobile-fueled suburbanization, and computers and telecommunication technologies have completely rewritten societal expectations. As the world becomes less and less familiar than the one people are used to, it not only looks alien but we also have a harder time knowing who to trust in it. Communities that are able to withstand such changes and adapt to new conditions can maintain their higher levels of trust. In these instances, transition can occur without too many terminal problems. However, communities that do not weather change well tend to suffer. These distrusting places are consequently battered more severely by change than those who have found ways to retain, grow, or transform trust.

A small case study of this anomic chaos is the deindustrializing northern cities of the US in the 1960s, 1970s, and 1980s. Neighborhoods that experienced disinvestment, unemployment, declining opportunity, and crime were caught in a downward spiral tough to escape from. Sociologist William Julius Wilson referred to neighborhood residents as "the truly disadvantaged".[63] These disproportionately Black and Latino neighborhoods had not been able to adapt to, let alone influence, forces outside their control. For each new problem, distrust increased, and people tended to grow more socially distant from each other. In part, greater joblessness, poor performing schools, decreasing property values, and desperation compounded, and residents were just as likely to place blame upon each other, as they were on the opaque forces of global capitalism, the reeling and withering welfare state, white supremacist dismissal, and empire decline. Additionally, crime spiked, as some unemployed residents preyed upon others around them. People with the economic means to leave these declining neighborhoods made the effort to do so, thus further destabilizing the neighborhood. As a consequence, people's ability—to say nothing of their desire—to trust each other diminished drastically. The neighborhood disruption from these cascading social problems resulted in a catastrophic loss of trust.[64]

Entrenched hierarchies appear to orient people toward pro-police attitudes: Individuals in stable countries, whether authoritarian or "democratic", tend to profess higher confidence in the police compared to countries with only short-term stability. Perhaps destabilized democracies invite critique, since there's finally a possibility of change. The criminologists responsible for this research study recommended that governments emphasize efficiency in order to improve confidence. But this is an uncritical, superficial suggestion—it may be more important to recognize that changing circumstances create opportunities for those seeking to fight for expanded justice and liberation, who can use the moment to undermine respect and trust in old, tired hierarchies.[65] "New democracies" tend to experience a "post-honeymoon decline" in political trust, as expectations become unfulfilled; such trust is reduced by the tolerance of corruption.[66] Thus, once people begin to correctly identify the circumstances facing them, they address their trust in hierarchies accordingly.

The principal problem and challenge we face is whether people can develop stable trust with their neighbors in times of crisis and intense change. For example, can people trust their co-workers in a unified struggle against their employer if they are at risk of being fired (or even an entire workplace being closed), which is still a regular occurrence in various American industries? Or if a pandemic like Covid-19 threatens the safety of those who physically attend a workplace? Asking such people to optimistically develop "open-hearts, despite the consequences"—or potentially "getting burned"—may be too demanding of people lacking societal privileges. Being trusting, strong, nimble, and flexible is a tall order in the face of rapid changes. Creating resilient trust in such times remains a formidable challenge. And it is not easily done through individual will alone, especially if one's life is on the line.

TRUST IS NECESSARY FOR SURVIVAL

Ultimately, we're social creatures. And despite myths of individualism, we need each other.[67] Remember, Ayn Rand and her ultra-individualistic philosophy were not just absurd but completely impossible.[68] Following such absurdity makes us lemmings prone to running off cliffs.[69] Let's consider all the reasons why trust is necessary for human survival.

Very few of us are capable of completely providing for ourselves, given our limited skill sets, and we would need quite large individual, territorial zones to do so too. Granted, I know how to garden, but I can't grow enough food for all my dietary needs, especially if I want to do anything else with the hours of my day. I can't produce the solar panels that could power the air conditioner (that I also can't build) to cool my house down so I don't suffer heatstroke during hot summers. Yes, that might not be *essential* to survival, but life would dramatically worsen in a trust-less future. We wouldn't just lose air conditioning but things like medicine and disease prevention, and other "luxuries" that allow us to generally live past "middle age" would all shrivel up in the absence of community and trust.

But, even more fundamentally, there must be some form of trust between children and parents (particularly mothers) or some other adults. If trust is absent, the species would quickly cease. If children do not have stability, predictability, and nurturing, they grow up without maturing, becoming scarred and incapable of higher-order human skills. There have been centuries' worth of examples of abused "feral children" who experienced devastating intellectual, developmental, and emotional impairment as a result of their treatment and isolation from non-nurturing adults.[70] But, while abuse can clearly damage our brains and "normal" development, abuse doesn't need to be as extreme to have destructive outcomes—it's helpful to remember that nurturing families don't just help children survive but to thrive. Individualistic parents who raise their children as consumers or obedient workers (in the family and for society) may group up lacking the ability to deeply trust others. Children need to be able to place trust in adults and violating such trust earlier in life can permanently cripple their adulthood. The flip side of this coin is the trust that elderly adults place in younger generations—old age would be short and brutish if the elderly cannot trust their descendants, or the community that follows them, to care for them.[71]

Beyond obvious provisioning and parental upbringing, we emotionally, psychologically, and physically need each other too. Stable, friendly relationships are essential for our emotional health, itself a prerequisite for a stress-free existence. Being afraid of others all the time simply heightens our stress and cortisol levels, leads to dangerous inflammation, and brings on catastrophic medical problems.[72] For example, innumerable studies have investigated why Black mothers have significantly higher rates of premature births, compared to white mothers. The emerging consensus has begun to highlight the impact that daily racism plays: Not being able to trust those around you (especially whites) to treat you fairly, kindly, appropriately, and so forth, tends to accumulate stress in Black women's bodies. This stress is chronic and cannot be "turned off" at nighttime, and it begins to saturate their bodies in unhealthy ways, leading to problems like premature birth.[73] Not being able to trust and not be trusted literally kills us.

Thus, even if survival were possible without trust—and it's not—we still couldn't *thrive*.

OVERCOMING FEAR

Disasters are scary; tragedies are heartbreaking; chaos is stressful. Dramatic weather phenomena, riots, wars, disease pandemics, and other events may inspire different human possibilities, but they are still very dangerous. An unclear future and the lack of guarantees tend to raise people's anxieties and stress, which can generate fear. Beyond these hardships, and the loss of life and destruction of the means of subsistence, the threats to our social fabric are great. Fear can disable us if not dealt with properly. Becoming isolated in our fear, we will remain fearful—just as with the isolation of depression or addiction. Fear will remain a serious threat to social trust.

Even in non-disaster situations, there's still fear to overcome. We may fear that social ostracism or humiliation will result from trusting certain people. We risk the chance that someone will disappoint us or, worse, take advantage and abuse our trust. Many of these fears are ghosts—figments of our overactive imaginations or socially generated psychosis—but they can still govern us, restricting how we act. Social norms and stigmas have an impressive capacity to convince people to willingly follow hierarchical rules and scripts, even absent any actual sanctions or consequences. Our affairs seem challenging to us when we're isolated and fearful.

It's unreasonable to demand that individuals "just" become more trusting, especially when they have a lifetime of inhibitions warning them otherwise. Instead of relying on an individual-centric strategy for enlarging societal trust, we should recognize this goal is *the responsibility of whole communities*—whatever form they take. Collective approaches to overcoming fear have the best chances for success. And, hopefully, such collective efforts can change our shared circumstances once disaster passes.

But how do we stymie fear? How can we collectively overcome the social problems that have helped to create fear as well as all the negative consequences that result from it? These are big questions and they are not simple to answer. I argue that the best strategic way forward is to accept the necessity of trust and pursue it with a radical vision of freedom and justice. We can build collective resilience to adversity. These matters are the subject of the next and final chapter.

DISASTER TRUST SUMMARIZED

Disasters can be devastating and they're likely inevitable. But disasters are survivable if social trust exists that binds people together when times get hard. Unfortunately, disasters—and the predictable cadre of individuals who would take advantage of such crises—tend to provoke social distrust. This makes a bad situation worse, by impairing a community's potential to collectively respond to their problems. Yet times of crisis and disaster illustrate the potential of humans to unite together around a common cause, spontaneously organize for the common good, and fight to build a better world afterward. The social norm breaking that occurs during these unusual times makes clear what people often don't like about the "normal" state of affairs and what kind of world we would like to deliver into existence. The experiences gained during natural disasters like floods, fires, and earthquakes are comparable to social crises like war, urban revolts, and pandemics—all show a different way to live. Intense feelings of commitment, trust, and solidarity emerge so vibrantly that they tend to provoke life-changing epiphanies. Trust is necessary for the latent potential, which emerges repeatedly under these conditions, to fully flower. And this potential contains lessons we should heed.

6

A Reason to Trust—Trust in Revolution: How We Can Strategically Use Trust

RADICAL TRUST EMPOWERS AND CREATES JUSTICE

I've been involved in enough social movements to see a wide spectrum of interpersonal trust. In some movements and organizations many people know each other, share common cultural references and interests, are emotionally present, and build trust by socializing and participating in leisure activities together. Sometimes these were people who had a common DIY aesthetic who joined Food Not Bombs or participated in Critical Mass bike rides together. Student activist groups were often unified around common experiences, age, social class, and political views. Anti-war activism or labor unions brought people together around shared values and visions of the future, as well as pragmatic collective interests. While not all such organizations have enjoyed the same degree of trust, and solidarity can be fickle, participants have usually found ways to make it work. Trust doesn't guarantee movement success, but it's an essential ingredient. Movements cannot thrive without widespread interpersonal trust and, usually, general social trust.

However, I've also witnessed what happens when trust is lacking or distrust is rampant in movements. Participation can be limited or low energy, with people attending briefly and not meeting outside of scheduled events. If inequalities have disrupted trust potential, participants tend to be guarded or cliquish, suspicious about fellow participants and only engaging with a handful of others. In a few organizations, malevolent actors have inserted themselves into the group, taken advantage of existing open trust, and subverted the organization from within. One student activist with delusions of grandeur even secretly rewrote an organization's constitution and submitted it to the school, thereby replacing its horizontal decision-making process with a hierarchical one led by a few executives (of which they became "president" as opposed to just a "facilitator"). Another activist was experiencing a mental health crisis that infused them with paranoia; they took manipulative revenge on their perceived "adversaries", in the process disrupting group activities and solidarity. Their subversion eroded trust; individuals being attacked didn't know who else supported them because many were afraid to stand up to the bad actor. And I've attended countless events where the earliest announcements intend to warn attendees of the likely presence of police informants or even undercover police. While this can sometimes bolster the anti-authoritarian emotions in a room, it surely also fractures trust potential.

For movements officially dedicated to the pursuit of empowerment and justice, the presence of trust can make all the difference between progress or failure, just as the presence of distrust—whether intentionally created by Machiavellian operators or confrontation loudmouths, or just accidentally formed—can forestall collaboration and the potential for making any gains. This all matters greatly because while there are many reasons to advocate greater social trust, there are two simple ones: empowerment and justice. Empowerment and justice are both wonderful conditions for individuals to experience, as well as for whole communities to have in ample supply. If we could have both, why not?

Granted, authoritarians know this and try to deceive us by misusing these words. Capitalists try to convince us that "empowerment" is something we exclusively experience as consumers alone. Thus, capitalists' narrow definitions only empower those with lots of money. Or defenders of the social welfare state simply consider "empowerment" as the ability to vote. We are told that "justice" is just a nefarious concept that communists use to trick everyone into thinking that we can share things. Actual state socialists do profess to be big fans of "justice", but just so long as its only about equalizing incomes, not sharing power. They usually want their statist power to be respected and their expertise deferred to; as the right is fond of reminding us, state socialists have killed large numbers of people who challenged them in pursuit of greater autonomy and freedoms. But, beyond these hierarchy-infused arguments against empowerment and justice, most people tend to like these values.

The clearest intersection of empowerment and justice can be found in the ideology of libertarian socialism—libertarians pursue empowerment, while socialism implies economic and social justice. The ideology of libertarian socialism modifies both of their parent ideologies (libertarianism and socialism), pointing out the weakness implicit in each's isolation. Russian revolutionary Mikhail Bakunin wisely offered nuance in regard to these two ideologies in his 1867 proposal to the League for Peace and Freedom: "liberty without socialism is privilege, injustice; and that socialism without liberty is slavery and brutality".[1]

A free society empowers people to express themselves more openly and live how they wish (i.e., libertarianism), and thus requires trust. If we trust each other, we are more interested in working to guarantee that everyone has what they need (i.e., socialism). These imply the best types of goals: libertarian trust in yourself against the state and other hierarchical institutions, and socialistic trust in your fellow equals. Social trust supports a society where people trust you to act appropriately and not infringe on their rights too (and thus not become a hierarchical authority yourself). Being able to gather and meet publicly increases general social trust. We can see each other, experience diversity, and figure out how to co-exist. Hiding in one's home tends to limit exposure to "the other" and reduce empathy. Having a truly open space in society for us to co-trust is essential for any effort for liberty and justice. And efforts to reduce access to public space are detrimental to freedom and therefore increase inequality.[2] Trust creates a society with more interdependence and consideration for others, thus helping justice to flower.

I think there is value in more explicitly extending Bakunin's logical style to the realm of trust. Just as liberty and justice are intertwined and must be balanced against each other, so must the two primary forms of trust we've described thus far—social and political trust. Therefore, I contend: Social solidarity with political trust is naivete and self-subjugation to the state; anti-authoritarianism without social trust is nihilism and paralysis.

Here, solidarity is the main weapon of those seeking justice (or socialism) and it requires social trust. In fact, solidarity necessitates a deep, committed trust in abstract others. Anti-authoritarianism is a tool of those seeking empowerment (or liberty), and it wholly rejects any statist or other form of hierarchical trust. Anti-authoritarianism is an essential feature of political distrust, just as it is an essential feature of social trust—we can trust each other, because we must distrust hierarchy. Thus, if we wield our social solidarity with others while we also trust the state, we are being obtuse, ultimately placing more faith in the hierarchical systems of the status quo to save us than we place in each other. If we subordinate ourselves to those systems, our solidarity is flanked and undermined. Opposing authority is ultimately fruitless if we lack hope in the potential of others around us. To reject all—hierarchy along with our fellow equals—would (in the extreme) be to give up on the future, and to collapse into a self-destructive mode of depression and hopelessness.[3]

A modern example of a pro-solidarity and empowerment-seeking project is FLOSS—free, libre, open-source software.[4] Free software embodies the opposite characteristics of proprietary software. Anyone is allowed to contribute to FLOSS software, because these contributions are expected to be well intended. Even though malicious (or just suboptimal) programming code could be added in this open process, advocates continue to trust FLOSS's overall arrangement that seeks maximum transparency, code auditing by outside programmers, and as many possible eyes and testers working with the software who are looking for weaknesses. This openness encourages the intervention of certain ultra-critical people who suspiciously seek to investigate the code "just in case" malicious elements have been inserted. Thus, FLOSS is founded on general trust in the FLOSS community, as well as a militant level of hostility toward those who would seek to obscure code and pervert the underlying honest intentions of software. FLOSS's anti-authoritarianism rejects the notion of software *ownership* or that single authorities should be able to dictate how others use software. FLOSS's solidarity is witnessed in the millions of programmers, testers, and users who contribute their labor without pay (usually), for this community's greater good.[5] It's a prime example of the effectiveness of commons-based peer-production that relies on decentralized production and self-management.[6]

A public-key encryption program like GPG is a specific example of FLOSS. This form of software encryption requires the exchange of "keys" between users, which allows them to send secure e-mails to each other. Public keys are publicly accessible and are used to scramble a message in such a way that only the person who has that key's private pair can decrypt it. This process relies on what are called "webs of trust", a system to authenticate the connection between an individual and their associated public key. With a good, strong "web of trust", encryption works well. Adversaries—be they governments, corporate actors, or personal enemies—must expend incredible computing resources to attack public-key encryption. Thus, social movement participants, human rights observers, and others facing the state's wrath have used public-key encryption to evade their adversary's prying eyes.[7] Even though this system is premised upon a web of trust to guarantee accurate key exchanging, it exists because there are ample anti-authoritarian reasons to distrust the intentions of malevolent actors who have access to monitor unencrypted internet traffic.[8] In order for people to be empowered and free in their communication, encryption requires a substantial degree of trust in the social systems at work behind key exchanges, as well as the elaborate encryption algorithms and protocols that software like GPG uses. If it were not FLOSS, weaknesses may remain undetected by the software's developers, only to be exploited by malevolent actors (like the National Security Agency) who use such "zero day" bugs to gain unpermitted access to people's communications.

To use a non-software example, building cross-race trust may be hard for many reasons. It's pretty clear what doesn't work: paternalism, subordination, suspicion, deviousness, and Machiavellian intent. There are far better ways to construct the foundations of coalition building: emphasizing common interests, co-scheming among fellow accomplices, and general comradery. Even though this trust is in the foreground, trust in systems of white supremacy, segregation, racial profiling and discrimination, and other bigotry and nastiness is counterproductive. It's infinitely wise to distrust in these disruptive, schism-inducing hierarchies and to focus trust upon the "other", whom we are encouraged—but shouldn't—to distrust. As political scientist Joel Olson argued, putting your faith in multiculturalism (wherein mere diversity is the end goal) or color-blindness (where difference is simply ignored) are both dead-end approaches; revolutionary anti-racism is the best strategy for overcoming white supremacy.[9] And while trust is a foundational requirement, it doesn't "just happen"; trust requires studious, deliberate, respectful, and outgoing nurturing. Experience is the best cauldron for creating such cross-race, anti-racist trust, where various groups (and especially those with greater privileges) take risks *together*.[10]

An applied example of such trust would be decolonization. By acknowledging that there are shared interests (e.g., the protection of the earth) between settlers and indigenous people, both sides can (literally) find common ground. For settlers to accept that indigenous lifeways are almost surely better than capitalist lifeways for the earth (and thus all humans who live here), both empowers settlers *and* indigenous people, but also works to resolve ongoing injustices.[11] Next, re-establishing indigenous sovereignty helps to ensure that future trust partners are social equals—not part of the same groups, but equal in terms of their power and standing. Decolonization undermines one of settler colonialism's "original sins" (i.e., indigenous genocide), but it also subverts the foundations of capitalist domination, wherein land is owned by private interests as opposed to by communities. While neither simple nor straightforward, decolonization is a solution to a thoroughly disruptive and violent force in society.[12] And the trust that it requires (and engenders) empowers disadvantaged groups to seek justice.

It is suggestive to look at how radical social movements operate. Prefigurative politics involve people creating the kind of world they want now, in the current moment, through the present decisions they make and actions they take.[13] Thus, movements not only act in ways that emphasize trust in others—and distrust in hierarchy—but also model future social patterns they hope to see more widely practiced in the future. In other words, if you want a more trusting society, you might as well start building trust, right now. And the best way to start reducing trust in brutal systems like capitalism or white supremacy is to start undermining them in this current moment via your own deliberate, vocal distrust. Your anti-authoritarianism will augment your solidarity.

Lastly, what some might call "selfishness" is ultimately okay in all this—despite coercive-collectivist whisperings otherwise. A white person participating in struggles for racial justice may alternatively be seen as altruistic or selfless—but they are *also* selfishly seeking a better, more full life for themselves too. Such a (supposedly) selfish life can be lived without compromises of their spirit, as they realize that their own freedom is contingent upon the freedom of others.[14] Thus, if an individual wants real, meaningful freedom in their own life, it's crucial to fight for everyone else's freedom too. This is just as "selfish" as it is "selfless". This accidentally works on the principle of the Golden Rule (described in greater detail below), in which people seek better treatment for themselves by treating others well first. Trust can thus be "paid forward" just as it can also be selfishly sought from others. The best way to become trusted is to be trustworthy to others.

A REASON TO TRUST

There are many reasons to trust others. We can witness the benefits of radical social trust whenever we have successful encounters and relationships with others. These experiences validate the contact hypothesis. Unfortunately, people with greater social privileges have more opportunities to have such experiences, as they tend to be surrounded by people who treat them better. As we are treated well by others, we are apt to do the same. This is often known as the Golden Rule—treat others as you would like to be treated. People who experience good treatment will reciprocate. Extending goodwill toward others makes us feel good; unsurprisingly, most people like to give and receive goodwill. It ought to be uncontroversial to suggest that reducing inequalities, domination, violence, or other disadvantages will surely result in better treatment of the average person in society.

It may be surprising to some that nearly every ethical tradition has a rough equivalent to the rule.[15] For example, in modern, liberal democracies, a dominant discourse of human rights is founded on a presumption that "all" can access the same rights. This may be an application of the rule, to the extent that such human rights operate universally and independently of citizenship, current residence, or other group memberships.[16] The very fact that we have such a discourse presumably justifies arguments in favor of social trust.

As described earlier, trust is mutually reinforcing. Being trusted generates the desire to return such trust. Trusting others generally leads them to trust you. If people trust you, you will also trust them. If I trust others not to do recklessly dangerous things, like shoot a gun in a crowded area, then I am surely safer than I would otherwise be, just as they are safer, too, because they also trust me to not shoot off a gun in a crowded area. Our mutual expectations of reasonableness make us trusting and trustworthy.

Trusting your fellow equals will result in less need to trust those in authority. This is another good reason to trust—it cuts-out the middleman. We become more aware of our collective capabilities because they are not filtered through the state's (or another authority's) authorization, pronouncements, or action. Once the claims of those in power are discredited—that we need police to prevent murder, politicians to guide our actions, or the wealthy to provide necessities—we can more fully appreciate that *we*—everyday people, *hoi polloi*—are the ones actually doing the important work for public safety, planning and action, and provisioning.

While there are lots of reasons to trust others, the most meaningful reasons cannot be easily quantified or categorized. Just as Raj Patel has argued that "value" is much more than the monetary price applied to something[17]—which might include what Marx called "use value" rather than mere "exchange value"—so, too, trust must be valued for its existential, abstract importance for humanity and the planet. We could try putting a price tag on how broad social trust could help us and, for example, coordinate a unified response to climate change by estimating the amount of money saved by mitigating property loss from catastrophes. But such estimates miss the most important thing about stopping climate change; the "value" of species survival, comfort, comradery, equity and justice, intergenerational confidence, and so on just shouldn't have a price placed on them. While doing so would literally value them, it also cheapens them too. Ethical behavior exists and thrives outside of the market.

Trust can help to build a resilient civil sphere. But what sort of civil sphere? According to sociologist Jeffrey Alexander, capitalism and the state are part of the "uncivil sphere", while the civil sphere is a safe place for the non-powerful to collaborate.[18] While insightful and inspiring—and he and others have extended this theorizing to how social movements "breach" the civil sphere to incorporate more and a wider diversity of voices[19]—Alexander's civil sphere is still ultimately premised upon a dialogue and mediation with capitalism and state, with the civil sphere seeking to mediate the uncivil sphere's harms. Given its immense power, such an uncivil sphere will remain a persistent threat to life and liberty so long as hierarchy is allowed to persist.[20] So, why tolerate its existence? Humans don't need the state or capitalist markets to trust, let alone survive. Why mitigate harm when it could instead be eliminated?

STRATEGIC PATHWAYS

If horizontalism is the ideal sociopolitical trust for society's masses to possess—and I've tried to make a strong argument that it is—then what do we do about the fact that most societies are *not* horizontalist in respect to trust? This fact reflects an undesirable situation, one with all the problems and challenges that much of this book has already outlined. The urgent task for those wishing to help reorient society toward greater horizontalism should involve determining how to convert those possessing each kind of sociopolitical trust into horizontalists. Thus, we should aim to move people toward horizontalist positions, despite how complicated this transformation will be. The work required is different for each population and category of trusters and distrusters.

Here, I'd like to return to my typology of sociopolitical trust, first introduced in Chapter 1. First, trusters already possess the needed social solidarity to work with their fellow peers. But they lack an anti-authoritarian impulse that is needed to critique and struggle against hierarchies. Trusters are apt to retain faith in the system's intentions and capacities. Thus, they must come to understand the futility of respecting hierarchies, and of hoping for, looking to, and placing trust in hierarchical institutions. Institutions are different—although they have some comparable features, they are not the same—thus, politicians and bosses are somewhat different from landlords, military and police commanders, or social and ideological abstractions like patriarchy and white supremacy. Raising trusters' level of criticism is challenging, as inspiring cynicism can have dangerous, unintended consequences. It's important to retain trusters' solidarity with others, while only losing trust in hierarchies. It would be devastating if, by fostering institutional cynicism, this simply transformed a truster into a distruster. Keeping trust in their fellow equals—perhaps by collaborating with them in their critique and opposition to hierarchies—is essential. Likely, experiences that sour trusters on hierarchy may include disappointment. Perhaps disappointment or perceived failures of allegedly "progressive" politicians will do much to build such anti-authoritarianism, as did the disappointment in Obama among his younger voter base from 2008. As the Great Recession proceeded with little intervention from his administration—stacked as it was with former (and future!) Goldman Sachs executives—these enthusiastic Obama supporters became disappointed with his inaction and lack of prosecution of Wall Street criminals, which fed into the Occupy Wall Street movement of 2011.[21] Obama's inaction on matters of racial justice also surely led to the Black Lives Matter movement.

Distrusters possess helpful anti-authoritarianism, which can resist temptations to believe or obey hierarchical orders. But they also lack crucial social trust and solidarity that can provide alternative allies, in the absence of hierarchy. Their pessimism about the state, capitalism, and other hierarchies unfortunately also extends to their neighbors and their fellow social equals too. Consequently, their rejection of trust in *anyone* can hamstring their options and abilities. Great dangers can result for distrusters who embrace conspiracy theories about "the system", which open up to placing trust in charismatic leaders (e.g., Trump or the originator of the QAnon conspiracy theory, "Q"). Additionally, nihilism about the future and generalizable distrust tend to reign for these individuals. They reasonably do not trust those in power to help them, but they also don't trust others to be on their side either. Closing themselves off to far more potential allies only darkens their perceptions of the future. Thus, improving their social trust is key—but focused upon general others; if this increased trust comes with improved political trust or trust in other elites, then they will lose their critical, anti-authoritarian edge. The challenging tightrope to walk is, once again, improving optimism in others while maintaining pessimism in the system. Demonstrating the benefits of trusting others may be the best way to do this. Ideally, having distrusters experience firsthand others' generosity and social willingness will be most impactful. Encouraging distrusters to participate in social movements—and other facets of civil society—where they can witness and experience solidarity can be important. Feeling the support of others, even if from perfect strangers, can have a transformative impact. And appreciating the collective strength and potential that comes from such collaboration can, over time, pull distrusters away from their social pessimism to a realm of greater social possibility.

Hierarchicalists are perhaps the people furthest from the horizontalist ideal. Their orientations are highly authoritarian, potentially even fascistic. Lacking social trust, they are social distrusters. In contrast to political and hierarchy distrusters, they are political and hierarchy trusters. Hierarchicalists could not be more distant and hostile to a horizontalist trust position. Their personality types, feelings of affinity with rulers, suspicions and fears about others, and innumerable other traits get in the way of changing their sociopolitical trust position. Consequently, a transition toward horizontalism may be incredibly difficult. There are some potential pathways, such as if they get "burned" by the powerful or having their faith in the fallibility of leaders challenged. Perhaps opportunities to witness a narcissistic leader be exposed for their selfishness, and how others can be often selfless, may work? Building small, critical reservoirs of horizontal social trust in others is challenging but necessary. Unfortunately, social trust is likely to be limited to immediate neighbors and people like them (who share coveted racial, ethnic, national, or class characteristics). This group may make the most sense to try to convert last, as they are the most entrenched opponents to horizontalism. In fact, the task may not simply be "a lot of work" for movements but may even prove fruitless. It may make more sense to try to marginalize and demobilize their group as active agents in society than confront them head-on (and use our valuable time to organize among trusters and distrusters). (Hierarchical movements—with clearly defined leaders who direct orders at the rank and file are not only inefficient but also susceptible to repression; if the state arrests or kills "the leader", the movement is as good as dead too. But horizontalist movements can survive such adversity.) Hierarchicalists' defense of the status quo and opposition to popular movements for justice and freedom make them formidable adversaries. Perhaps simply discouraging their opposition to progressive social change is enough, so they can no longer obstruct such movements.

There's a lot to say about how this typology can aid the understanding of social change agents' work. How can organizers and activists help nudge along their fellow peers to stronger, horizontalist trust positions? There are twelve conceivable pathways between these four groups, which are complicated and pose their own unique problems (see Figure 6.1). Each pathway requires an awareness of specific features of the origin trust position and the destination trust position. For radicals interested in justice and freedom, the task is

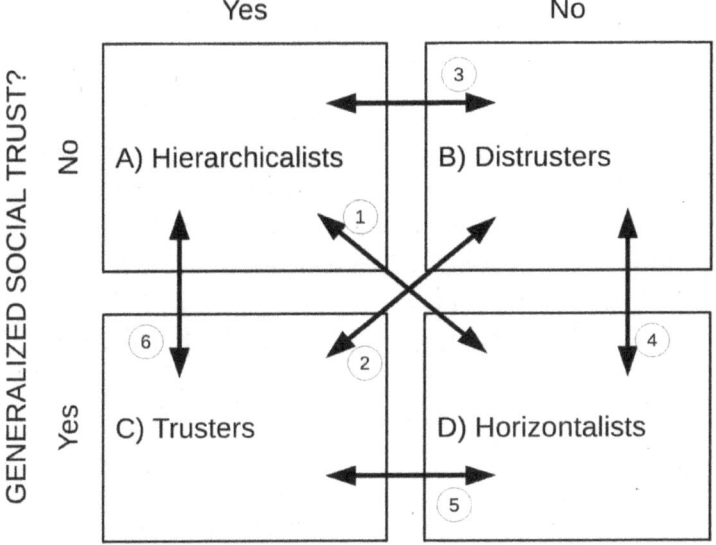

Figure 6.1 Relational Typology of Institutional Confidence and Social Trust

to propel people toward horizontalism and prevent the slide away from it. Thus, only some of these pathways are advantageous.

To describe each pathway in detail, and what strategies would be necessary for those interested or invested in such work, would take a considerable amount of time and effort. Instead, here, I briefly describe each potentially bidirectional pathway, noting its essential features. A further elaboration will have to be the charge of others.[22] (1) Moving between hierarchicalism and horizontalism would require the dramatic flowering—this being the starkest transformation of all—either into a progressive or into a statist reactionary. (2) The chasm between distrusters and trusters is also wide. The key changes necessary to move from one of these trust orientations toward the other would either be a general explosion in optimism or an explosion of pessimism. (3) Other transformations are a bit less extreme, such as moves between hierarchicalism and distrust; both maintain their low social trust but must either lose faith in a hero

or savior or develop the worship of a hero or savior. (4) Distrusters and horizontalists share an allergy to political and hierarchical
trust but differ in their social trust orientations; here, the transition
between them would necessitate either the development of hope
in their fellow human beings or the respective loss of such faith in
their fellows. (5) Trusters and horizontalists are both keen on social
trust, differing in their attitudes toward political trust; horizontalists
require a loss of faith in the political system while trusters require
the creation of belief in a new system. Finally, (6) hierarchicalists
and trusters both have higher political trust. One transformation
would require finding value in their fellow humans while the other
would result from being "burned" by their fellow humans.

ALTERNATIVES

Although it may be unclear what we can do differently, there are
actually many alternative examples that offer paths toward radical
trust. Viewed in isolation, some of them may seem very small or
anecdotal. But if considered together, these alternatives constitute a
more substantial, comprehensive collection of strategies. To explore
a few of these alternatives, I'll focus on anti-state, anti-capitalist, and
anti-organized violence manifestations.

In the place of the state—which is an organized coalition of elite
interests who choose to retain their power over non-elites—we
could supplement official political channels with trust in face-to-
face settings. Building local power in organizational activities may
seem small, but, carried to its logical conclusion—and with an
appropriate amount of federation and up-scaling to higher levels of
society—these could supplant the state's main coordinating functions. In such settings, direct democracy (practiced in a variety
of forms) could exist in place of hierarchically wielded authority.[23] Principled, horizontalist organizations and projects can
foster radical trust—antagonistic anti-authoritarianism directed
externally and cooperative solidarity among non-elites. There are
numerous examples of community-based power to turn to. To
select just one, Argentina's neighborhood assemblies during the

2001–2002 uprising allowed Buenos Aires neighbors to formally and informally collaborate, decide their futures, and wield community power in a vacuum left by successive resignations within the national government.[24] Other examples include such decentralized and federated social structures as the Zapatistas of Chiapas, Mexico, and the Kurds of Rojava.[25]

While capitalist economic forms seem equally hegemonic, there are innumerable anti-capitalist alternatives we can draw inspiration and lessons from. Trust thrives in cooperative economic settings— more so than in corporate workplaces and markets. Worker-owned and worker-managed cooperatives exist in an amazing amount of variety (some being less liberatory than others, to be sure).[26] During times of crisis, mutual aid projects often form: the Black Panthers' survival programs (pending revolution), post-fire or post-hurricane efforts, or the Argentinean Movimientos de Trabajadores Desempleados (unemployed workers movement), which created small crafts industries and community gardens. Arguably the most natural and historic model of anti-capitalist economic activity is the gift economy—people sharing things they need whenever they feel like it and whenever the need arises. Those who have more share with those who have less. Why? Because it makes people feel good to do so.[27] Solidarity is rewarding.

In place of the organized violence of police and militaries—who don't achieve security or safety—alternative steps can be taken every day to keep communities safe. From simply calling on neighbors for solidarity in combative or dangerous situations, to the trust fostered in community-based security efforts.[28] The work of Brian Martin, who has studied the ways—often officially and practically "nonviolent"—to keep people safe, provides a helpful road-map for pursuing stability without violent, hierarchically organized actors.[29] Movements regularly provide for their own safety, as seen in defensive formations within the US civil rights movements,[30] modern-day antifascist activists,[31] or the defensive culture of the Aymara people of Bolivia who have risen up during crises to popularly protect their communities.[32] Of course, more egalitarian and empowering societies are safer too.

For each of the above brief examples, there are countless points of potential intervention and participation. We're still in the earliest stages of experimentation and creation but can aspire to expand such models more widely. Surely some people will be skeptical of efforts to comprehensively transform society. Such radicalism—while arguably necessary, may seem too improbable in the short-term. But these efforts at small reforms can serve as good starting places for those more dramatic, deep, and radical long-term changes. While pursuing these reforms, we'll get a better sense of how possible more radical changes might be. We shouldn't expect radical trust to simply emerge on its own. It'll take work.

For those who are more committed to revolution, there's a hundred places to begin and no absence of issues and causes to struggle around, to investigate, or dream about. As Crimethinc has argued, "to change everything, start anywhere".[33] Learning from history can counsel us in how to apply some of the above alternative options. But, our collective imaginations, lived daily practice, and engaged conversations will do even more for our revolutionary aspirations.

With the considerable growth of time spent online, mistrust and conspiracies have also spread. Since the internet can be a cesspool, reflecting some of the worst tendencies of human interaction, it takes principled organization and action to hold the craziness at bay.[34] For example, following the peak of billionaire Elon Musk-initiated despotism and paranoia at Twitter (which he purchased in 2022), users fled to alternative social media platforms, including the decentralized Fediverse's Mastodon network.[35] Within the Fediverse—a name for a "federated universe" of computer systems that can all equally communicate and freely share information (unlike behind the corporate, "walled gardens" of most hierarchical social media, like Twitter, Facebook, and Instagram)—Mastodon was created, in part, to keep fascists and other hostile groups from interacting with the main network. Any system server ("instance") can de-federate (the equivalent of people in a conversation refusing to acknowledge or speak to someone causing problems) with any other; this has allowed a values-based "covenant" to emerge where only "trustworthy" instances would be officially listed. To be on the list, instances had to pledge "active moderation against racism, sexism, homophobia, and transphobia". The covenant proclaims that Mastodon users "must have the confidence that they are joining a safe space, free from white supremacy, antisemitism and trans-phobia" that is regularly found on hierarchical platforms.[36] This covenant and the wider culture within the Mastodon network has led to the de-federation of far-right instances. Such an instance, called Gab, was de-federated, thus practically blocking it from wide-spread participation with the Mastodon network, thereby limiting their influence. Mastodon's early adopters included queer and trans people and sex workers, who desired greater security and protec-tions against bigots but also content warnings, blocking tools, and other resources not offered by hierarchical social media platforms.

And it's worth considering what a truly transformative alter-native would look like, in the most extreme of circumstances. What can horizontalist trust offer someone with highly conflict-ing values, such as a modern-day white supremacist? How can someone who—either consciously or unconsciously—values the lives, worth, contributions, and culture of white people more than any other race, be shown the merits of trusting people of color too? Not everyone will be willing to undertake this type of work; in par-ticular, this would likely provide distasteful or stressful to many people of color, who have spent a lifetime being targeted by such individuals. But to really change society means making it possible for all people to change. It's clear that past efforts at racial trans-formation have not been as effective as they should have been. For example, the civil rights movement of the 1950s and 1960s often strategically prioritized the assertion and guarantee of *de jure* rights for Black Americans. In demanding fair treatment from the white power structure, it was hoped that changed behaviors would then lead to changed attitudes. While that may have happened for some, it's quite clear that not enough soul searching occurred. Many white people simply learned to hide (or speak more quietly) their bigot-ries. And with the arrival of the first Black president, "racism" was declared dead and a "post-racial" order begun. How can supposedly "color-blind" Americans, who continue to harbor all sorts of regressive racial attitudes and stereotypes, be expected to trust people of color who choose to share their experiences? When a Black person tells a white person that they were mistreated by a police officer, is that white person likely to believe them? I believe the ingenious innovation of Black Lives Matter is the prioritization of values over mere rights or treatment. Consequently, it's necessary for revolutionary movements to not simply fight white supremacy but also to seek ways of transforming white supremacists—lest the personnel keep the practices alive. There are intervention programs that work with avowed white supremacists, counseling and mentoring extremists, to help them abandon their racist beliefs and shitty politics. But something much more ambitious must also occur for the many millions who still harbor authoritarian and bigoted values but who haven't (yet) tattooed themselves with white supremacist symbols. Alternatives must offer choices and reasonable pathways for everyone.

DUAL POWER AND MUTUAL AID

While "dual power" is an idea often attributed to Vladimir Lenin, thankfully many non-Leninists have adopted and further developed it.[37] Dual power involves working toward the horizontal and liberatory ends of accomplishing every necessary human task. There are essential needs that everyone has: food, shelter and safety, health care, and community. The principles of dual power encourage people to find ways to acquire these necessities without capitalism, patriarchy, white supremacy, or the state. Dual power would involve, for example, envisioning health care without capitalism, envisioning community without patriarchy, safety without white supremacy, and envisioning emergency food and shelter without state intervention. Acquiring resources and needed services in this way poses a serious threat to both the legitimacy and necessity of hierarchical institutions. The growing presence of these challenging forms of horizontal social relations represents a "dual power" within society, one that could actually compete with long-lasting hierarchies—

even on grounds of efficiency—and maybe even ultimately displace them. Dual power should thus be understood as revolutionary.

We can provide for our own needs. Anthropological examples drawn from many millennia suggest that, for most of human history, many societies found ways of doing everything they needed without even a minimum of hierarchy.[38] Why should present-day societies' large scale or technological sophistication prohibit egalitarian relations? Arguably, nothing about size or complexity should foreclose the potential for egalitarianism. Thus, if this is true, modern-day dual power could be nurtured to pose a serious threat to hierarchy. But all this necessitates undermining hierarchical political trust and building horizontal social trust. To escape hierarchy's pull, people must en masse distrust these avenues—be they paltry Temporary Assistance for Needy Families (i.e., "food stamps") provisioning, insurance company-mediated health funding, racist policing, or patriarchal-based family, relationships, and community. To build horizontal alternatives requires building trust in each other. Because if dual power is to be built and ultimately challenge hierarchy, *we* (and not some disinterested third-party) are the people who will have to offer food, medical care, safety, and community. We need to have the confidence to do this well and know that we can do it for each other, without judgment. And this all requires deep, radical social trust.

Communities of horizontal social trust can become powerful enough to supplant hierarchical trust, thereby democratizing social structures, making relations more just, and helping people's life chances be more liberatory—although it's neither guaranteed nor easy to do so. Where people begin, live, and finish in life can be dramatically transformed and filled with greater potential via such social trust. This process involves breaking free of hierarchy's centripetal force, and making the old ways seem inefficient, ugly, less desirable, and unethical—*which they are*. Living with greater solidarity and in communion empowers communities like nothing else. As Mexican revolutionary Praxedis Guerrero wrote in 1910, "Solidarity with others is protection for ourselves".[39]

This future involves the creation of the mutual aid found in non-coercive relations of give-and-take and reciprocity. Community members "have each other's back" if and when it is needed. Such mutual aid may seem almost too volatile to achieve or handle—indeed it's difficult to envision how we can go about building this kind of horizontal trust and exchange. At its core, mutual aid is a relational practice that demonstrates how human communities primarily survive. Cooperative relations of mutual aid help communities survive external threats and invasions and protect against the ravages of natural extremes and disasters. But, importantly, mutual aid is how communities flourish too. According to the influential evolutionary paleontologist Stephen Jay Gould, mutual aid is an important pathway for species' survival, as important as competition.[40] The simplest example of such organic communities are "free" groups on social media, where members give things away at no cost and allow people to request items they need or want. As David Graeber has observed, humans tend to enjoy giving gifts as much as they like receiving gifts—and that this can form the basis of social solidarity.[41]

Social thinkers like Herbert Spencer and Thomas Huxley developed a reactionary "social Darwinism", based on Jean-Baptiste Lamarck and later buttressed by a selective reading of Charles Darwin's research.[42] In contrast, the geographer and revolutionary Peter Kropotkin demonstrated mutual aid is essential for not only prehistoric, ancient, and modern humans, but even many non-human animal species. And non-horizontal relations—such as authoritarianism, states, and capitalist markets—actively impede and disrupt our capacities to offer mutual aid to others. Authoritarianism, whether found in a specific, hierarchical individual leader or simply distributed in the hearts and minds of everyday people, supplants our empathetic and engaged impulses to be of assistance to others, replacing it with apathy, disconnection, and social distrust.[43]

Building mutual aid communities in the buffer spaces of capitalism and state is an ideal place to start pushing back against hierarchicalism. Two US-based examples—the Black Panther Party and Common Ground—exemplify how this has been done and suggest the importance of trust in accomplishing short-term and long-term goals. Both worked to strengthen feelings of (and preferences for) horizontal trust, as well as providing opportunities to practice it, thereby undermining the perception that hierarchical trust was needed. First, the Black Panther Party's "survival programs pending revolution" aimed to address immediate needs in Black communities.[44] The Democratic administrations in the 1960s, and their Great Society programs, tended to overlook poor, urban Blacks (despite lip-service otherwise).[45] Therefore, the Black Panthers sought to immediately address their community's needs using their own labor and resources. The survival programs included free breakfast for children, medical clinics, transportation for people visiting imprisoned family members, armed community self-defense, and many others. These survival programs were (and still are) necessary in the short-term, but they also provided the nucleus for a future, horizontal community that is empowered, and doesn't need authority figures or their hierarchies. By witnessing the actual benefits of trusting each other, future possibilities opened for individual observers and program recipients.

Second, the Common Ground project emerged in the wake of Hurricane Katrina's devastation of New Orleans, Louisiana, in 2005, providing medical care, legal assistance, self-defense from armed vigilantes, and home-gutting and renovation for poor residents whose homes were destroyed and lives disrupted. Common Ground advocates initiated projects—and in some ways reintroduced, as former-Black Panthers were active in Common Ground—community self-reliance and empowerment to neighborhoods like Algiers and the Lower Ninth Ward. Supporting Common Ground's mission of immediate care and long-term transformation required social trust among Common Ground volunteers, and trust between Common Ground and the communities they worked in. This mission also necessitated a hostile, distrustful orientation of Common Ground toward the forces of social control—police, real estate developers, politicians, armed white vigilantes, and hierarchical "aid" agencies (including the Federal Emergency Management

Administration and the Red Cross)—that sought to suppress residents' aspirations.[46]

Mutual aid is a traditional component of indigenous movements resisting settler colonialism and global capitalism. Notably, the Mayan-led Zapatista movement of Chiapas, Mexico, relies upon communal-land agreements and directly democratic decision-making structures, all of which rest upon a fertile bed of historical social trust. Similarly, the APPO (Popular Assembly of the Peoples of Oaxaca) in Oaxaca required considerable mutual aid to survive a months-long siege as Oaxacans squared off with both federal police and right-wing vigilantes. Similar mutual aid was central to the active functioning of the Očhéthi Šakówiŋ Camp at Standing Rock, North Dakota, where indigenous activists attempted to blockade the Keystone XL pipeline—eventually provoking the Obama administration to temporarily suspend construction.[47]

Even an ostensibly non-political example of mutual aid is illustrative. Football (soccer) teams tend to inspire passionate comradery among fans of the same team. Sometimes this can result in so-called "hooliganism" and directionless, horizontal fan-on-fan violence. But the longevity of fandom and shared experiences (especially during the "adversity" of a poorly performing team) are solidarity-inducing forces. Fans tend to reject with great hostility efforts by private owners to manipulate their team or the sport, and the corrupt International Federation of Association Football (FIFA) is universally despised and enjoys zero trust from fans. Team solidarity sometimes intersects with social class and politics in potent ways: Turkish footballers were core participants during the 2013 Gezi Park occupation in Istanbul. Their previous experiences fighting off police and their impressive unity were essential for defending the encampment from eviction.[48] Caring for others, even for the fans of other teams, during the occupation was made possible by their acquired skills of mutual aid and solidarity. These footballers make clear that, given the right circumstances, large communities can converge together around a common cause and defend their interests despite their differences.

FORMS AND PURPOSES OF RADICAL TRUST
IN MOVEMENTS

Trust helps movements to accomplish many of their goals, in the best possible ways. Movements should—and often do—prioritize acquiring, nurturing, and utilizing trust.[49] Trust facilitates potent, individually and collectively empowering movements. In a previous study, published in the *International Journal of Comparative Sociology*, I showed how increased social trust and decreased institutional confidence in parliaments and the police increased protest across 43 diverse countries.[50] Here, I'll describe a few of the forms and purposes served by trust within movements, including constructive learning and consciousness-raising, resistance and protection, internal strength, and the capacity for both organizing and insurrection.

Political trust is positively associated with institutionalized participation *and* negatively associated with non-institutionalized participation (i.e., political trusters vote more and protest less).[51] This pattern holds for European citizens who distrust representative systems (and protest more)[52] and more globally too.[53] Interpersonal trust, on the other hand, serves as a personal and social capital resource that fosters collective action and protest.[54] Thus, political distrust and interpersonal trust are both affiliated with extra-institutional politics.[55]

Movements help their participants to transform their identities, ideologies, and emotions. This is done through constructive learning and consciousness-raising that can take innumerable forms. Movement participants share knowledge horizontally through a variety of forums and processes that are sometimes called "teach-ins" and "skill-shares". Individuals—acting in good faith—help each other to understand things going on in the wider world and to learn about new techniques for waging collective struggle. Movements also construct popular political education initiatives. Free skools are venues in which anyone can teach a class and anyone can come to learn something; participants trust the intentions of both teacher and learner.[56] Reading groups (or book clubs) are projects that focus participants' attention upon the ideas contained in certain readings meant to individually and collectively push those participants to advance and challenge their analysis. Alternatively, open forums are a popular strategy for permitting those assembled to vent their rage at injustices and share ideas about practical next steps in a campaign or struggle. Finally, movement participants regularly meet with close friends and comrades in formal or informal settings to build trust and come to a stronger, clearer agreement on things. Such consciousness-raising sessions are a staple of movement building (most famously used in the US's second-wave feminist movement).[57] And, internet-based social media facilitates the lightning-quick relay of news, analyses, and information. To the extent that parties within these aforementioned forms (i.e., the learners, teachers, or sharers) are trustworthy, then the movement-oriented transformations are more likely to be deeper and fuller.

Movements work to resist unjust practices and to protect the lives of people and other life forms on earth. Given the often-risky nature of these actions (and their potentially or strictly illegal qualities), trust is an imperative resource; shared trust among those taking risks together helps to protect each participant, the collectivity, and the movement at large from repression. Conspiracies to protect those facing the state's wrath—such as deportation or arrest—require great trust. For example, thousands of antifascist families helped to hide Jews and other people whom the Nazis sought to exterminate during the Holocaust of World War II. This was a high-stakes effort, since protecting Jewish people would put their concealers at risk too. But these families knew lives were imperiled and so they acted. Each party—the concealers and the concealed—had to trust each other. Concealers had to trust that Jews would not inadvertently reveal their location, while Jews entrusted their protectors to not turn them over to Nazi forces for rewards. Both were also hopeful that gentile neighbors would not inform Nazis. The Danish resistance's campaign to evacuate Jews required incredible trust among the Danish population. The Danes were not only united in their resistance to the Nazi occupation of Denmark but also conspired to conceal and ultimately provide safe passage for some 7,000 Jewish citizens to neutral Sweden.[58]

The American abolitionist movement not only opposed the institution of chattel slavery with words and public demonstrations, but also actively undermined it by depriving it of its lifeblood. The Underground Railroad was a network of safe locations ("stations") that fugitive Black slaves could use during their trek north out of slave territory. The abolitionist movement created vigilance committees that coordinated the Railroad's infrastructure, consisting of hundreds of allies and stations. Immense trust was required among the core members of the vigilance committees—that their fellows would not reveal secrets to slave-catchers or make sloppy mistakes—as well as among the fugitives themselves and those who provided them protection. If slaves were caught, abolitionists attempted rescues from jail cells or courtrooms, or provided legal defense to those captured. When mistakes were made (which was rare) or slave-catchers got lucky, consequences were dire: re-enslavement for runaway Blacks or imprisonment for vigilance committee members (or even enslavement if those members were themselves Black).[59]

Another dimension of protection involves resistance to housing evictions. It requires considerable social trust to show up to protect someone else's home, especially if you don't know the residents. Siding with residents because they are members of a community against landlords, developers, or city officials is a decision made in a context where poor people unable to pay rent have resorted to squatting abandoned buildings, or when the state moves against political dissidents.[60] Great Depression-era communist activists often encouraged people to help move their neighbors' belongings back into their home after a sheriff eviction. However, neighbors did not always have the practical experience, politicization, and, likely, trust necessary to take that action, even though it would surely benefit the stability of their community in the long run. Providing sanctuary to immigrants and refugees, conscientious objectors to war, and others also requires trust. Churches have served as sites for people needing protection from police and immigration officials seeking their arrest. Vietnam War draft dodgers and Central

American refugees relied upon networks of activists willing to hide such individuals, even in their own homes, to physically and politically protect them.[61]

It's also worth noting that trust can enhance protest participation, particularly out-group trust. This means that people who trust those not in "their" group (i.e., out-group) are more apt to protest. Research using a large, international sample found that this kind of trust was an important factor, while in-group trust (i.e., trusting those in their group) was either an insignificant factor or even had the reverse effect upon attending "peaceful demonstrations".[62] Participants' distrust in political institutions—like parliaments and police—strongly motivates protest.[63] According to a European study, protesters who distrusted parliament were substituting their protest in place of party politics, while trusters who protested were supplementing their support for party politics.[64]

Trust also serves as a source for internal strength, propping up a movement and the organizations that compose that movement. The core of most movements are affinity groups—whether officially conceived of as such or just informally. These groups are premised on long-term trust, social compatibility and stable friendship, shared goals and values, and an opaqueness to outside observers, all which make them resistant to external surveillance and suppression. Affinity groups unite individuals around a common purpose, even if that purpose has risky, controversial, and maybe even questionable legality.[65] An example of an affinity group is the so-called Citizens' Commission to Investigate the FBI, who raided an FBI field office at night, only to discover that it contained documents pertaining to a secretive, not-yet-known government subversion program nicknamed COINTELPRO. The Citizens' Commission released information about COINTELPRO to the press and the anti-war movement, and strong internal solidarity kept their identities secret for decades, thus preventing legal repercussions for their burglary.[66]

Movement trust sometimes wanes overtime or is simply lacking. For example, the FBI engineered what is known as the Green Scare in response to the radical activism of the Earth Liberation Front (ELF) in the 1990s and 2000s. Unlike the Citizens' Commission,

ELF participants eventually lacked the internal solidarity necessary to maintain a trusting security culture, which would have consisted of a refusal to share information about ELF activities with outsiders (especially law enforcement). The Green Scare revealed weaknesses in the trusting ties between ELF activists, especially when the state applied pressure and long jail sentences were threatened against already-arrested participants.[67] In contrast, radical organizers often advocate for "jail solidarity" with those arrested, encouraging people to not participate with the legal attacks against them, by refusing to give their names, not willingly accepting processing, not speaking to police (with or without a lawyer present), and absolutely refusing to implicate anyone else in any charges. Trust is particularly central in resistance to grand juries seeking to prosecute radical activism, wherein people are compelled to testify against their will and can be held in contempt of court for their refusal.[68]

Activists in the Indian farmer and Hong Kong democracy movements have created strong internal bonds of trust to help their movements persist through hardships like state repression, while holding diffused trust in strangers overseas who can act in solidarity to support them. This advocacy was the ostensible purpose of Peoples' Global Action (PGA); this network coordinated international solidarity actions against global capitalism and was reliant upon radical trust.

Internal movement strength also relies on cooperative relations fueled by trust. Trust builds power and enables more to be accomplished collectively than by individuals alone. Worker-owned and worker-managed cooperative organizations are an example of this principle in action. Cooperatives have been used extensively to provide food and housing, produce countless goods and services, and acquire other resources. According to sociologist Joyce Rothschild, the core principles of cooperatives are collective authority, minimal rules, personalistic or moralistic social control, communal ideals, normative and solidarity incentives, egalitarianism, and horizontal relations.[69] Cooperatives may not always be anti-capitalist, but they can help build solidarity and facilitate resource-acquisition for movements.

Finally, trust empowers social movements to pursue their strategies of organizing and insurrection. Organizing is the strategy of bringing people together for the purpose of collective action; this differs from "activism", wherein individuals directly do their political advocacy work. Organizers attempt to help *others* manifest their own will—by instigating their initial collaboration and providing some essential tools for their struggle. Organizing can exist in authoritarian contexts, but the most potent kind is anti-authoritarian.[70] Community organizing requires finding commonality with others (e.g., neighbors), a task made easier by pre-existing social trust. Creating a sense of obligation and expectation among community members connects them in a potent way—which trust facilitates—that "unorganized" communities lack.

Organizing takes place in a direct and immediate fashion. Traditionally, people have found ways to make decisions in a quasi-democratic fashion without the need for dilution and hierarchy. The strategy often taken in movements has been for small groups to select a spokesperson who promises to directly represent the collective's views—not the spokesperson's views—to a higher-order gathering of other spokespersons. This is typically called a spokes-council. Spokespersons (or spokes) must have the trust of the other members of their group in order to act in good faith within the spokes-council. If the spoke has not been acting in good faith or conveying the group's views accurately, it will hopefully become clear to the small groups (which are often affinity groups). Thus, groups reserve the right to recall and replace their spokespersons within a spokes-council.

Some trust exists in the immediate situation of a movement's moment-to-moment interactions. If movement participants are confident that fellow participants "have their back" (and are, in fact, correct in their assumption), they are empowered to take risks and push the envelope in a way impossible otherwise. For example, police regularly exceed their legal mandates and target certain individuals at protest events for harassment and arrest. If a strong sense of generalized trust exists in a movement, its participants may attempt to "de-arrest" one of their comrades who has been detained by police.

Well-organized and trusting movements may have universal attitudes that anyone's freedom from police force is an important thing to risk your own arrest to guarantee. Trusting that people will grab *you* back from police also implies that they are trusting you to do the same if the situation demands. Such militant tactics are also relevant for antifascism. During street mobilizations confronting a fascist or far-right rally, antifascists may find themselves facing Nazis brandishing knives—as people did at rallies in Anaheim and Sacramento, California, in 2016. Knowing that those who march by your side are going to do their best to protect you is incredibly important. If fellow marchers are watching your fascist nemesis and making sure nothing happens to each other, the overall goals of the movement (e.g., shutting down fascist attempts to organize) can be furthered. Antifascism in the era of social media (and Trump) has meant being wary of "sock-puppet" user accounts of claimed "antifa" who are not worthy of trust.[71] Fascists (or trolls who tolerate or sympathize with fascism) who pretend to be "antifa" for the purposes of slandering or "doxxing" real antifascist organizers attempt to undermine the radical trust that exists in antifascist movements.[72]

One of the most dramatic forms of insurrectionary activity in movements takes place when a wide swath of society's members, workers, or a neighborhood's residents choose to withdraw their support for the governing order.[73] This has most commonly occurred in the context of great societal conflict, wherein workers— historically the industrial class—refuse en masse to work. The "general strike" is often reverentially discussed in movements, due to its powerful meaning and for how rarely it occurs. In a general strike, the entire class of workers has each other's back—you go on strike and support your fellow workers, and they do the same for you. To even declare a strike (especially a general strike)—with the honest belief that it can result in a favorable end—requires incredible trust with your fellow workers and neighbors. Specifically, participants must trust that there is a shared commitment to each other and that everyone has an interest in deep, long-term goals. General strikes presume that individual mobility in a class-based society is too piecemeal, costly, and unjust, and thus class-wide mobility, or independence from and beyond capitalism, is ideal. General strikes are uncommon in most societies—a series of such strikes in the US during the 1946 "strike wave" (occurring in Camden, NJ; Hartford, CT; Houston, TX; Lancaster, PA; Oakland, CA; Pittsburgh, PA; Rochester, NY; and Stamford, CT) led to the anti-labor Taft–Hartley Act of 1947, which explicitly banned sympathy or "secondary strikes".[74] However, Greece has experienced them rather frequently—since the 2008 economic crisis, Greek workers have used general strikes to propel mass resistance to austerity policies and create space for further forms of resistance.[75] These coordinated insurrections necessitate deep, radical trust, which must be grown and nurtured across multiple generations. Participants in the global justice movement, which used the Direct Action Network to coordinate the shutdown of Seattle's World Trade Organization conference in 1999, referenced the city's cultural legacy of the 1919 general strike in Seattle, arguing for the abstract inheritance of radical, insurrectionary, and class solidarity across the twentieth century.

Without hope in a better future—beyond the possibility of immediate improvement—progressive social change faces formidable challenge. Hope is a fragile commodity for individuals, but it is in greater supply within social movements. Rebecca Solnit argues in *Hope in the Dark* that movements have had a considerable impact in recent human history and that their potential remains crucial. While a naive faith that things will always improve is illogical and reckless, rational optimism remains a key priority for movements.[76] Why act unless there is a possibility that those actions will bear positive fruit?

RADICAL RESOCIALIZATION

Many people are socialized, often through their immediate experiences, to not trust others, especially those presented as potential competitors. As a consequence, revolutionary change requires resocialization to create new expectations that can enable new, collectively empowered experiences. Resocialization is distinct from reprogramming; it isn't simply forcing someone to change their mind, tricking them, or manipulation without their knowledge or consent. Thus, unlike in cults, resocialization is not indoctrination. When successful, resocialization is reasonable, logical, demonstrative, and efficacious. People ought to recognize the merits of transforming their distrustful attitudes about others into trusting attitudes. Being able to clearly see the source of their heretofore distrustfulness will help to make this transition, as well as understanding the merits of being more trustful. However, it is equally crucial to also see the merit in remaining distrustful of hierarchical institutions. It's unhelpful for resocialization to encourage hierarchical trust, because, as we've discussed, hierarchical trust negates many of the benefits of social trust. Resocialization can focus on action—getting people to change behavior. But the most reliable form of resocialization addresses values. Hierarchicalism comes with disagreeable values that produce problematic trusting patterns; it's premised upon a belief in meritocracy, authority, innately evil human nature, selfishness, and competition. To resocialize a hierarchicalist as a horizontalist would require replacing such values with new values, such as egalitarianism, voluntary association, a critical appraisal of potential human goodness, and cooperation—all rooted in justice and freedom.

The main agents of socialization for children—the family, friends, school, and media—also have a role to play in resocialization. But often these institutions also require radical reorientation. A family that raises children to respect hierarchy needs to itself be resocialized, just as friends (or the groups of available friends) must change, schools must be re-tooled to be liberatory, and media radicalized toward anti-authoritarian priorities. It's naive to expect these often-hierarchical institutions (with the exception of friends) to assist in radical trust resocialization, since these are the very agents that produce socially distrustful and hierarchy-respecting individuals in the first place. For example, hierarchy-respecting families will tend to produce children with anti-radical trust, just as the children of dysfunctional parents (those who are barely or poorly serving in the role of caregiver) will scarcely know what trust is. Thus, resocialization must occur on a societal level, too, not just among individuals. If individuals are the sole targets of resocialization then we miss all the social forces that are molding people in the first place. Thus, revolutionary change necessitates change of these institutional actors of socialization.

So, how to regain people's trust? Consider a serious, challenging example: What should communities do after a sexual assault has occurred in its midst? Such an event quickly disrupts any illusions of unanimous trust, displaying an undercurrent of distrust and mistrust—and rightfully so. If people, particularly women, have assumed that those around them are respectful of bodily integrity but then find out that someone has been violated—and that others may have helped to conceal the assault and even defend the accused perpetrator—this will surely reduce trust.[77] Again, pleading for greater trust in these circumstances is not only premature, but largely inappropriate. In the US, large, bureaucratic organizations—ranging from the Catholic Church and the military to universities and the Boy Scouts—have faced massive scandals for widespread predation and cover-ups.

Restorative justice is a general approach many have adopted to address this kind of situation. The principles of restorative justice presume that people cannot easily forgive (let alone individually and collectively move past) the wrongs done against them unless the perpetrator apologizes and attempts to repair the situation. Ideally, the conditions that led to the wrong ought to be addressed, too, to prevent a future wrong from recurring. For example, in order to repair the distrust that emerges in a community where an assault has occurred, steps need to be taken that make the assaulter legitimately more trustworthy somehow. This may require a variety of actions, ranging from educating the perpetrator about their actions and making them go through a community-led process to repair the damage they created, to banishing them from that community. Of course, raising trust is important, but it's not more important than papering over an assault and asking people to mistrust in unsafe conditions when there has been no satisfactory effort to fix the problems that exist. And the least important (and maybe most harmful) thing is to simply demand that the person who was victimized begin trusting again. As trust is a social phenomenon, it's not up to an individual to "fix" their poor trust; it's up to a community to make greater trust possible and likely. In other words, the challenge falls to the perpetrator and the community to make things right, not the survivor.[78] Some initially criticized restorative justice for the assumption (premised on the word "restore") that all that was required was a return to the status quo, which was likely unequal and unjust. Usually, proponents argue for the need to *create* justice, regardless of whether or not it previously existed.[79] Thus, the emphasis upon *transformative* justice.

For individuals, resocialization will likely involve learning how to see past the isolated behaviors of a few bad apples—seeing past examples of victimization, backstabbing, or lying. Of course, the problem is not a few "bad" apples, but the rotting, festering barrel that such apples begin to rot within.[80] Being able to reaffirm that most people have generally good human potential is an essential realization. But, again, the necessary steps have a social cost. The intellectualization required to understand the low probability of evil behavior is one thing; it's a whole other challenge to get over the emotional overload that typically drowns out our rationality. This is a key problem with resocialization—knowledgeable people often assume that the strength of logic alone will be enough to convince someone to act differently. But emotions are typically more powerful, visceral, and persuasive for people. This doesn't imply we must jettison all logical argument, but it can't be the only way to sway people: New experiences, positive emotions, appeal to values, and other (mostly non-rational) techniques are just as, if not more, important.

There are two primary pathways that resocialization occurs in. There is informal or latent resocialization, and formal or manifest resocialization. The former is unintentional, while the latter is intentional. First, although the overt purpose of informal resocialization is not to explicitly resocialize individuals, this end is nonetheless accomplished. Often people simply observe others acting differently and become familiar and comfortable with new practices. Due to lived experience—for example, working in a radical social movement organization—people come to know new ways of being.

While the resulting resocialization is not the individual's goal or even necessarily the organization's, it still occurs. Other mundane, daily interactions can also retrain an individual's expectations; this is a social process that encourages the individual to adapt to certain collective needs or expectations.

Second, most commonly, however, movements very deliberately try to help individuals to change themselves. Indeed, both reform and revolutionary social movements do this, as do purely redemptive or alternative movements that just target individual action. Here, resocialization is the activity's overt purpose. Education is an ideal example of intentional resocialization. By definition, education aims to teach people something they did not previously know, assuming this will modify an individual's future behavior. For movements, practices like skill-sharing events, teach-ins, conferences, or organizations like free skools attempt to institutionalize learning opportunities inside movement communities. Like many movement participants, I've attended numerous teach-ins, meant to inform wide publics about important topics, and participated in multiple reading groups intended to afford individuals the opportunity to discuss provocative ideas. Such practices consciously provide new knowledge experiences to people (e.g., how to de-arrest a friend from police, avoid mass surveillance, organize collectively, or practice good emotional health), thus encouraging different future action and adherence to new norms.[81]

TRUST IN REVOLUTION

"Revolution" is a heavy word, subject to much abuse. Corporations promote their products as revolutionary, while conservatives of all stripes heap scorn upon revolution (except for the revolutions that created *their* perfect society). In the midst of this confusion, many still believe that revolution is a good, important goal depending on the values that drive it. Revolution can be understood as a continuous combination of revolt and reform. Depending on the pace of the revolution, this combination could be rather long and seemingly endless. Or the revolution's primary events could occur within days. Either way, revolution is a fairly complex process that oscillates between explosive efforts to attack society's principal institutions, followed by pointed—although usually limited—efforts to modify particular characteristics of that society. Revolt, then reform, and repeat. This process moves fast, then slow. The more explosive the revolt and the more far-reaching the reforms, the greater the revolution. It is popularly driven and appears chaotic, as the revolts are leaderless and the reforms begrudging. No one person or group can truly control a revolution.[82] Rulers acquiesce and relinquish bits or all of their power to a wider group of others.

Unsurprisingly, trust is a key feature of revolution. Generalizable trust during the revolt cycle is needed in the streets and is found among the insurrectionists. During the reform cycle, trust dims a bit, as the former insurrectionists skeptically assess the status quo's efforts and promises for change. Rebels are usually distrustful of elite promises and remain doubtful that their wildest dreams and demands will be fulfilled. But rebels may retain hope for something positive to emerge in the long-term. Revolution not only necessitates trust but is also a prerequisite for trust. If we want to create revolution, we need to trust. If we want to trust more than we do now, we need to revolutionize that which stands in the way of greater trust. Like many features of trust, this is a paradoxical chicken-versus-egg conundrum. We must work toward both continuously and in tandem. This vision of "revolution" is not one of unbridled chaos or dog-eat-dog competition but a collective struggle toward societal transformation. Further, revolution is not revolution—at least of the dramatic "people-marching-in-the-streets and tearing-down-statues" sense—if most people retain trust in society's dominant institutions. No revolution is possible (or necessary, apparently) if widespread trust remains in the system. Perhaps extensive change in this context could be pro-system "evolution", but not revolution.

There's a lot to consider with revolution, but two radical organizational forms—very different in type, scale, and purpose—convey the relevance and differing modalities of trust: affinity groups and general assemblies. The former are specific and closed in-group trusting formations, while the latter are abstracted and open out-group trust formations.

First, affinity groups feature very high levels of interpersonal trust. Members know each other well and thus are intimately familiar with each other's backgrounds, interests, and limits. They know their fellows aren't police attempting to spy on or disrupt the group. While authorities benefit from or seek to discourage social trust in order to enhance political trust in the state, affinity groups are resistant to external efforts to foster social distrust. Affinity groups are small enough to create strong bonds of trust based on commonality. The Spanish term *grupo de afinidad* was meant to describe lifelong bonds between people that transcended the power of the church, monarchy, state and republic, and capitalism, thus making them resilient in the face of attack by those hierarchical institutions. According to Murray Bookchin, the affinity group was the nuclei of Spanish anarchist resistance to fascism during the Spanish Revolution (1936–1939).[83] Affinity groups allow small groups of people to autonomously take the initiative within larger configurations (like assemblies). They are resistant to the loss of a "leader" because of their horizontalist decision-making structure and since all members can be leaders. In some respects, affinity groups are similar to leaderless resistance formations (including terrorist cells), albeit usually with less socially destructive or violent aims, of course. Affinity groups are self-managed and are thus autonomous from other affinity groups; members' allegiances are to each other and the group's values and goals, not to wider organizational configurations. Consensus decision-making within such groups requires strong interpersonal trust—deliberations are open and transparent to all members. Members must act honestly and be sincere with their intentions; contrast this with voting in representative democracies where the "secret ballot" is of prime importance. Secrecy is unnecessary within an affinity group (where all are presumably sympathetic and have each other's interests at heart)—members do not need protection from those who might condemn or attack people for their ideas or contributions, as is necessary in society at large, where interpersonal trust is typically much lower. Affinity groups have been used throughout the twentieth and twenty-first centuries, in settings as diverse as the anti-nuclear occupations of Germany and the US, the anti-WTO and anti-IMF mobilizations from 1998 through 2001, the anti-Iraq War movement, and Black Lives Matter, among others.

Second, general assemblies are larger and more heterogeneous formations. In an assembly, people must at a minimum trust that others have good intentions, have faith in the power and wisdom of the collective mind and will of the assembly, and work to encourage accurate and honest statements within the assembly. The trust found in assemblies is diffused, as the setting is diverse—it's the opposite of an affinity groups' homogeneity. Assembly participants must presume that there are diverse—probably even contradictory—interests involved and still must somehow find a way to manage their collaboration. Assemblies can be established in a lot of ways, be structured variously, and make decisions diversely. Consequently, historical examples of assemblies are unlikely to be completely comparable. Assembly participants try to trust each other, even though their fellow participants are likely rather diverse. For example, the documentary film *The Take* (about the occupied factory movement of Argentina) showed auto-parts workers interviewed who claimed that regular, routine voting at their cooperative workplace, in an assembly, meant that workers got used to "winning" (i.e., agreeing with the decisions) as well as "losing" (i.e., wanting a different decision to pass), but people manage this mixed outcome by learning to trust the general will and wisdom of their fellow workers.[84] Trusting the "general will" in assembly-like conditions which aren't truly democratic or horizontal will lead to poor outcomes. For example, the Mondragón corporation in the Basque region of Spain (which is theoretically a "cooperative") has yearly worker meetings; but these workers are not truly equal, as they are paid different salaries and because there are managers who direct lower-status workers.[85] This inequality pollutes the nature of the assembly, harming trust. Additionally, some popular organizations create coordinating or central committees that are directed by a small portion of members and not the mass; these representation forms are less authentically democratic and will likely lead to a disconnect and growing distrust between the rank and file and leadership. Even when such committees bring proposals to an assembly to be voted upon, average participants will often be skeptical of the process if the basic terms of agreement are predetermined beforehand. This is a slightly more populist version of voting in a representative democracy (e.g., non-candidate ballot initiatives; thus, more of a "direct democracy", but with flaws), where important preliminary decisions have already been made that narrow the scope of debate, limiting participants' power.[86] If individuals—perhaps members of an affinity group—choose to act outside of the essential "will" or decisions of an assembly, they prefer to do so as to not come into direct conflict with that assembly or to bring down the state's wrath upon the assembly without its consent. If an assembly can trust affinity groups to not endanger the wider collective process, that can improve trust, via deeper interrelated connections. Assemblies have appeared in movements and historical revolutions as diverse as the Paris Commune, the Mexican Revolution, the Gwangju Uprising, or the Oaxacan Commune.

Bringing affinity groups together within general assemblies links the rich, face-to-face participation of affinity groups with the large, diverse, and broadly legitimizing strength of general assemblies. The former is resistant to external subversion since it is based on long-term, dense trust relations among members, while the latter is resistant to the concealment of action since everyone gets to witness the decision-making process. The two revolutionary forms are still at odds with each other, as affinity groups seek autonomy, while assemblies create broader consensus.[87] While revolution is messy, its potential is more fertile when planted in beds of deep, radical trust. Affinity groups and assemblies reflect the principles of radical trust: believing in the collective strength and solidarity of your peers, while rejecting the meddling and suppressive influence of dominant, hierarchical institutions.

Trust also matters in less-than-deliberate contexts, like spontaneously unfolding situations that precipitate revolutionary situations (recall the earlier discussion of urban revolts in Chapter 5). It is important for people in such situations to be able to expect that others will follow and respect radical, emergent norms, allowing some to further push the envelope. Having each other's backs, retrieving comrades from the state's clutches, attacking symbols of violent authority, standing in solidarity with anyone and everyone who needs it, and facing collective threats together are some situations that can emerge quickly without warning—and strong bonds of trust can help guarantee that others will do what's needed. To see this from an opposite perspective—elites within the social system who have their privileges threatened during uprisings—consider Gustave LeBon's claim that people's experiences in crowds was the result of a "contagion" effect, wherein people are infected with crazy ideas not their own, and thus act foolishly.[88] While LeBon's fear-mongering was provoked by the terror he saw in the French Revolution, there *is* collective wisdom to be found in people's physical experiences in quickly developing and spontaneous settings, like protests. If you witness a good idea—like someone else de-arresting a comrade (or future co-defendant) from a violent police officer—you may instantly feel compelled to contribute your support to this type of action. Thus, given the right conditions, many people are willing to destroy property that facilitates or simply represents hierarchical domination—like military weaponry, auto-dealerships, oil pipelines, or police precincts and Columbus statues, following the example of groups like the Plowshares, Catholic Workers, ELF, water defenders, or the Minneapolis rebels of 2020. Those who take such radical actions may or may not have completely considered their actions (although most surely have), but they took those actions because they had trust in those who would follow behind them. In particular, direct actionists trust that if they are arrested that they will be defended by others in the movement—many nameless people who will write letters of support, attend rallies, lobby, and coordinate a legal and movement defense on their behalf. Understood this way, the confidence and strength that an individual person feels is not merely felt within their own body but is the aggregation of strength from those who feel affinity with them, express solidarity with them, and act in their interests if they face repression.

When people gather together in public, trust tends to grow. A rough egalitarianism can emerge when open-ended encounters are encouraged. Witnesses can observe open expressions of trust, see how others manage to trust, and then—in part due to peer pressure—see the merits of adopting those trustful orientations themselves. These public spaces, whether just on street corners or community gardens, or public squares or occupations, flip the concealed, secretive world of distrustful private interactions on their head.[89] Instead, people can experience the intentions (which are mostly benign and benevolent) of their peers and learn how to collectively trust. Of course, these experiences don't need to occur in stationary crowds, locked in place—instead they can emulate the actions of Hong Kong freedom fighters and "be like water", always moving and able to penetrate any obstacles in their path. There is no better teacher than experience and as a social struggle develops, popular movements that stay in the streets not only lose their fear and social distrust but also gain expertise and strength.

Revolution often finds its genesis in a "commune". While everyone who interacts with other humans is part of a society, very few today belong to a commune. When people are part of a collectivist community of large scale—which resists outside forces seeking to crush it, all while pursuing common purpose, justice, and freedom—this is a commune. There have been many such examples in the modern period, but almost none have survived any considerable length of time; many lasted just days, while a few survived a handful of years.[90] But all ended, often with great bloodshed unleashed by hierarchical institutions that sought to crush their commune enemy. One of the modern period's first important communes was the Paris Commune—a month and-a-half-long experiment in social justice and freedom within the confines of Paris during a period of political instability. From the very start, communards used their working-class solidarity to organize resistance to the Versailles forces who gathered outside the city limits, laid siege to Paris, and attacked the Commune relentlessly. Unfortunately, the Paris Commune ended in incredible violence, with perhaps 30,000 killed. Still, the Paris Commune is legendary in France's collective memory.[91] The longest-lived non-indigenous commune is likely the anarchist-led resistance to Franco's fascistic coup in Spain from 1936 through 1939. In particular, the initial period of rebellion in Barcelona leading to the so-called May Days of 1937 saw immense, popular trust emerge among the Catalonian communards.[92] Later rebellions also created communes, such as South Korea's Gwangju commune in 1980,[93] the uprising in the Mexican state of Oaxaca in 2006, which the corrupt governor and federal police couldn't control, and the rather small and localized communes in public spaces that quickly rippled outward across their countries, such as Beijing in 1989[94] and Cairo's Tahrir Square in 2011.[95] Communes involve many things, but most importantly they feature people learning to collectively solve problems in adverse situations. A good example regards community self-defense offered by the building of barricades. This classically French tactic not only facilitates greater social trust among the poor but also empowered poor Parisians to solve their own problems behind the barricade walls while they fought the state.[96] The most recent commune of note exists in what's known as Western Kurdistan, in Syria; the Kurds of Rojava collaborated with other ethnic populations (including Alevi, Arabs, Armenians, Assyrians, Êzîdî, and Turkmens) to maintain their autonomy from the fascistic government of Bashar al-Assad, constant cross-border invasions by Turkey, imperial incursions and stratagems by Russia and the US, and brutal violence by Islamists like the Islamic State and al-Nusra Front. The Rojava commune filled the entire geographic scale of its society with layers of participation and interaction, organizing around values of feminism and ecological consciousness.[97]

Sometimes these communes break out of their plaza, neighborhood, city, or region and become country-wide revolutions. Revolutionary conditions are rarely just exploited by progressive forces seeking greater freedom and justice, but also by reactionaries or others intent upon expanding their own power at others' expense. This is surely the story behind the revolutions in Mexico 1910, Russia 1917, Spain 1936, and Egypt 2011, where other anti-systemic (but authoritarian) movements or other elite factions gained the upper hand over popular, democratic organizations like assemblies, soviets, or councils.[98]

Revolution primarily wipes clean contemporary conditions, rewriting them anew. The wiping process can include what has often been called abolition in different times and places. Like the efforts to abolish slavery in previous centuries—the most famous application of the term abolition—there are some things of which absolutely nothing is worth preserving. It was worth envisioning, and struggling for over a century, a world without the terrible crime of slavery. And it is worth envisioning a world without all other manner of violent hierarchies, even if this seems like a time-wasting naive fantasy. Every hierarchical institution that this book has described that impairs our capacities to be more fully empowered and just, and thus generates massive distrust, ought to be considered on the list of things to be done away with. To explicitly name some of these institutions, why preserve the military-industrial complex? What is worth saving in patriarchy that can be better accomplished through more egalitarian gender, familial, and social relations? The thoroughly corrupted institution of modern policing, which was tainted with the stink of white supremacy ever since the first slave patrol began earning a tax-funded, publicly subsidized wage, also needs to go. Any good that policing accomplishes can be done better, without its brutality, graft, thuggery, and fascism.[99] Many modern-day abolitionists apply this logic to the prison-industrial complex, arguing that the entire penal system (not just the state's foot soldiers, who serve as armed government bureaucrats, administering street-corner justice—but the lawyers, judges, and jailers too) is rotten to the core and must be discarded to history's banal list of bad ideas.[100]

Relevant to our purposes, the hierarchical institutions targeted for abolition induce terribly debilitating distrust and contribute very little positive trust to society. Every "necessary" thing these hierarchies seem to accomplish either doesn't really need to occur or exist, or can simply be done in a better way that is less coercive, violent, or unequal. Revolution could transform how things are done, dramatically changing everyday life. From a strategic movement perspective, unless abolition advocacy is on the table, nearly every suggested course of action will remain terminally reformist and could at best only result in half measures.[101] Why not "shoot for the stars", aiming for abolition, and thus accomplish the revolution (in trust, yes, but in other important ways too) that offers the best promises for a good society? In the least intimidating terms possible, revolution is the means to a good society. Since we don't have that good society now, revolution is necessary.

HOW TO TRUST MORE

Let's finish with some prescriptive ideas for building up social trust, without mistrust in authority figures. Individuals can take the following actions on a day-by-day basis, but they're also meant to be pursued collectively. This is surely an abbreviated, incomplete list. I assume that you, the reader, have your ideas by now about how to pursue this course—and I encourage you to do so!

First, there are innumerable individual actions worthy of our time and labor. While the much-hyped "random acts of kindness" fad in the US often seems kitschy and can be rather pro-status quo, it can be very meaningful. Putting yourself "out there", being vulnerable, and risking possible exploitation is a cognitive, emotional, and cathartic leap that's hard to take. Acting purely—with all the authenticity implied by actual altruism—is powerful and catalyzing. Join an organization to give your time and labor to something worthwhile, if only to feel the experience and anticipate the rewards of such collaboration. Meeting new people who are unlike you can build empathy—a sense of cross-class, cross-race, cross-national solidarity and affinity we don't experience unless we traverse geographical, cultural, and psychological segregation.[102] And learning new things, even if outside of our actual areas of interest, forces our mind to have new thoughts and "go somewhere" unfamiliar. That unfamiliarity takes us out of our comfort zones, illustrating that others who already know these things are pretty amazing too. Generating respect for difference helps build radical trust; advocating for people whose lives, appearances, or expressions transcend the norm (e.g., trans people) can broaden the range of acceptable ways of being in the world. Thus, people can adopt or reject whatever rigid or traditional roles they choose and be who they would like to be. Individuals can build social trust and engage in solidarity through simply acts. Be a participant: Join (or create) a collaborative project, campaign, organization, and discuss trust with others ("what should we do to establish trust between ourselves?").[103] And serve as an amplifier: Communicate with (and especially listen to) others and ask questions. Share what you learn with others who don't have the same opportunities to participate in such communications.

Of course, there's a definite weakness in focusing on individuals as the locus for building social trust. It's an unfair prescription to ask so much of individuals who have the right to be skeptical of broadening their trust horizons. Instead, it should be the responsibility and domain of movements to help individuals create habits of radical trust, to support, encourage, and model how to go beyond our distrustful personal lives. Relying on collective efforts is not only reasonable but it's actually the best means to grow as individuals. As Dorothy Day put her life's mission: We ought to make it easier for people to be good to each other.[104] Thus, let's create *social* institutions in which it is easier to trust our peers.

Collective action within organizational structures offers the best opportunity for building horizontal social trust. In particular, organizational missions focused on the expansion of freedom and justice are worth supporting. For example, seeking restorative or transformative justice in place of cancellation or punishment—which are neither just nor constructive—does not mean simply returning to the status quo but emphasizing the creation of freedom and justice, usually in place of social conditions that were constrained and smothering, divisive and unequal.[105] When appropriate, creating trust between "offender" and "victim" doesn't only help repair social relations but also generates a more egalitarian society in which trust is easier. The current "deviance response system", masquerading under the inaccurate moniker of the "criminal justice system" simply generates distrustful citizens who fear "criminals". Disadvantaged people are criminalized and locked away when caught doing things that most everyone else has also done (but gotten away with), without any attempt to re-establish trust between them. In both transformative justice organizations and the wider society, we ought to eliminate top-down leadership, discuss with others how to avoid hierarchy and centralization in practice, debate how to best live democratically with each other, and consider how this requires greater trust but also a skepticism toward the alleged "natural inclinations" of trusting those with power and privilege. In our collective environments, we ought to create socializing opportunities where people can gather, find common ground, and build common experiences and reference points—even if it means "forcing" ourselves to get together somewhere past our preferences for the comfortable familiarity of best friends and family. And in the environment of our communities—whether real world or online—we need to find ways to *act* together, as it brings us closer together and illustrates the possibilities for further trust. How many people have found themselves at a protest, or discovered an organization in the midst of a campaign, become awestruck or catalyzed, and then stuck around for years on the exuberance of that first encounter? *This* is the kind of experience to nurture and multiply.

There are many societal actions possible too. The establishment of stable and safe communities has long been a goal throughout the world in the modern era. How to keep residents of a neighborhood in place (thus maintaining stability and community) but still free to move? Preventing evictions and racial profiling by developers, realtors, police, and politicians will allow a natural diversity to emerge and prevail. Creating interest groups that can act on behalf of that neighborhood in its entirety (and not just some interests) will allow it to defend itself, gain a collective sense of itself, and grow its power. Non-state-based community assemblies that use horizontal methods of consensus building and collaboration are a model for such interest groups. Disrupting the unidirectional propaganda mediums known as mass media will help liberate people from confused and contradictory notions: campaigns to turn off TVs, de-charter corporate TV and radio stations, ostracize corporate "news", and develop strategies to marginalize media conglomerates online. Social media, too, while seemingly collaborative and appealing to our social natures, is often subtly manipulative, fueled by corporate and political advertising and deception. In its absence, decentralized and autonomous social networks need to grow, free of walls between corporate-owned computer networks—ActivityPub, Mastodon, and other federated protocols and platforms could be suitable alternatives.

Although mainstream therapy tends to be bourgeois and individualistic, there are still good reasons to talk through our problems with others. "Fixing" ourselves individually and personally is worthwhile, but it need not be individualistic. In fact, liberatory group "therapy", such as soma therapy, may be just as helpful. Soma is an anarchist approach to therapy, created by the psychiatrist Roberto Freire, and originally intended to combat the negative, traumatic consequences of Brazil's military dictatorship, torture, and political alienation. It combines a physically embodied and interactive style—adapted from the African martial art Capoeira Angola, the pleasure-based psychological theories of Wilhelm Reich, and anarchist philosophy. Soma aims to build meaningful bonds with others, bonds that are physically and emotionally rooted. Trust is built through group-based physical experiences and expressions of honesty and intimacy.[106]

While we are somewhat responsible for our circumstances, we should still stop blaming individuals for society's problems. Someone who is "mentally ill" had a lot of help to become that. Treating individuals as "abnormal" is problematic, as social forces made them that way. We won't be able to trust each other completely until we realize that society's structure makes us distrustful. Society's alleged "normalcy" actually results in pathological normalcy. In non-psychological terms, normal conditions—like widespread pollution, pesticide use, and toxic consumer products—lead to systemic social problems, like high cancer rates. Even though individuals are treated for cancer, they are not individually pathological. As Erich Fromm argued, a healthier world needs radically transformed social relations and correction to its pathological normalcy.[107] Elites benefit from the focus on treating individuals and ignoring the systemic pathologies that cause problems. In other words, we should heed C. Wright Mills's advocacy to hone our "sociological imaginations" that help people identify the social problems lurking behind and provoking our personal troubles.[108] Investing time in learning about inequality and hierarchy by reading sociology could be helpful—it could give perspective that will explain the social forces that result in people disappointing us or why some things are untrustworthy. Then popular education needs to distribute and proliferate this essential analysis.

By joining and participating in different kinds of groups, circles, and networks, as well as developing "generic affiliations"—and encouraging others to do the same—we will enhance our capacities to trust. If enough people do this, they will create identities that are sympathetic with other identities, thus generating trust. For example, when people join various networks, organizations, or projects within a wider field of movement, they may not always agree or get along, but the overlap and compatibilities can lead them to trust each other.[109] Trust is highest among those who belong to more voluntary associations, although it's less clear which is the cause and which the effect.[110] Local "welcoming committees" could have the sole purpose of building bridges between social movements' participants and non-participants. This work is akin to classic community organizing, with an emphasis upon establishing principled, value-based relations of trust with others. Efforts can include social activities, cultural work, social networking, leisure, and popular education. Indeed, many social movements include this kind of trust-building—welcoming committees are just less focused on protest and resistance. This will be more challenging for certain distrustful groups, such as rural dwellers, who often have less opportunity for diverse social experiences.

The most challenging path to building social trust may require the most looking within. We ought to embrace the necessary contradictions of trust: being aware of and on-guard for mistrust and distrust but still being open to and actively seeking trust. This is hard. Being grounded, not guarded. Critical, not cynical. Pessimistically optimistic. It's hard to expect the best of people, but be willing to receive something a bit less than that sometimes. We'll find that people "rise to the occasion" more often than not. But we need to be able to appropriately react to and accept when they don't. We need to be able to recover from disappointments and double-crosses, and remain committed to each other (in the abstract We), to society, and revolutionary change.

Patience is not always easy, but it's important to not always jump to conclusions or make judgments before attempting to understand other people and their perspectives. Call-out culture makes an individual's mistakes or failings so devastating that they lose the trust of their peers. It's hard to imagine a constructive, humane, functioning society wherein people aren't allowed to make mistakes (even bad ones).[111] We ought to remember Malcolm X's admonition to be forgiving of others' ignorance, because there was a time when we also didn't know everything.[112]

Finally, if it hasn't been clear yet, massive community building and organizing is not only needed to expand trust but also to simply guarantee a society that tends toward justice and freedom. Building public spaces to gather in, engage, and cross-fertilize—especially spaces that are multi-ethnic and tolerant of class-sedition—is a must. Tearing down the things that divide people physically and emotionally can only help in this regard; things like billboards, multi-lane roads, walls, and so on have got to go. Celebrating ourselves during festivals that popularize *tabula rasa* behaviors gives just the right kind of opportunity to challenge authority and re-enforce social trust; for example, the politicized medieval carnival turned power relations upside down and shook them vigorously.[113] While it's possible to have a thriving civil sphere and still lack justice and freedom, it's increasingly difficult. The civil sphere may lack broad, radical trust, but breaching efforts meant to force open the civil sphere to be more inclusive and empowering can do the trick.[114]

THE FUTURE OF RADICAL TRUST

I consider myself to be, generally, an optimistic person. Despite the perilous state of the world, I believe we have the ability to solve our social and ecological problems. Movement experiences have effectively convinced me of all the amazing things we are collectively capable of. But I must admit that the Covid-19 pandemic has challenged my own radical trust, even if only a bit. While outpourings of solidarity and mutual aid initially appeared nearly everywhere, it was eventually replaced (particularly in the US) by selfish individualism. I have become aware that many of my neighbors have little incentive to keep me safe and healthy by masking or vaccinations, especially if it inconveniences them. However, as opposed to interpreting this frustrating awareness as a systemic flaw of human nature, it's quite clearly the logical consequence of an individualistic, consumeristic society, where priorities are established by the wealthy and powerful. Emergency safety nets were canceled, workplace safety provisions eliminated, mask mandates dropped, public health messaging watered down, and the pandemic was declared "over"! In the two years following US President Biden's September 2022 declaration, there were—based on rather incomplete record-keeping—a minimum of 167 million new cases of Covid-19 globally and at least one-half million deaths, according to World Health Organization data.[115] These elites have decided that the most important thing is to get workers back to work, so that capitalism can resume its slow death grind. The crisis's chaos wasn't simply disrupting business as usual but also had the potential to overturn the unequal status quo. In other words, while I've become acutely aware of how I trust others a bit less, I'm even more convinced that hierarchical institutions have set the stage for this social distrust. They have no real problem with millions of us dying preventable deaths if it means that profit keeps rolling in and the powerful stay in charge.

Trust in each other is necessary to maintain mere survival and to pursue another world. But such trust is definitely challenging to nurture. The endless drumbeat of "trust us, trust us!" coming from authority figures is both a centripetal-force black hole and a soothing lullaby opiate. To break free of authority we need centrifugal force and detoxification. Of course, trust isn't the only thing we need, either—we also need resources, less ecological devastation, more humane social priorities, and a few dozen other things too. None of this is easy or guaranteed. There are exceptions to aspirational standards of radical trust everywhere—some of your neighbors probably *shouldn't* be trusted in some instances, and individuals occupying positions of authority can accidentally do the right thing or be convinced to violate their oaths to hierarchical institutions.

Since trust is about relationships, we need to prioritize collective steps—that we take together, ideally in vital social movements—toward radical trust. This isn't and shouldn't be the only goal of movements, but if radical trust is part of our long-term strategizing, then it's an important improvement over pure instrumentality. We need movements that prioritize generating highly conscious community outreach with a radical orientation toward organizing, the "mainstreaming" of radical values and ideas using formal educational venues and propaganda, and creating the opportunities to experience and practice radical trust impulses all the time and everywhere.

The radical trust principles I've described in these pages can serve as a guide for movement building. If this book helps to start important conversations about how to pivot our priorities, recalibrate our analytical lenses about what and who we trust (or not), and generate strategies for solving this paradox, then it'll have accomplished my goals. Of course, this future is *ours* and we'll have to figure out how to create it together. I trust us.

Notes

INTRODUCTION

1. See the General Social Survey, https://gssdataexplorer.norc.org/
2. Jones & O'Donnell 2010.
3. In one of the US's closest cousins—the United Kingdom— approximately one-fourth distrust others, while approximately 17 percent, optimistically, wanted "help to trust more" (Freeman & Loe 2023). Also, see a decent overview—although rather liberal and pro-capitalist—by Keefer and Scartascini (2022) about low trust in Latin America and the Caribbean.
4. A common tactic during the first Trump presidency was for the far right to converge on supposedly liberal bastions—e.g., Berkeley, California, and Portland, Oregon—believing, with good reason, that if they can establish an organized presence there and rule the streets, then they could do so anywhere in the US.
5. St. Clair & Frank 2012.
6. Desilver 2021. Despite over one-third of Americans not voting, this record high was widely celebrated in the US media, with (as always) little concern about why millions didn't even bother.
7. Sanders & Riccardi 2025.
8. Cheney's policy toward Iraq and Kissinger's toward (to select just one example) Cambodia not only violated international law but were violent, long-term attacks against those societies.
9. Buttigieg 2021.
10. For a critique of saviorism, see Flaherty 2016.
11. Theoharis 2018.
12. Sims & Grigsby 2019.
13. In the seventh wave of the World Values Survey, of sixty-six countries analyzed, an average of 79 percent of respondents trusted their families "completely", while 91 percent of respondents trusted their neighbors at least "somewhat" if not "completely".
14. It's not uncommon for trust scholars to emphasize the role of both trust and distrust concurrently (e.g., Lindenberg 2000) but usually then advocate *for* trust and *against* distrust, in general.

15. Scott 2012: xxi. In some ways, this book is a declaration of an anarchist trust. The phrase "quality of mind" echoes the orientation of C. Wright Mills's (1959) sociological imagination.
16. Tilly 2005: 87–88.

CHAPTER 1   US AND OTHER PEOPLE: WHAT TRUST IS

1. Franks 2018; Williams 2011.
2. hooks 2000a.
3. Levine (2018) defines anti-authoritarianism as a rejection of illegitimate authority (not necessarily *all* authority).
4. A person is not moral because they are religious but because they belong to a society that shares values and norms (Durkheim 1973).
5. See Engels's letter to Franz Mehring (Engels 1893): www.marxists.org/archive/marx/works/1893/letters/93_07_14.htm
6. Kaufman 2003; Stephens et al. 2012.
7. Simmel 1969.
8. Indeed, although it's not Simmel's primary argument, the "other" is exploited by authoritarians.
9. Kropotkin 2006. He was casually rejecting the statism of social democracy and greed of individualism (Kinna 1995).
10. J. Coleman 1990.
11. Emerson 1962.
12. Fromm 1956.
13. Also, see Gilman-Opalsky 2020 and hooks 2000b.
14. Montgomery & bergman 2017: 131.
15. Montgomery & begrman 2017: 133.
16. As Morris (2018) notes, Kropotkin would interpret this Enlightenment-era slogan as flawed insofar as it services capitalism and not economic justice, thus negating both equality and ultimately liberty.
17. Top-down statist solidarity in the form of social welfare and redistributive policies.
18. Kip 2016.
19. Wagner & Berger 1985.
20. Indeed, legal contracts typically invoke state power, which brings the potential for coercion and violence. Obviously, "trust" is absent when one or more parties require weapons to enforce proper interaction.
21. Graeber 2011.
22. Kääriäinen & Sirén 2012.
23. Tönnies 2001.
24. Kropotkin 2006.
25. Hardin 2002.

26. After a scandalous event occurs—like the police shooting of a Black person—police often talk about re-establishing trust with citizens. This overlooks several key facts. First, it assumes that trust previously existed between African Americans and the police. Second, it prioritizes Black people changing their attitudes so as to trust the untrustworthy, rather than prioritizing that the police stop killing people. Finally, by their actions, the police have shown that their interests do not align with Black communities and so they *are* untrustworthy.

27. Bamyeh 2009.

28. Olson 2004.

29. Graeber 2011.

30. Bogardus 1947.

31. L. McKay et al. 2023.

32. K. Cook 2015: 125.

33. Stirner 1963. See a sociological framing of Stirner in Simon 2014.

34. Graeber 2011.

35. Cellular phones, the internet, and social media are replicating and exaggerating some of these trends, while some characteristics may serve as counterweights. Chayko 2014.

36. Stagnating male wages have meant that female family members have had to make up the slack in heterosexual relationships, while most men have not compensated by adopting an equal share of household labor. Thus, many women now work a "second shift": paid, low-wage employment alongside still mostly full-time, unpaid domestic labor at home (Hochschild 1989).

37. See Furness 2010 and Kunstler 1993 for more about the negative impacts of car culture.

38. Graham 2015. Also, see Leier 2006 and Eckhardt 2016.

39. The international research came from my 2009 unpublished dissertation analyzing the World Values Survey, while the US analysis used the GSS (Williams 2020).

40. Crepaz et al. 2017.

41. Guo et al. 2022.

42. Hamamura et al. 2017.

43. Since the polity is simply one institution within broader society, political trust may be subordinate to social trust. But studies have provided mixed results when modeling individual social trust's effect upon political trust. While some studies have found a positive effect (Catterberg & Moreno 2006; Peng 2013; Roßteutscher 2010), others have found no relationship (Cook & Gronke 2005; Damico et al. 2000), and even a negative effect (Kim 2005). The opposite approach views the

political sphere as the dominant, directing feature of society, setting the ground for civil society's potential for social trust. Here, the statistical association for political predicting social trust is wholly positive, within samples focused on both the US (Keele 2007; Irwin & Berigan 2013) and elsewhere (Freitag & Bühlmann 2009; Robbins 2011; Rothstein & Stolle 2008). The effect is consistent, whether measured as confidence in police (Freitag & Bühlmann 2009; Robbins 2011), local and national government (Irwin & Berigan 2013; Tao et al. 2014), or multiple institutions together (Rothstein & Stolle 2008).

44. Williams 2020.

45. For those who find the labels "horizontalists" and "hierarchicalists" cumbersome—and that may even be most readers—you can instead use the short-hand of "anti-authoritarians" and "authoritarians" (respectively), if you like. But these terms usually describe singularly a political orientation toward centralized power, and a I prefer the original terms' depiction of the direction that trust goes in: laterally or toward the top.

46. Gärtner & Prado 2016.

47. Alexander 2006.

48. Williams 2020.

49. Libertarians in the US differ from "libertarians" elsewhere in the world. American use of the term almost exclusively references pro-capitalist state-minimalists, and has been consciously appropriated from left-wing anarchists (Rothbard 2007: 83).

50. Rand 1992.

51. There are hints of antisemitism to some anti-urbane theories of how society's policies and values have been perverted by immigrants and intellectuals (with Jewish people historically serving as the boogeymen).

52. Kropotkin 2006. Or, according to sociologist John Lofland (1988), classic anarchism argued that "Leaders corrupt group life and should not be allowed. If they do appear, they should be distrusted" (p. 5).

53. Arendt 1966.

54. The labels for the "horizontalist" and "hierarchicalist" categories are partly inspired by Offe (1999), who described horizontal and vertical trust (akin to masses and elites). However, I eschew these specific terms for two main reasons. First, horizontal and vertical were meant to describe the simple direction of trust, not its exclusivity vis-à-vis the other direction. Second, horizontalism references a specific term in popular usage by anti-authoritarian movements throughout Latin America (*horizontalidad*), meant to consciously reject political trust, electoral action, and party politics (Sitrin 2006). Likewise, hierarchi-

calist appropriately describes not just a vertical relationship, but an exclusively vertical form of trust.

55. See Gerth & Mills 1946.
56. See Collins 2005.
57. As a disclaimer: The typical survey measurements of political trust are worded as "confidence in ____ institution", which may have more to do with respondents' perception of them as trustworthy, rather than respondents trust in them. Thus, while interesting, the empirical analysis above should be tentative and tested with future analysis and better data. See Williams 2020 for more methodological details and analysis.
58. Jamil 2023: 180.
59. Tava 2023.
60. Efremenko & Evseeva 2012.
61. Stjernø 2004.
62. Thome 1999.
63. Scott 1999b: 273.
64. Hunt-Hendrix & Taylor 2024.
65. Milstein 2014.
66. Baker 2023: 68–69.
67. Levine 2018.
68. Gordon 2007: 12.
69. Sitrin 2006: 3.
70. Witoszek 2019.
71. Dixon 2014: 6–7. Anti-authoritarianism is one of Dixon's "four anti's", also including anti-capitalism, anti-oppression, and anti-imperialism.
72. Luhmann 1979.
73. Oxford English Dictionary 2017.
74. Carey 2017: 9.

CHAPTER 2 WHO DO YOU TRUST?
SOME OF THE WAYS THAT TRUST WORKS

1. For a larger exploration of nation as "imagined community", see Anderson 2016.
2. Associated Press 1992.
3. Bogardus 1947.
4. T. Smith 2009.
5. Boch (2020) proposes separating groups whose speech is simply controversial from actual hate speech to assess tolerance. Upon doing so, there has been an increase in Americans who tolerate any speech,

while tolerance of hate speech has decreased among certain groups (e.g., college graduates).

6. Surprisingly, "segregation" for immigrants within "ethnic enclaves" of fellow nationals may actually be beneficial for their social capital, networks, and mutual aid—as opposed to being integrated in native-born neighborhoods but socially isolated from those most like them (Portes & Zhou 1993).

7. The infamous MS-13 gang (see Steven Osuna's 2020 article describing the other ways in which US-funded civil war in El Salvador, neoliberal globalization, and US sponsorship of authoritarian policing in El Salvador has also contributed to the gang's "moral panic").

8. Zimmer 2015.

9. Apoifis 2016.

10. Boffey & Tondo 2019.

11. Said 1979.

12. Few Americans know much about Islam or personally know any Muslims, and Islamophobic attitudes have become politically polarized (see Mohamed 2021).

13. Dahab & Omori 2019; Jones & Unsworth 2004; Sherkat & Lehman 2018.

14. Mohamed 2016.

15. Williams 2021.

16. Ellingson 2001.

17. See Brown 1970.

18. Brecher 1997.

19. A highly abbreviated list: Korea, Iran, Vietnam, and Cuba (US); and Czechoslovakia, Hungary, and Afghanistan (USSR).

20. Blum 1995.

21. Bell 1980.

22. Cobb-Reiley 1988; Hong 1992.

23. In fact, contemporary FBI documents claim that classic age anarchists were principled, working-class, and committed to their struggles, while alleging the contemporary anarchist movement is none of those things (see Williams 2017: 34).

24. See Brodkin 1998; Gugilemo & Salerno 2003; and Roediger 2005.

25. This is a lie because not only were Black slaves not content but they also actively subverted their master's control through both confrontational and passive methods. See Horne 2016 and Mullin 1972.

26. For more on racial differentiation, see Delgado & Stefancic 2017.

27. Glassner 1999.

28. Bartholomew & Reumschüssel 2018; Lee & Martinez 2009.

29. A. Chomsky 2007.

30. Lipka & Martínez 2014.
31. Zuckerman 2009.
32. Durkheim [1912] 2001.
33. Coyle 2016.
34. See this classroom-based exercise that illustrates how regularly Americans break laws—with little actual consequence (Reichel 1975; Woodall 2017).
35. See field of critical criminology (e.g., Cohen 1988).
36. K. Williams 2015.
37. Eigenberg 1989.
38. Vitale 2017.
39. Simmel 1969.
40. Grenier 2005; Vine 2015.
41. Asal & Rethemeyer 2008.
42. Zinn 1997: 645.
43. Interview with Charlie Rose (Graeber 2006).
44. Aguilera 2021.
45. Data drawn from the 2024 GSS (regarding US Congress) and the seventh wave of the World Values Survey (regarding police). Implications regarding trust in police is explored in Williams (2024a).
46. Scott 2009.
47. Delhey et al. 2011.
48. N. Chomsky 2015.
49. Laursen 2012.
50. Glassner 1999.
51. See Rossides 1972.
52. Zheng 2015.
53. Mainstream political theorists consistently advocate for political trust (and against political distrust), as people "must trust *their* legislators to have their best interests in mind" (Lenard 2008: 328, emphasis added)—but is it actually true that legislators in capitalist representative systems do (or even can) hold diverse constituency's interests at heart? This seems incredibly naive and inefficient.
54. See Parker 1995.
55. This is surely the academic meaning of "political trust"; in my reading, it should more appropriately be "state trust" or "trust in hierarchy".
56. Oliver & Wood 2014. Also see Merlan 2019.
57. Burris and Staples (2012) point to a very real "transnational capitalist class", strongest within the North Atlantic region.
58. Rosenblum & Muirhead 2019.
59. Denton 2012.
60. Domhoff 2014.

61. Stanley 2018.
62. Schilke & Huang 2018.
63. Kennedy 2020.

CHAPTER 3 THE CANCER OF HIERARCHY: HOW SOCIAL TRUST GETS FUCKED UP

1. du Plessis et al. 2023: 585.
2. Messner et al. (2015) argue that most American men are either passive enablers or passive critics of sexual victimizers. Only a minority of anti-sexist men are active, vocal opponents.
3. Haas & Deseran 1981.
4. Glassner 1999.
5. Callanan 2012; Lowry et al. 2003; Romer et al. 2003.
6. Herman & Chomsky 1988.
7. Pager & Quillian 2005.
8. Quillian 2006.
9. David & Derthick 2014.
10. Aptheker 1969.
11. See Shirley & Stafford 2015. See, also, the anti-state tendency to flee toward zones where "friction" is too high for state forces to pursue (Scott 2009).
12. Alimahomed-Wilson 2016; Bonacich 1976; Roediger 2005.
13. Milstein 2015.
14. Evangelist 2022.
15. Measured by their "F-Scale". Adorno et al. 1950.
16. Gatto et al. 2010; Rubinstein 2006.
17. Way & Patten 2013.
18. Altemeyer 1998, 2004.
19. Boykoff 2007.
20. Churchill & Vander Wall 2002.
21. Cunningham 2005.
22. Bruce 2010.
23. Ladhani 2011.
24. The "panopticon" is a physically built surveillance system, originally designed by Jeremy Bentham, that social theorist Michel Foucault (1995) famously argued can also be understood as a technique for getting others to discipline themselves, even in the absence of an authority's presence.
25. Witness high distrust of politicians throughout Latin America (Power & Jamison 2005).

26. Basu 2021; Ganguly 2023.
27. See Williams 2015 for the definitive history on police in America.
28. See Foucault 1995; Orwell 1949.
29. For example, one Massachusetts drug task force employed more than 2000 informants, who conducted almost half of all drug transactions (Natapoff 2009).
30. Massey & Denton 1988. The DI is a measure of "evenness"; other distributional traits include exposure, concentration, centralization, and clustering, and these can be measured by an impressive twenty different indices (of which DI is only one).
31. Social Science Data Analysis Network 2000.
32. Rothwell 2012; Uslaner 2011.
33. See Allport 1954; Pettigrew & Tropp 2006.
34. Thomsen & Rafiqi 2019; Visintin et al. 2019.
35. Dangl 2010. Also, Ross 2016.
36. Scott 1999a.
37. Greenwald 2014.
38. To be clear, "crypto" is intended in its original meaning—cryptographic techniques and tools to scramble data—and does not refer to what has, regrettably, become more common, as a narrowly specified form of digital currency.
39. See Schneier 2015.
40. Vine 2015.
41. Blum 1995; Hämäläinen 2023.
42. The countries whose residents ranked the US as the world's biggest threat included Argentina, Australia, Brazil, China, Finland, Germany, Indonesia, Mexico, Peru, Russia, South Africa, Spain, Turkey, and others. And to be completely clear, these results are from the Obama era (i.e., pre-Trump). See Zuesse 2017.
43. See Paley 2014.
44. Gauchat 2012. It's important to note that distrust in science runs deep in US society and some scholars, such as the cognitive scientists Sloman and Fernbach (2018), have uncritically argued for raising such trust (e.g., in climate science or vaccines, but also corporate-controlled genetically engineered foods).
45. Krastev 2013.
46. See Goldfield 1989 and Moody 1988 regarding business unionism and the example of US state cooptation of the Black freedom struggle (Allen 1969; H. Haines 1984).
47. Parenti 2000.
48. This finding is so banal and taken for granted that it rarely features prominently in cutting-edge criminology research.

49. Violent victimization in particular has a significant, negative impact on generalized social trust (Janssen et al. 2021).
50. As pointed out by Graeber (2015), people who are doing nothing "wrong" are more apt to protest police mistreatment, thus leading to police escalation of force.
51. Wilson 1987.
52. Gilens 1999.
53. Garcia 2023.
54. Patriarchy also encourages distrust in members of one's own sex too.
55. Martin (1998) writes productively on the topic of information resistance and liberation.
56. Graeber 2006.
57. See Landry et al. 2022; Savage 2007.
58. Robinson 2021, 2022.
59. For a fascinating exploration of darkness and nighttime, see Palmer 2000.
60. Ahrens & Aldana 2012.
61. Interpersonal conflict negatively impacts social trust (Bell et al. 2019; Delhey & Newton 2003).
62. See Hari 2015; Maté 2013.
63. Lilley et al. 2012.
64. Climate chaos fears may be leading to a rise in youth depression (see Gianfredi et al. 2024).
65. Best 1990.
66. Walsh et al. 2016. Also see Shutt et al. 2004.
67. Terrell et al. 2000.
68. Marya & Patel 2021.
69. Electronic Security Association 2020.
70. Passett 2023.
71. Semuels 2023.
72. Jiobu & Curry 2001.
73. Advertisements found in a century's worth of *The American Rifleman* magazine changed from emphasizing sport shooting and hunting to self-defense (see Yamane et al. 2018).
74. Dunbar-Ortiz 2018.
75. Depetris-Chauvin 2015.
76. Reich & Barth 2017.
77. Hicks et al. 2023.
78. Associated Press 1987.
79. Lavin 2021; Zuboff 2020.
80. Logan 2002.
81. US News 2020.

82. Arendt 1966.
83. Given the nature of patriarchal societies throughout the world, these leaders are usually male.
84. Note: the *right* to own property (i.e., possibility), not the *guarantee to* property.
85. Greenfield 2011.
86. N. Chomsky 2017.
87. I. McKay 2019.
88. Noted by Wallerstein 2003, among others.
89. J. Osuna et al. 2021.
90. Stanley 2018.
91. Social democracy and welfare states can be seen as weak versions of state communism.
92. See China's "cultural revolution"; Liu 2016.
93. See Lerner 1986 for more on the history of patriarchy.
94. Lorber 2005.
95. Yu 2006.
96. See S. Smith 2010 for explanations of the lower levels of social trust from people of color.
97. Bonilla-Silva 2003.
98. Regarding the effects of colonialism in Uganda, see Kizito 2017 and Rodriguez 2017; regarding the impact of American churches, see K. Ward 2015.
99. Coaffee 2004.
100. Wallerstein 2003.
101. Horrox 2009.
102. Gordon & Grietzer 2013.
103. See Holtzman & Sharpe 2014 and Benshoff & Griffin 2021 for detailed analyses of flattened cultural representation.
104. Climent & Coll-Florit 2021.
105. Chermak et al. 2024.
106. Cooper & Kroeger 2017.
107. Back in 2000, a full 50 percent of all psychology graduates worked in for-profit enterprises, in areas such as "marketing research, social work, labor relations or management and productivity improvement" (Schwartz 2000).

CHAPTER 4   MISPLACED TRUST:
BEING SMART ABOUT TRUST

1. Notably higher among Republicans, indicating perhaps a somewhat reflexive trust for the Republican president George W. Bush. See Williams & Slusser 2014.

2. Incredibly, one officer grabbed me, jammed his finger in my chest, and accused *me* of assault on his fellow officer.

3. It should be stated that Obama's 2008 slogan "Hope" was merely a blank slate upon which voters wrote their own aspirations. Obama left his own platform and values relatively unarticulated and vague.

4. St. Clair 2016.

5. Messner et al. 2015 points to the small minority of men who sexually assault, but the sizable minority of men who endorse such assault, facilitate it, and provide ideological cover and defense for it.

6. Barack Obama was the first exception to this rule, of course; but this exception does not negate the overall pattern.

7. Claimed by Muirhead & Rosenblum 2019.

8. "It is a well-known fact that those people who most want to rule people are, ipso facto, those least suited to do it ... anyone who is capable of getting themselves made President should on no account be allowed to do the job" (Adams 1994: 278).

9. It might not warrant mention here, but these things have *literally* been uttered by Trump, who again is the penultimate example of an untrustworthy elite. The internet is replete with video clips of Trump uttering "Trust me ..." as a stylized way of emphasizing that what he's saying is both important and true (although the latter is rarely the case).

10. See Isaac 2001; Wimberly et al. 2024.

11. Similar critiques have been lobbied against US government regulatory agencies, such as the Environmental Protection Agency (often dubbed by environmentalists as "Every Polluters' Advocate") for its toothless enforcement of pollution laws, underfunded mandates, and orientation toward punishment rather that prevention.

12. DSM-5: 313.81 (F91.3) (American Psychiatric Association 2013).

13. Levine 2012.

14. The DSM's page length and total number of diagnosable disorders has grown with each successive edition. Either psychological disorders are actually expanding in society or human "understanding" about them is changing. Medicalization has been a central critique of medical sociologists for decades, but Conrad (2005) argues that commercial and market interests are now a greater engine of medicalization than professionals.

15. According to the "principle of least interest", power is afforded to the exchange partner who needed the relationship the least (Waller & Hill 1951). Also see Blau 1964.

16. Kropotkin 2006: 182.

17. Also reflected in interviews conducted with Christian spiritual leaders, whose emotions and ego intervened on their "altruistic" decision-making (Poloma & Hood 2008: 179–180).

18. Gilens & Page 2014.

19. The reasons for this sell-out are mostly irrelevant. It's easy to imagine how it happened: He wasn't really a radical socialist; he began to identify more with his new elite peers than those who elected him; EU leaders made him empathize with them personally; the EU personally threatened him or threatened all of Greece (and thus he caved to defend them); and so on (see Economakis 2019; Polychroniou 2016).

20. Dangl 2010.

21. It's also crucial to note that Clinton embraced many conservative positions and policies, ranging from law enforcement and prisons, the death penalty, social welfare reduction, and others (e.g., O'Connor 2002).

22. St. Clair 2016.

23. Granted, some Sanders supporters did this and had (and continue to have) a social movement orientation, but they are exceptions to the rule. Elections in the US are fundamentally candidate-centric, not issue-centric.

24. Amaral 2016; Dikaios & Tsagkroni 2021; Mariette 2022.

25. Garcia 2014.

26. Urban 2013.

27. Lalich 2004.

28. Flaherty 2016.

29. Birn & Richter 2018.

30. Girdiharadas 2018.

31. Barsamian 2014: 146.

32. Milstein 2015.

33. Just as one example, consider the *hundreds* of cop movies where police "get their man", despite bending rules, brutality, and ultimately righteousness. Even in cop movies where some of their fellows are corrupt, there are nearly always good cops who save the day that the audience can cheer for.

34. See Williams 2024a.

35. Graeber 2015.

36. Gatto & Dambrun 2012; Haley & Sidanius 2005.

37. Even though you are likely to find more people of color who distrust police, that is not guaranteed. In fact, some poor people want more police in their community because they believe it makes them safe against crime and criminals. Radicals may be tempted to rate such pro-police beliefs as reactionary, but caution is warranted. Poor people

of color longing for more policing is not necessarily a sign of their fascistic tendencies or indicative of authoritarian sycophants, but rather it indicates they are desperate people who perceive that they lack a collective means to make their communities safer. They wonder if, in the absence of strong social trust and capital, perhaps the police could help?

38. Price 2011. For example, "peace" in Afghanistan is not a benevolent American gift, but helpful for fossil fuel extraction by Western corporations.

39. There are some limitations to this, because it eventually reduces consumer trust. But manipulation is still a key part of this relationship.

40. See Michael Messner's research on anti-sexual violence movements and how only the minority of men engage in such actions, while sizable majorities both defend them or quietly oppose them. Only a vocal minority actively struggles against such practices (Messner et al. 2015).

41. Dauvergne & Lebaron 2014; A. Smith 2007.

42. Rodríguez 2007.

43. Durkheim 1997.

44. There is much time-tested experience with eviction defense, from Brazil's landless workers movement, Central European squatters, or the UK "poll tax rebellion", in which everyday people intimidated agents of the state to back off evictions of those poor Britons who refused to pay a punishing tax (see D. Burns 1992).

45. This is common in cults and hostage situations, wherein someone captured and held against their will comes to identify with their captors (the so-called "Stockholm Syndrome"). Incidentally, this "syndrome" is rare and contested by experts.

46. Flaherty 2016.

47. Apparently, mirrors are only for checking the status of one's hair, not for double-checking one's morality or humility.

48. Bourdieu 1977.

49. Spring 1998.

50. Marcuse 2002.

51. Association of National Advertisers 2015, 2022.

52. Buttigieg 2021: 44.

53. See Spring 1998.

54. Beard 1998; Domhoff 2014; Fresia 1988; Lynd 1967.

55. Horne 2016.

56. Piven 2006.

57. Beard 1998; Ovetz 2022.

58. Fresia 1988: 16; Zinn 1995.

59. Locke [1689] 1988.
60. Hertel & Groh-Samberg 2019.
61. See Klein 2023.
62. Mills 1959.
63. Gramsci 1971.
64. Fukuyama 1995. Kohn (2008) makes a similar argument, opening his treatise entitled *Trust: Self-Interest and the Common Good* by declaring that an "agreement has been reached about how humankind can best make a profitable living, with a single economic orthodoxy established around the world" (p. vii). Ironically, the world economic recession hadn't yet hit and Kohn's conclusion about capitalism's universal acceptance is far from certain.
65. Graeber 2011.
66. Perhaps most notably Simmel's (1969) and Coser's (1998) observations of cooperation and conflict.
67. See examples of this in Adamic 2008 and Brecher 1997.
68. Van Meter 2017.
69. A fascinating, critical analysis of comparable international solidarity work offers similar critiques and additional challenges (Ryan 2011).
70. Stokes 2009.
71. Western-style development programs in the post-World War II era were justified by a "modernization" rhetoric, in which poor countries acquired infrastructure that allowed them to compete in global markets just as wealthy countries did. Problematically, this claim overlooks how various instruments—often implemented by the US- and UK-dominated International Monetary Fund and World Bank—actually kept poor countries underdeveloped and dependent upon and subservient to Western economic interests, while developing a local economic elite.
72. See O'Rourke 2018.
73. See Hessick 2007.
74. Harrell 2012.
75. Ample examples of Obama falling short of his constituency's expectations regarding race can be found in Ali 2012; Jacobs 2012; and K.-Y. Taylor 2016.
76. Omi and Winant (1986) have argued that prior to 1964 (and with the brief exception of Reconstruction), America was a white dictatorship. And, since 1964 (the year of the Civil Rights Act), the US has remained a white hegemony: dominated by whites and de facto inequality, despite de jure equality. Thus, even when the US formally renounced white supremacy, its institutions (and citizens) continued to act in ways that perpetuated racial domination and inequality.

77. Based on the 2006 and 2010 results of the GSS, comparing "confed" variable's "hardly any" confidence in "executive branch of federal government" (as distrust) to "partyid" variable's partisan categories (strong, not strong, and near affiliations for each party).

78. See the impressive left anthology critical of Obama's first term in St. Clair and Frank 2012.

79. Thus Max Weber's (1958) caution about legal-rational authority's embodiment in bureaucratic systems—an "iron cage"—and the relentless strength they possess.

CHAPTER 5 TRUST, DISASTER, AND CHANGING CIRCUMSTANCES: TRUST'S VOLATILITY

1. On another occasion, I found myself walking outside in the midst of a severe blizzard. I was offered car rides to my destination by complete strangers. Similar things have happened in the aftermath of accidents or car breakdowns. Of course, not everyone stops to ask if you're okay, but a surprising number of people do, and they really *do* care and are willing to help. See Purkis 2022 for more on hitchhiking.

2. See crow 2014; Firth 2022; Solnit 2009.

3. Solnit 2009.

4. Williams 2019.

5. Turner 1967.

6. Collins 2005; Durkheim 1997.

7. Zimbardo 2007.

8. Interview in documentary film *The Corporation* (Achbar & Abbott 2003).

9. There's evidence that people have taken away an extreme lesson from Milgram's work, that people are highly obedient to authority, to the point that they would often willingly torture others (despite any inflicted insight they may face in the future). In fact, it appears likely that many test subjects understood the experiments to be fake and artificial (see Perry et al. 2020).

10. crow 2014.

11. Klein 2007.

12. C. Ward 1996.

13. Becker 1997.

14. Khodyakov 2007.

15. Jem Cohen's *Instrument* 1999.

16. Olson 1965: 131.

17. See Potiker et al. 2022 for just such an analysis of non-state spaces, including anarchist and anarchistic participation.
18. The Spanish Revolution literature is vast, but here are some fundamental starting points for the curious: Evans 2020; Leval 2018; Mintz 2013; Paz 2011; and Richards 2019.
19. Olson 1965: 131.
20. Scott (1999a) argues that such long-term planning is fruitless and inane and ignores all the real ways that people live in their own communities, of which the state and its planners do not truly understand (or fundamentally care about).
21. Campbell 2024.
22. James 1956; Martin 1996.
23. Olson 1965.
24. See Ostrom's 1990 critique.
25. According to Giddens (1990), a primary consequence of modernity is a "risk society", in which the guidance of experts is essential. In order for society to function smoothly, experts must be trusted and trustworthy. This seems most relevant in the cases of public health experts, climate scientists, and others whose insights are important for the survival of humanity.
26. See Leier 2006 and Bakunin 1970.
27. Stanley 2018.
28. Martin 2008: 10.
29. There are exceptions to the urban-based revolution, as illustrated by Chiapas, Mexico's indigenous Zapatista revolutionary movement.
30. Gamson 1971.
31. Case 2022.
32. Illustrative examples of these include the 1905 pogroms in Russia's "pale of settlement", the US's "red summer" of 1919 or the 1921 Tulsa, Oklahoma, race massacre, and the 1947 Amritsar massacre during the India–Pakistan Partition. Also not considered here are the somewhat frequent "riots" led by celebratory (and often inebriated) fans after sporting events.
33. This possibility—and strategies for it—are discussed in the final chapter.
34. For example, see Schwarz & Sagris 2010.
35. Traugott 2010.
36. An excellent example is the Paris Commune of 1871 (Merriman 2014).
37. LeBon 1925. For more on LeBon, see Reicher 2002.
38. Templeton et al. 2024.

39. Piven 2006. Note that "mob" here does not refer to "the mafia" or organized crime, per se, but an insurrectionary popular mass of people.

40. Orwell 1952. He describes formalities like *usted* dropping from speech, replaced by the informal *tú*.

41. Guillamón 2014.

42. Tanaka-Gútiez 2020.

43. Newburn et al. 2018.

44. Solnit 2009.

45. Pearl Harbor is not an exception to this rule, either, as it was a military base on a colonial holding (Hawaii) that was attacked in the midst of a multi-year escalation across the Pacific Ocean between Japan and the US. See Immerwahr 2019 for more on the "hidden" American empire.

46. As discussed elsewhere in this book, much of this diminished trust stems from active subversion by the US government, principally the FBI's COINTELPRO.

47. Mills 1959.

48. Scott (2009) describes resistance to the draft in his work focused on Southeast Asia's Zomia, *The Art of Not Being Governed*. Cross-national sabotage (of sorts) has existed among soldiers, too, such as the infamous sports games played between various opposing European forces, especially during holidays (see Kohn 2008).

49. The US radical Catholic left engaged in numerous acts of civil disobedience during the late Vietnam War—most notably raids on draft board offices, where records were stolen and destroyed. These and other direct actions stymied the US military's ability to recruit soldiers (Cortright 2005; Glick 2020).

50. See Rinaldi & Keating 2004 for a great overview of efforts to monkey-wrench the Vietnam War.

51. Knapp et al. 2016.

52. Cockerham 2017.

53. Their "strong leadership" demands reflexive trust, despite their recklessness and foolishness in face of a pandemic.

54. Firth 2022.

55. See Graeber 2018.

56. Solnit 2009.

57. For first-hand description of the perils and consequences of outside volunteers and solidarity work, see Ryan 2011 and crow 2014. Also see Luft 2008 and Medwinter 2021.

58. Hager 2022; Pestana 2013.

59. According to the Red Cross's 2017 Annual Report, their net assets were nearly $1.2 billion, receiving $660 million in financial contri-

NOTES

butions that year. www.redcross.org/content/dam/redcross/National/
pdfs/annual-reports/Annual-Report-2017.pdf

60. Holguin 2002; Mascarenas & Valles 2019. Such practices are fairly common within the nonprofit industrial complex (see Raventós & Wark 2018; A. Smith 2007).

61. Garrison 2024.

62. It's important to note that most people who donate items to Goodwill for their resale and profit, trust that the donation will directly help to fund a person who has such disabilities. See Carter 2018 and ProPublica 2024.

63. Wilson 1987, also see Marable 1983 and Massey & Denton 1998.

64. See complicated links between individualism and solidarity, as per social trust, with Raudenbush 2016.

65. Cao et al. 2012.

66. Catterberg & Moreno 2006. Additionally, countries that had experienced "colored revolutions", were more apt to later have less social trust and more political trust (Ishiyama & Pechenina 2016), establishing conditions that would appear to be greatly incompatible with further social movement mobilization.

67. Callero 2009.

68. See J. Burns 2009; Wolfe 2012.

69. Unfortunately, this colloquial saying insults the intelligence of this mammal, which does not commit mass suicide. But it's still a colorful metaphor and conveys meaning well.

70. Unlike popular depictions in fictional works like Kipling's *The Jungle Book*, most examples of "feral children" are likely the result of conscious neglect, not abandonment. The infamous child abuse and isolation experienced by "Genie" (b. 1957) in the US is a classic modern example of this pattern.

71. Unfortunately, adult children and their parents underestimate their own future care needs (Walz & Mitchell 2007).

72. Marya & Patel 2021.

73. Gavin et al. 2011.

CHAPTER 6 A REASON TO TRUST—TRUST IN REVOLUTION: HOW WE CAN STRATEGICALLY USE TRUST

1. Bakunin 1867. I've previously argued that libertarian socialism is the core ideological underpinning of modern-day anarchism (Williams 2017), a claim also echoed by Kristian Williams 2018.

2. Shepard & Smithsimon 2011.

3. Crucially, Katsiaficas (2018) defines the New Left's values squarely in this range too: justice and freedom.

4. Many advocates simply use the acronym FOSS (minus the L). But, given the copious ambiguity about the English word "free", the added "libre" emphasizes freedom, as opposed to the unfortunately more popular meaning of free—gratis (i.e., without monetary cost). Trusting something to remain cost-free is fine, but trusting that it will continue to respect your freedoms is more impressive.

5. Coleman 2013.

6. Benkler 2006.

7. The steeper learning curve to GPG has limited its proliferation, especially compared to mobile phone-ready applications—e.g., Signal and WhatsApp—that are end-to-end encrypted instead.

8. Greenwald 2014.

9. Olson 2004.

10. A notable example here is antifascist organizing (see Vysotsky 2020).

11. Social justice movements ignore colonialism to their own detriment (Fortier 2017).

12. See works like Churchill 2005; Dunbar-Ortiz 2014; and Fortier 2017.

13. Creasap 2021; Yates 2015.

14. Surely there are more complex reasons motivating the participation of white anti-racists (or male feminists or middle-class anti-capitalists), which may involve ego-glorification, boredom, or self-righteousness. Those are "selfish" reasons of a less trusting character.

15. Blackburn 2001.

16. Problems arise in the liberal framework when resources, statuses, and power aren't equally accessible. In a class society anyone *can* become affluent, but most *don't*. Thus, rights are not the only thing we require.

17. Patel 2010.

18. Alexander 2006.

19. Alexander et al. 2020.

20. Williams 2024b.

21. See K.-Y. Taylor 2016.

22. This is a challenging exercise that participants in social movement organizations could strategize about.

23. Polletta 2002.

24. Sitrin 2006.

25. These and other non-state spaces—and their covariates—are summarized in Potiker et al. 2022.

26. The Spanish Mondragón has veered off its egalitarian path (Benello 1996; Greenberg 1986; Rothschild & Whitt 1986; P. Taylor 1994).

27. Graeber 2011.

28. Rose City Copwatch 2008.
29. Martin 1993.
30. Cobb 2015; Umoja 2014.
31. Vysotsky 2015.
32. Zibechi 2010.
33. "To Change Everything: An Anarchist Appeal", https://crimethinc. com/tce
34. Lavin 2021; Merlan 2021. Other craziness includes Meta CEO Mark Zuckerberg's 2025 declaration that Facebook would abandon fact-checking on its platform, likely both to court the incoming Trump presidency and to save employee costs.
35. More than one-fifth of American users left (Hern 2024).
36. Mastodon 2024.
37. For example, Jame Mumm's (2002) famous underground essay "Active Revolution: Organizing, Base Building, and Dual Power". https:// theanarchistlibrary.org/library/an-organizer-active-revolution
38. Barclay 1990.
39. Guerrero 2018: 114.
40. Gould 1988.
41. Graeber 2011.
42. V. Haines 1991.
43. See Kropotkin's (2006) masterpiece, *Mutual Aid: A Factor in Evolution*. Hari (2018) argues that social disconnection is behind much of the recent spike in anxiety and depression.
44. While popularly known as the Black Panther Party's "survival programs", the "pending revolution" part is crucial to acknowledge, as these weren't just projects to make Black life marginally better but were the means to *survive* until a broad revolution could overthrow American capitalism and white supremacy. See Abu-Jamal 2016.
45. For an impressive account of how everyday Black people pushed—or some might say revolted—during this period for greater social safety net support, see Piven & Cloward 1979.
46. crow (2014). It should be noted that the presence of certain toxic individuals—including a paid FBI informant—in these communities did undermine radical trust within Common Ground.
47. Estes 2019.
48. Eken 2014; Turan & Özçetin 2019.
49. For an overview of social movements, see Williams 2025a.
50. Williams 2023.
51. Hooghe & Marien 2013.
52. Braun & Hutter 2016.
53. Williams 2023.

54. Benson & Rochon 2004.
55. Kaase 1999.
56. Ehrlich 1991; Shantz 2017.
57. Freedman 2014; Rosenthal 1984.
58. Lampe 2014; Werner 2004.
59. Foner 2015; Wells 2020.
60. D. Burns 1992; Rameau 2013; van der Steen et al. 2014.
61. C. Smith 1996.
62. Suh & Reynolds-Stenson 2018.
63. See Williams 2020.
64. van Stekelenburg & Klandermans 2017.
65. See Sakai 2014.
66. Medsger 2014.
67. Potter 2011.
68. Ratner & Ratner 2000.
69. Rothschild-Whitt 1979.
70. Dixon 2014.
71. Sock-puppets are fake simulations, pretending to be something they are not. "Antifa" is simply an abbreviation for antifascist, and despite government and media paranoia otherwise, is not necessarily an organization.
72. Doxxing aims to reveal online individuals' private information (names, addresses, employers).
73. What Sharp (1973) calls non-cooperation, with one higher and riskier category of action called intervention.
74. See Lipsitz 1994.
75. Schwarz & Sagris 2010; Vradis & Dalakoglou 2011.
76. Solnit 2016.
77. Transparency and education motivated an activist community I was part of in northeast Ohio, where just such an assault occurred in 2003, to organize a well-attended conference, during which many attendees revealed that they, too, had experienced assault (although not from the same perpetrator).
78. Of course, survivors often choose to participate in such efforts, too, but such a restorative burden is not theirs alone.
79. This follows the logic of the classic chant "No justice, no peace!" Liberals and others in the mainstream often presume that "peace" meant the lack of overt, physical violence, while radicals have been quick to point out that injustice is a subtle but real form of violence that must be dealt with before true peace can be established. To demand peace without justice is to advocate for a return to quiet acceptance of injustice.

80. To extend the apple barrel analogy, the barrel requires better ventilation, cooler temperatures, and periodic cleaning to remove bacteria or other organisms that threaten to spread rot. Likewise, movement organizations can benefit from greater transparency, better and safer spaces, and constant collective education to be aware of emergent concerns or threats to the group.

81. Resocialization is discussed extensively in Williams 2011.

82. Thus, things often referred to as "revolutions" that resemble dictatorships (e.g., "the Bolshevik revolution") are more likely top-down coups.

83. Bookchin 2004.

84. Lewis & Klein 2004.

85. Greenberg 1986; P. Taylor 1994.

86. See Williams 2025b.

87. An anarchist critique of assemblies and democracy can be found in Crimethinc 2017.

88. LeBon 1925.

89. See Shepard & Smithsimon 2011.

90. The analysis in Potiker et al. 2022 assesses just what conditions matter for long-term anti-state spaces: the nature and source of repression.

91. Merriman 2014.

92. Guillamón 2020.

93. Katsiaficas 2013.

94. See Calhoun 1994.

95. Bamyeh 2013.

96. Traugott 2010.

97. Knapp et al. 2016.

98. See Potiker et al. 2022 for an analysis of how repression—from states or purported left allies—reduce commune survival.

99. See Vitale 2017 and K. Williams 2015.

100. See the reach of abolitionist influences in today's anti-authoritarian movements in Dixon 2014.

101. See Schenwar & Law's 2020 critique of these alternatives, which can be even *worse*.

102. Fascists are an illustrative counterfactual. In other words, would you really want to go out of your way to befriend fascists who are unlikely to be swayed by logic, compassion, or your better example? That's probably a waste of time, but if you feel up for it, go ahead. People *do* leave far-right movements and they need support in doing so. Non-leaders are more likely to de-convert than leaders, but even leaders can give up too.

103. Membership in interconnected voluntary associations improves generalized social trust, while isolated associations decrease trust (Paxton 2007). And analysis on trust in cities like Istanbul and Moscow support a "cosmopolitization thesis", wherein those who associate more widely are also more trusting of their fellow citizens (Secor & O'Loughlin 2005).
104. Day 1954.
105. See brown 2020.
106. Ogo 2008.
107. Fromm 2011. Also, Ratner 2018.
108. Mills 1959.
109. Light 2015.
110. Anheier & Kendall 2002.
111. brown's (2020) critique of "cancel culture" is illuminating here.
112. Conyers & Smallwood 2008.
113. See Ehrenreich 2006 and Williams 2018 on ecstatic rituals.
114. Breaching described in Alexander et al. 2020.
115. World Health Organization 2024.

References

Abu-Jamal, Mumia. 2016. *We Want Freedom: A Life in The Black Panther Party*. New York: Common Notions.

Achbar, Mark and Jennifer Abbott. 2002. *The Corporation*. New York: Zeitgeist Films.

Adamic, Louis. 2008. *Dynamite: The Story of Class Violence in America*. Oakland, CA: AK Press.

Adams, Douglas. 1994. *The More than Complete Hitchhiker's Guide: Complete and Unabridged*. New York: Wings.

Adorno, Theodor, Else Frenkel-Brunswik, Daniel Levinson, and Nevitt Sanford. 1950. *The Authoritarian Personality: Studies in Prejudice*. New York: Harper & Row.

Aguilera, Jasmine. 2021. "'An Epidemic of Misinformation': New Report Finds Trust in Social Institutions Diminished Further in 2020". *Time*, January 13. https://time.com/5929252/edelman-trust-barometer-2021/

Ahrens, Courtney E. and Erendira Aldana. 2012. "The Ties That Bind: Understanding the Impact of Sexual Assault Disclosure on Survivors' Relationships with Friends, Family and Partners". *Journal of Trauma & Dissociation*, 13: 226–243.

Alexander, Jeffrey C. 2006. *The Civil Sphere*. Oxford: Oxford University Press.

Alexander, Jeffrey C., Trevor Stack, and Farhad Khosrokhavar. 2020. *Breaching the Civil Order: Radicalism and the Civil Sphere*. Cambridge: Cambridge University Press.

Ali, Wajahat. 2012. "Obama's Immigration Reforms" (pp. 67–70) in *Hopeless: Barack Obama and the Politics of Illusion*, edited by J. St. Clair and J. Frank. Oakland, CA: AK Press.

Alimahomed-Wilson, Jake. 2016. *Solidarity Forever? Race, Gender, and Unionism on the Ports of Southern California*. Lanham, MD: Lexington.

Allen, Robert L. 1969. *Black Awakening in Capitalist America: An Analytic History*. Garden City, NJ: Doubleday.

Allport, Gordon W. 1954. *The Nature of Prejudice*. Cambridge, MA: Perseus.

Altemeyer, Bob. 1998. "The Other 'Authoritarian Personality'" (pp. 85–106) in *Advances in Experimental Social Psychology*, edited by M. Zanna. San Diego, CA: Academic Press.

Altemeyer, Bob. 2004. "Highly Dominating, Highly Authoritarian Personalities". *The Journal of Social Psychology*, 144 (4): 421–447.

Amaral, Aaron. 2016. "The Struggle against Syriza's Austerity Program". *New Politics*, 16 (1). https://newpol.org/issue_post/struggle-against-syrizas-austerity-program/

American Psychiatric Association. 2013. *Diagnostic Statistical Manual of Mental Disorders*, 5th ed. Arlington, VA: APA.

Anderson, Benedict. 2016. *Imagined Communities: Reflections on the Origin and Spread of Nationalism*. London: Verso.

Anheier, Helmut and Jeremy Kendall. 2002. "Interpersonal Trust and Voluntary Associations: Examining Three Approaches". *British Journal of Sociology*, 53 (3), September: 343–362.

Apoifis, Nicholas. 2016. *Anarchy in Athens: An Ethnography of Militancy, Emotions and Violence*. Manchester: Manchester University Press.

Aptheker, Herbert. 1969. *American Negro Slave Revolts*. New York: International Publishers.

Arendt, Hannah. 1966. *The Origins of Totalitarianism*. New York: Harcourt, Brace & World.

Asal, Victor and R. Karl Rethemeyer. 2008. "Dilettantes, Ideologues, and the Weak: Terrorists Who Don't Kill". *Conflict Management & Peace Science*, 25 (3): 244–263.

Associated Press. 1987. "26 Countries Selling Arms to Both Sides in Gulf War". June 18. www.latimes.com/archives/la-xpm-1987-06-18-mn-8000-story.html

Associated Press. 1992. "Robertson Letter Attacks Feminists". August 26. www.nytimes.com/1992/08/26/us/robertson-letter-attacks-feminists.html

Association of National Advertisers. 2015. "New Study Confirms Advertising as Key Driver of U.S. Economy". www.ana.net/content/show/id/37679

Association of National Advertisers. 2022. "Study from the Advertising Coalition Finds Advertising Drives $7.1 Trillion in U.S. Sales". www.ana.net/content/show/id/pr-2022-05-advertising-drives-sales

Baker, Zoe. 2023. *Means and Ends: The Revolutionary Practice of Anarchism in Europe and the United States*. Chico, CA: AK Press.

Bakunin, Mikhail. 1867. *Federalism, Socialism, Anti-Theologism*. www.marxists.org/reference/archive/bakunin/works/various/reasons-of-state.htm

Bakunin, Michael [Mikhail]. 1970. *God and the State*. New York: Dover.

Bamyeh, Mohammed A. 2009. *Anarchy as Order: The History and Future of Civic Humanity*. Lanham, MA: Rowman & Littlefield.

Bamyeh, Mohammed. 2013. "Anarchist Method, Liberal Intention, Authoritarian Lesson: The Arab Spring between Three Enlightenments". *Constellations: An International Journal of Critical & Democratic Theory*, 20 (2): 188–202.

Barclay, Harold. 1990. *People without Government: An Anthropology of Anarchy*. Seattle, WA: Left Bank Books.

Barsamian, David. 2004. *Louder Than Bombs: Interviews from the Progressive Magazine*. Boston: South End Press.

Bartholomew, Robert E. and Anja E. Reumschüssel. 2018. *American Intolerance: Our Dark History of Demonizing Immigrants*. Amherst, NY: Prometheus Books.

Basu, Deepankar. 2021. "Majoritarian Politics and Hate Crimes against Religious Minorities: Evidence from India, 2009–2018". *World Development*, 146: 105540.

Beard, Charles A. 1998. *An Economic Interpretation of the Constitution of the United States*. New Brunswick, NJ: Transaction.

Becker, Howard. 1997. *Outsiders: Studies in the Sociology of Deviance*. New York: Free Press.

Bell, Derrick A. 1980. "*Brown v. Board of Education* and the Interest Convergence Dilemma". *Harvard Law Review*, 93 (3): 518–533.

Bell, Victoria, Benjamin Robinson, Cornelius Katona, Anne-Kathrin Fett and Sukhi Shergill. 2019. "When Trust Is Lost: The Impact of Interpersonal Trauma on Social Interactions". *Psychological Medicine*, 49 (6): 1041–1046.

Benello, George. 1996. "The Challenge of Mondragon" (pp. 211–220) in *Reinventing Anarchy, Again*, edited by H. J. Ehrlich. Edinburgh: AK Press.

Benkler, Yochai. 2006. *The Wealth of Networks: How Social Reproduction Transforms Markets and Freedom*. New Haven: Yale University Press.

Benshoff, Harry M. and Sean Griffin. 2021. *America on Film: Representing Race, Class, Gender and Sexuality at the Movies*, 3rd ed. Hoboken, NJ: Wiley-Blackwell.

Benson, Michelle and Thomas R. Rochon. 2004. "Interpersonal Trust and the Magnitude of Protest: A Micro and Macro Level Approach". *Comparative Political Studies*, 37 (4): 435–457.

Best, Joel. 1990. *Threatened Children: Rhetoric and Concern about Child-Victims*. Chicago, IL: University of Chicago Press.

Birn, Anne-Emanuelle and Judith Richter. 2018. "U.S. Philanthrocapitalism and the Global Health Agenda: The Rockefeller and Gates Foundations, Past and Present" (pp. 155–174) in *Health Care under the Knife: Moving beyond Capitalism for Our Health*, edited by H. Waitzkin. New York: Monthly Review.

Blackburn, Simon. 2001. *Ethics: A Very Short Introduction*. Oxford: Oxford University Press.

Blau, Peter. 1964. *Exchange and Power in Social Life*. New York: Wiley.

Blum, William. 1995. *Killing Hope: U.S. Military and CIA Interventions since World War II*. Monroe, ME: Common Courage Press.

Boch, Anna. 2020. "Increasing American Political Tolerance: A Framework Excluding Hate Speech". *Socius: Sociological Research for a Dynamic World*, 6: 1–12.

Boffey Daniel and Lorenzo Tondo. 2019. "Captain of Migrant Rescue Ship Says Italy 'Criminalising Solidarity'". *The Guardian*, June 15. www.theguardian.com/world/2019/jun/15/captain-of-migrant-rescue-ship-says-italy-criminalising-solidarity

Bogardus, Emory S. 1947. "Measurement of Personal-Group Relations". *Sociometry*, 10: 306–311.

Bonacich, Edna. 1976. "Advanced Capitalism and Black/White Race Relations in the United States: A Split Labor Market Interpretation". *American Sociological Review*, 41: 34–51.

Bonilla-Silva, Eduardo. 2003. *Racism without Racists: Color-Blind Racism and the Persistence of Racial Inequality in the United States*. Lanham, MD: Rowman & Littlefield.

Bookchin, Murray. 2004. *Post-Scarcity Anarchism*. Edinburgh: AK Press.

Bourdieu, Pierre. 1977. *Reproduction in Education, Society and Culture*. New York: Sage.

Boykoff, Jules. 2007. *Beyond Bullets: The Suppression of Dissent in the United States*. Oakland, CA: AK Press.

Braun, Daniela and Swen Hutter. 2016. "Political Trust, Extra-Institutional Participation and the Openness of Political Systems". *International Political Science Review*, 37 (2): 151–165.

Brecher, Jeremy. 1997. *Strike!* Cambridge, MA: South End Press.

Brodkin, Karen. 1998. *How Jews Became White Folks and What That Says about Race in America*. Piscataway, NJ: Rutgers University Press.

brown, adrienne marie. 2020. *We Will Not Cancel Us: And Other Dreams of Transformative Justice*. Chico, CA: AK Press.

Brown, Dee. 1970. *Bury My Heart at Wounded Knee: An Indian History of the American West*. New York: Henry Holt.

Bruce, Gary. 2010. *The Firm: The Inside Story of the Stasi*. Oxford: Oxford University Press.

Burns, Danny. 1992. *Poll Tax Rebellion*. London: AK Press.

Burns, Jennifer. 2009. *Goddess of the Market: Ayn Rand and the American Right*. New York: Oxford University Press.

Burris, Val and Clifford L. Staples. 2012. "In Search of a Transnational Capitalist Class: Alternative Methods for Comparing Director Interlocks within and between Nations and Regions". *International Journal of Comparative Sociology*, 53 (4): 323–342.

Buttigieg, Pete. 2021. *Trust: America's Best Chance.* New York: Liveright.

Calhoun, Craig. 1994. *Neither Gods Nor Emperors: Students and the Struggle for Democracy in China.* Berkeley: University of California Press.

Callanan, Valerie J. 2012. "Media Consumption, Perceptions of Crime Risk and Fear of Crime: Examining Race/Ethnic Differences". *Sociological Perspectives*, 55 (1): 93–115.

Callero, Peter L. 2009. *The Myth of Individualism: How Social Forces Shape Our Lives.* Lanham, MD: Rowman & Littlefield.

Campbell, Travis. 2024. "Black Lives Matter's Effect on Police Lethal Use of Force". *Journal of Urban Economics*, 141: 103587.

Cao, Liqun, Yung-Lien Lai, and Ruohui Zhao. 2012. "Shades of Blue: Confidence in the Police in the World". *Journal of Criminal Justice*, 40: 40–49.

Carey, Matthew. 2017. *Mistrust: An Ethnographic Theory.* Chicago, IL: Hau Books.

Carter, Maria. 2018. "Has Goodwill Become Too Greedy? The Truth about What the Organization Does with Its $5.7 Billion in Revenue". *CountryLiving*, February 28. www.countryliving.com/shopping/a18198848/is-goodwill-a-nonprofit/

Case, Benjamin S. 2022. *Street Rebellion: Resistance beyond Violence and Nonviolence.* Chico, CA: AK Press.

Catterberg, Gabriella and Alejandro Moreno. 2006. "The Individual Bases of Political Trust: Trends in New and Established Democracies". *International Journal of Public Opinion Research*, 18 (1): 31–48.

Chayko, Mary. 2014. "Techno-Social Life: The Internet, Digital Technology, and Social Connectedness". *Sociology Compass*, 8 (7): 976–991.

Chermak, Steven, Matthew DeMichele, Jeff Gruenewald, Michael Jensen, Raven Lewis, and Basia E. Lopez. 2024. "What NIJ Research Tells Us about Domestic Terrorism". *National Institute of Justice Journal*, 285. https://nij.ojp.gov/topics/articles/what-nij-research-tells-us-about-domestic-terrorism

Chomsky, Aviva. 2007. *"They Take Our Jobs!" and 20 Other Myths about Immigration.* Boston, MA: Beacon.

Chomsky, Noam. 2015. *Propaganda and the Public Mind.* Chicago, IL: Haymarket.

Chomsky, Noam. 2017. *Requiem for the American Dream: The 10 Principles of Concentration of Wealth and Power.* New York: Seven Stories Press.

Churchill, Ward. 2005. *Since Predator Came: Notes from the Struggle for American Indian Liberation.* Oakland, CA: AK Press.

Churchill, Ward and Jim Vander Wall. 2002. *Agents of Repression: The FBI's Secret Wars against the Black Panther Party and the American Indian Movement*. Cambridge, MA: South End Press.

Climent, Salvador and Marta Coll-Florit. 2021. "All You Need Is Love: Metaphors of Love in 1946–2016 Billboard Year-End Number One Songs". *Text & Talk*, 41 (3): 469–491.

Coaffee, Jon. 2004. "Rings of Steel, Rights of Concrete and Rings of Confidence: Designing our Terrorism in Central London Pre and Post September 11th". *International Journal of Urban and Regional Research*, 28 (1): 201–211.

Cobb, Charles E. 2015. *This Nonviolent Stuff'll Get You Killed: How Guns Made the Civil Rights Movement Possible*. Durham, NC: Duke University Press.

Cobb-Reiley, Linda. 1988. "Aliens and Alien Ideas: The Suppression of Anarchists and the Anarchist Press in America, 1901–1914". *Journalism History*, 15 (2–3): 50–59.

Cockerham, William C. 2017. *Medical Sociology*. New York: Routledge.

Cohen, Jem. 1999. *Instrument*. Documentary. Washington, DC: Dischord Records.

Cohen, Stanley. 1988. *Against Criminology*. New Brunswick, NJ: Transaction Books.

Coleman, E. Gabriella. 2013. *Coding Freedom: The Ethics and Aesthetics of Hacking*. Princeton, NJ: Princeton University Press.

Coleman, James S. 1990. *Foundations of Social Theory*. Cambridge, MA: Belknap.

Collins, Randall. 2005. "The Durkheimian Movement in France and in World Sociology" (pp. 101–135) in *The Cambridge Companion to Durkheim*, edited by J. C. Alexander and P. Smith. Cambridge: Cambridge University Press.

Conrad, Peter. 2005. "The Shifting Engines of Medicalization". *Journal of Health and Social Behavior*, 46 (1): 3–14.

Conyers, James L. and Andrew P. Smallwood. 2008. *Malcolm X: A Historical Reader*. Durham, NC: Carolina Academic Press.

Cook, Karen S. 2015. "Institutions, Trust, and Social Order" (pp. 125–144) in *Order on the Edge of Chaos: Social Psychology and the Problem of Social Order*, edited by E. J. Lawler, S. R. Thye, and J. Yoon. Cambridge: Cambridge University Press.

Cook, Timothy E. and Paul Gronke. 2005. "The Skeptical American: Revisiting the Meanings of Trust in Government and Confidence in Institutions". *The Journal of Politics*, 67 (3): 784–803.

Cooper, David and Teresa Kroeger. 2017. "Employers Steal Billions from Workers' Paychecks Each Year". Economic Policy Institute, May 10.

www.epi.org/publication/employers-steal-billions-from-workers-paychecks-each-year/

Cortright, David. 2005. *Soldiers in Revolt: GI Resistance during the Vietnam War*. Chicago, IL: Haymarket.

Coser, Lewis. 1998. *The Functions of Social Conflict*. London: Routledge.

Coyle, Michael J. 2016. "Penal Abolition as the End of Criminal Behavior". *Journal of Social Justice*, 6: 1–23.

Creasap, Kimberly. 2021. "'Building Future Politics': Projectivity and Pre-figuration Politics in a Swedish Context". *Social Movement Studies*, 20 (5): 567–583.

Crepaz, Markus M. L., Karen Bodnaruk Jazayeri, and Jonathan Polk. 2017. "What's Trust Got to Do with It? The Effects of In-Group and Out-Group Trust on Conventional and Unconventional Political Partic-ipation". *Social Science Quarterly*, 98 (1): 261–281.

Crimethinc. 2017. *From Democracy to Freedom: The Difference between Government and Self-Determination*. Salem, MA: Crimethinc.

crow, scott. 2014. *Black Flags and Windmills: Hope, Anarchy, and the Common Ground Collective*. Oakland, CA: PM Press.

Cunningham, David. 2005. *There's Something Happening Here: The New Left, the Klan, and FBI Counterintelligence*. Berkeley: University of California Press.

Dahab, Ramsey and Marisa Omori. 2019. "Homegrown Foreigners: How Christian Nationalism and Nativist Attitudes Impact Muslim Civil Lib-erties". *Ethnic and Racial Studies*, 42 (10): 1727–1746.

Damico, Alfonso J., Margaret Conway, and Sandra Bowman Damico. 2000. "Patterns of Political Trust and Mistrust: Three Moments in the Lives of Democratic Citizens". *Polity*, 32 (3): 377–400.

Dangl, Benjamin. 2010. *Dancing with Dynamite: Social Movements and States in Latin America*. Oakland, CA: AK Press.

Dauvergne, Peter and Genevieve Lebaron. 2014. *Protest Inc.: The Corpora-tization of Activism*. Cambridge: Polity.

David, E. J. R. and Annie O. Derthick. 2014. "What Is Internalized Oppression, and So What?" (pp. 1–30) in *Internalized Oppression: The Psychology of Marginalized Group*, edited by E. J. R. David. New York: Springer.

Day, Helen Caldwell. 1954. *Not without Tears*. New York: Sheed & Ward.

Delgado, Richard and Jean Stefancic. 2017. *Critical Race Theory: An Intro-duction*. New York: New York University Press.

Delhey, Jan, Kenneth Newton, and Christian Welzel. 2011. "How General Is Trust in 'Most People'? Solving the Radius of Trust Problem". *American Sociological Review*, 76 (5): 786–807.

Delhey, Jan and Kenneth Newton. 2003. "Who Trusts? The Origins of Social Trust in Seven Societies". *European Societies*, 5 (2): 93–137.

Denton, Sally. 2012. *The Plots against the President: FDR, a Nation in Crisis, and the Rise of the American Right*. London: Bloomsbury.

Depetris-Chauvin, Emilio. 2015. "Fear of Obama: An Empirical Study of the Demand for Guns and the U.S. 2008 Presidential Election". *Journal of Public Economics*, 130: 66–79.

Desilver, Drew. 2021. "Turnout Soared in 2020 as Nearly Two-Thirds of Eligible U.S. Voters Cast Ballots for President". Pew Research Center, January 28. www.pewresearch.org/fact-tank/2021/01/28/turnout-soared-in-2020-as-nearly-two-thirds-of-eligible-u-s-voters-cast-ballots-for-president/

Dikaios, George and Vasiliki Tsagkroni. 2021. "Failing to Build a Network as Policy Entrepreneurs: Greek Politicians Negotiating with the EU During the First Quarter of SYRIZA in Government". *Contemporary Politics*, 27 (5): 611–630.

Dixon, Chris. 2014. *Another Politics: Talking across Today's Transformative Movements*. Berkeley: University of California Press.

Domhoff, G. William. 2014. *Who Rules America? The Triumph of the Corporate Rich*. New York: McGraw-Hill.

Dunbar-Ortiz, Roxanne. 2014. *An Indigenous Peoples' History of the United States*. Boston, MA: Beacon Press

Dunbar-Ortiz, Roxanne. 2018. *Loaded: A Disarming History of the Second Amendment*. San Francisco, CA: City Lights.

du Plessis, Christilene, My Hoang Bao Nguyen, Trevor A. Foulk, and Michael Schaerer. 2023. "Relative Power and Interpersonal Trust". *Journal of Personality and Social Psychology*, 124 (3): 567–592.

Durkheim, Émile. 1973. *Emile Durkheim on Morality and Society*. Chicago, IL: University of Chicago Press.

Durkheim, Émile. 1997. *The Division of Labor in Society*. New York, NY: Free Press.

Durkheim, Émile. [1912] 2001. *The Elementary Forms of the Religious Life*. Oxford: Oxford University Press.

Eckhardt, Wolfgang. 2016. *The First Socialist Schism: Bakunin vs. Marx in the International Working Men's Association*. Oakland, CA: PM Press.

Economakis, Evel. 2019. "How Syriza Lost the Left". *Dissent*, July 3. www.dissentmagazine.org/online_articles/how-syriza-lost-the-left-upcoming-greek-elections/

Efremenko, Dmitry and Yaroslava Evseeva. 2012. "Studies of Social Solidarity in Russia: Tradition and Modern Trends". *American Sociologist*, 43 (4): 349–365.

Ehrenreich, Barbara. 2006. *Dancing in the Streets: A History of Collective Joy*. New York: Metropolitan.

Ehrlich, Howard J. 1991. "Notes from an Anarchist Sociologist: May 1989" (pp. 233–248) in *Radical Sociologists and the Movement: Experiences, Lessons, and Legacies*, edited by M. Oppenheimer, M. J. Murray, and R. F. Levine. Philadelphia, PA: Temple University Press.

Eigenberg, Helen. 1989. "Male Rape: An Empirical Examination of Correctional Officers' Attitudes toward Rape in Prison". *The Prison Journal*, 69 (2): 39–56.

Eken, Bülent. 2014. "The Politics of the Gezi Park Resistance: Against Memory and Identity". *South Atlantic Quarterly*, 113 (2): 427–436.

Electronic Security Association. 2020. "About ESA". https://esaweb.org/about/

Ellingson, Ter. 2001. *The Myth of the Noble Savage*. Berkeley: University of California Press.

Emerson, Richard M. 1962. "Power-Dependence Relations". *American Sociological Review*, 27 (1): 31–41.

Engels, Friedrich. 1893. "Letter to Franz Mehring". www.marxists.org/archive/mehring/1893/histmat/app.htm

Estes, Nick. 2019. *Our History in the Future: Standing Rock versus the Dakota Access Pipeline and the Long Tradition of Indigenous Resistance*. London: Verso.

Evangelist, Michael. 2022. "Narrow Racial Differences in Trust: How Discrimination Shapes Trust in a Racialized Society". *Social Problems*, 69 (4): 1109–1136.

Evans, Danny. 2020. *Revolution and the State: Anarchism in the Spanish Civil War, 1936–1939*. Chico, CA: AK Press.

Firth, Rhiannon. 2022. *Disaster Anarchy: Mutual Aid and Radical Action*. London: Pluto Press.

Flaherty, Jordan. 2016. *No More Heroes: Grassroots Challenges to the Savior Mentality*. Chico, CA: AK Press.

Foner, Eric. 2015. *Gateway to Freedom: The Hidden History of the Underground Railroad*. New York: Norton.

Fortier, Craig. 2017. *Unsettling the Commons: Social Movements within, against, and beyond Settler Colonialism*. Winnipeg, Manitoba: Arbeiter Ring.

Foucault, Michel. 1995. *Discipline and Punish: The Birth of the Prison*. New York: Vintage.

Franks, Benjamin. 2018. "Prefiguration" (pp. 28–43) in *Anarchism: A Conceptual Approach*, edited by B. Franks, N. Jun, and L. Williams. New York: Routledge.

Freedman, Janet L. 2014. *Reclaiming the Feminist Vision: Consciousness-Raising and Small Group Practice*. Jefferson, NC: McFarland & Co.

Freeman, Daniel and Bao Shen Loe. 2023. "Explaining Paranoia: Cognitive and Social Processes in the Occurrence of Extreme Mistrust". *BMJ Mental Health*, 26 (1): 1–8.

Freitag, Markus and Marc Bühlmann. 2009. "Crafting Trust: The Role of Political Institutions in a Comparative Perspective". *Comparative Political Studies*, 42 (12): 1537–1566.

Fresia, Jerry. 1988. *Toward an American Revolution: Exposing the Constitution and Other Illusions*. Boston, MA: South End Press.

Fromm, Erich. 1956. *The Art of Loving*. New York: Harper & Brothers.

Fromm, Erich. 2011. *The Pathology of Normalcy*. New York: Lantern.

Fukuyama, Francis. 1995. *Trust: The Social Virtues and the Creation of Prosperity*. New York: Free Press.

Furness, Zach. 2010. *One Less Car: Bicycling and the Politics of Automobility*. Philadelphia, PA: Temple University Press.

Gamson, William A. 1971. "Political Trust and Its Ramifications" (pp. 41–55) in *Social Psychology and Political Behavior*, edited by G. Abcarian and J. W. Soule. Columbus, OH: Charles E. Merrill.

Ganguly, Meenakshi. 2023. "Discriminatory Policies Trigger Religious Violence in India". *Human Rights Watch*. www.hrw.org/news/2023/08/03/discriminatory-policies-trigger-religious-violence-india

Garcia, Manon. 2023. *We Are Not Born Submissive: How Patriarchy Shapes Women's Lives*. Princeton, NJ: Princeton University Press.

Garcia, Matthew. 2014. *From the Jaws of Victory: The Triumph and Tragedy of Cesar Chavez and the Farm Worker Movement*. Berkeley: University of California Press.

Garrison, Steve. 2024. "Haiti Earthquake Victims, Donors Claim Red Cross Used Earthquake Donations for Personal Use". *Courthouse News Service*, November 25. www.courthousenews.com/haiti-earthquake-victims-donors-claim-red-cross-used-earthquake-donations-for-personal-use/

Gärtner, Svenja and Svante Prado. 2016. "Unlocking the Social Trap: Inequality, Trust and the Scandinavian Welfare State". *Social Science History*, 40 (1): 33–62.

Gatto, Juliette and Michaël Dambrun. 2012. "Authoritarianism, Social Dominance, and Prejudice Among Junior Police Officers: The Role of the Normative Context". *Social Psychology*, 43 (2): 61–66.

Gatto, Juliette, Michaël Dambrun, Christian Kerbrat, and Pierre De Oliveria. 2010. "Prejudice in the Police: On the Processes Underlying the Effects of Selection and Group Socialisation". *European Journal of Social Psychology*, 40 (2): 252–269.

Gauchat, Gordon. 2012. "Politicization of Science in the Public Sphere: A Study of Public Trust in the United States, 1974–2010". *American Sociological Review*, 77 (2): 167–187.

Gavin, Amelia R., Nancy Grote, Kyaien O. Conner, and Taurmini Fentress. 2011. "Racial Discrimination and Preterm Birth among African American Women: The Important Role of Posttraumatic Stress Disorder". *Journal of Health Disparities Research and Practice*, 11 (4): 91–109.

Gerth, Hans and C. Wright Mills. 1946. *From Max Weber: Essays in Sociology*. New York: University of Oxford Press.

Gianfredi, Vincenza, Francesco Mazziotta, Giovanna Clerici, Elisa Astorri, Francesco Oliani, Martina Cappellina, Alessandro Catalini, Bernardo Maria Dell'Osso, Fabrizio Ernesto Pregliasco, Silvana Castaldi, and Beatrice Benatti. 2024. "Climate Change Perception and Mental Health: Results from a Systematic Review of the Literature". *European Journal of Investigation in Health, Psychology, & Education*, 14 (1): 215–229.

Giddens, Anthony. 1990. *The Consequences of Modernity*. Cambridge: Polity.

Gilens, Martin. 1999. *Why Americans Hate Welfare: Race, Media, and the Politics of Antipoverty Policy*. Chicago, IL: University of Chicago Press.

Gilens, Martin and Benjamin I. Page. 2014. "Testing Theories of American Politics: Elites, Interest Groups and Average Citizens". *Perspectives on Politics*, 12 (3): 564–581.

Gilman-Opalsky, Richard. 2020. *The Communism of Love: An Inquiry into the Poverty of Exchange Value*. Chico, CA: AK Press.

Girdiharadas, Anand. 2018. *Winners Take All: The Elite Charade of Changing the World*. New York: Alfred A. Knopf.

Glassner, Barry. 1999. *The Culture of Fear: Why Americans Are Afraid of the Wrong Things*. New York, NY: Basic.

Glick, Ted. 2020. *Burglar for Peace: Lessons Learned in the Catholic Left's Resistance to the Vietnam War*. Oakland, CA: PM Press.

Goldfield, Michael. 1989. *The Decline of Organized Labor in the United States*. Chicago, IL: University of Chicago Press.

Gordon, Uri. 2007. *Anarchy Alive! Anti-Authoritarian Politics from Practice to Theory*. London: Pluto.

Gordon, Uri and Ohal Grietzer. 2013. *Anarchists against the Wall*. Chico, CA: AK Press.

Gould, Stephen J. 1988. "Kropotkin Was No Crackpot". *Natural History*, 97 (7): 12–21.

Graeber, David. 2006. "A Conversation with Anarchist David Graeber". www.youtube.com/watch?v=PVDkkOAOtVo

Graeber, David. 2011. *Debt: The First 5000 Years*. New York: Melville.

Graeber, David. 2015. *Utopia of Rules: On Technology, Stupidity, and the Secret Joys of Bureaucracy*. New York: Melville.

Graeber, David. 2018. *Bullshit Jobs: A Theory*. New York: Simon & Schuster.

Graham, Robert. 2015. *We Don't Fear Anarchy—We Invoke It: The First International and the Origins of the Anarchist Movement*. Oakland, CA: AK Press.

Gramsci, Antonio. 1971. *Selections from the Prison Notebooks of Antonio Gramsci*. New York: International Publishers.

Greenberg, Edward S. 1986. *Workplace Democracy: The Political Effects of Participation*. Ithaca: Cornell University Press.

Greenfield, Kent. 2011. *The Myth of Choice: Personal Responsibility in a World of Limits*. New Haven, CT: Yale University Press.

Greenwald, Glenn. 2014. *No Place to Hide: Edward Snowden, the NSA, and the US Surveillance State*. New York: Metropolitan.

Grenier, John. 2005. *The First Way of War: American War Making on the Frontier, 1607–1814*. Cambridge: Cambridge University Press.

Guerrero, Praxedis G. 2018. *I Am Action: Literary and Combat Articles, Thoughts, and Revolutionary Chronicles*. Chico, CA: AK Press.

Guglielmo, Jennifer and Salvatore Salerno. 2003. *Are Italians White: How Race Is Made in America*. New York: Routledge.

Guillamón, Agustín. 2014. *Ready for Revolution: The CNT Defense Committees in Barcelona, 1933–1938*. Oakland, CA: AK Press.

Guillamón, Agustín. 2020. *Insurrection: The Bloody Events of May 1937 in Barcelona*. Chico, CA: AK Press.

Guo, Qingke, Wang Zheng, Jinkun Shen, Taian Huang, and Kuanbin Ma. 2022. "Social Trust More Strongly Associated with Well-Being in Individualistic Societies". *Personality and Individual Differences*, 188: 1–8.

Haas, David F. and Forrest A. Deseran. 1981. "Trust and Symbolic Exchange". *Social Psychology Quarterly*, 44 (1): 3–13.

Hager, Anselm. 2022. "Protestant Missionaries Are Associated with Reduced Community Cohesion". *Sociology of Religion*, 83 (2): 252–279.

Haines, Herbert H. 1984. "Black Radicalization and the Funding of Civil Rights: 1957–1970". *Social Problems*, 32 (1): 31–43.

Haines, Valerie A. 1991. "Spencer, Darwin, and the Question of Reciprocal Influence". *Journal of the History of Biology*, 24 (3): 409–431.

Haley, Hillary and Jim Sidanius. 2005. "Person-Organization Congruence and the Maintenance of Group-Based Social Hierarchy: A Social Dominance Perspective". *Group Processes & Intergroup Relations*, 8 (2): 185–203.

Hämäläinen, Pekka. 2023. *Indigenous Continent: The Epic Contest for North America*. New York: Liveright.

Hamamura, Takeshi, Liman Man Wai Li, and Derwin Chan. 2017. "The Association between Generalized Trust and Physical and Psychological Health across Societies". *Social Indicators Research*, 134: 277–286.

Hardin, Russell. 2002. *Trust and Trustworthiness*. New York: Russell Sage Foundation.

Hari, Johann. 2015. *Chasing the Scream: The First and Last Days of the War on Drugs*. New York: Bloomsbury.

Hari, Johann. 2018. *Lost Connections: Uncovering the Real Causes of Depression—and the Unexpected Solutions*. New York: Bloomsbury.

Harrell, Erika. 2012. "Violent Victimization Committed by Strangers, 1993–2010". Washington, DC: US Department of Justice. Special Report #NCJ-239424.

Herman, Edward S. and Noam Chomsky. 1988. *Manufacturing Consent: The Political Economy of the Mass Media*. New York: Pantheon.

Hern, Alex. 2024. "Twitter Usage in US 'Fallen by a Fifth' since Elon Musk's Takeover". *The Guardian*, March 26. www.theguardian.com/technology/2024/mar/26/twitter-usage-in-us-fallen-by-a-fifth-since-elon-musks-takeover

Hertel, Florian R. and Olaf Groh-Samberg. 2019. "The Relation between Inequality and Intergenerational Class Mobility in 39 Countries". *American Sociological Review*, 84 (6): 1099–1133.

Hessick, Carissa Byrne. 2007. "Violence between Lovers, Strangers, and Friends". *Washington University Law Review*, 85 (2): 343–407.

Hicks, Brian M., Catherine Vitro, Elizabeth Johnson, Carter Sherman, Mary M. Heitzeg, C. Emily Durbin, and Edelyn Verona. 2023. "Who Bought a Gun during the COVID-19 Pandemic in the United States? Associations with QAnon Beliefs, Right-Wing Political Attitudes, Intimate Partner Violence, Antisocial Behavior, Suicidality, and Mental Health and Substance Use Problems". *PLOS One*, 18 (8): e0290770.

Hochschild, Arlie Russell. 1989. *The Second Shift: Working Parents and the Revolution at Home*. New York: Viking.

Holguin, Jamie. 2002. "Red Faces at the Red Cross". CBS News. www.cbsnews.com/news/red-faces-at-the-red-cross/

Holtzman, Linda and Leon Sharpe. 2014. *Media Message: What Film, Television, and Popular Music Teach Us about Race, Class, Gender, and Sexual Orientation*, 2nd ed. New York: Routledge.

Hong, Nathaniel. 1992. "Constructing the Anarchist Beast in American Periodical Literature, 1880–1903". *Critical Studies in Mass Communication*, 9 (1): 110–130.

Hooghe, Marc and Sofie Marien. 2013. "A Comparative of the Relation between Political Trust and Forms of Political Participation in Europe". *European Societies*, 15 (1): 131–152.

hooks, bell. 2000a. *Feminism Is for Everybody: Passionate Politics*. Boston, MA: South End Press.

hooks, bell. 2000b. *All about Love: New Visions*. New York: Harper.

Horne, Gerald. 2016. *The Counter-Revolution of 1776: Slave Resistance and the Origins of the United States of America*. New York: New York University Press.

Horrox, James. 2009. *A Living Revolution: Anarchism in the Kibbutz Movement*. Oakland, CA: AK Press.

Hunt-Hendrix, Leah and Astra Taylor. 2024. *Solidarity: The Past, Present, and Future of a World-Changing Idea*. New York: Pantheon.

Immerwahr, Daniel. 2019. *How to Hide an Empire: A Short History of the Greater United States*. New York: Farrar, Straus and Giroux.

Irwin, Kyle and Nick Berigan. 2013. "Trust, Culture, and Cooperation: A Social Dilemma Analysis of Pro-Environmental Behaviors". *The Sociological Quarterly*, 54: 424–449.

Isaac, Jeffrey C. 2001. "Thinking about the Antisweatshop Movement: A Proposal for Modesty". *Dissent*, 48 (4): 100–108.

Ishiyama, John and Anna Pechenina. 2016. "Colored Revolutions, Interpersonal Trust, and Confidence in Institutions: The Consequences of Mass Uprisings". *Social Science Quarterly*, 97 (3): 748–770.

Jacobs, Ron. 2012. "From Oscar Grant to Barack Obama" (pp. 29–30) in *Hopeless: Barack Obama and the Politics of Illusion*, edited by J. St. Clair and J. Frank. Oakland, CA: AK Press.

James, C. L. R. 1956. "Every Cook Can Govern: A Study of Democracy in Ancient Greece, Its Meaning for Today". *Correspondence*, 2 (12).

Jamil, Cayce. 2023. "Cohesion and Solidarity in Consistent and Inconsistent Status Structures". *Advances in Group Processes*, 40: 161–184.

Janssen, Heleen J., Dietrich Oberwittler, and Goeran Koeber. 2021. "Victimization and Its Consequences for Well-Being: A Between- and Within-Person Analysis". *Journal of Quantitative Criminology*, 37: 101–140.

Jiobu, Robert M. and Timothy J. Curry. 2001. "Lack of Confidence in the Federal Government and the Ownership of Firearms". *Social Science Quarterly*, 82 (1): 77–88.

Jones, Bryn and Mike O'Donnell. 2010. *Sixties Radicalism and Social Movement Activism: Retreat or Resurgence?* London: Anthem Press.

Jones, Stephen H. and Amy Unsworth. 2024. "Two Islamophobias? Racism and Religion as Distinct but Mutually Supportive Dimensions of Anti-Muslim Prejudice". *British Journal of Sociology*, 75 (1): 5–22.

Kääriäinen, Juha and Reino Sirén. 2012. "Do the Police Trust in Citizens? European Comparisons". *European Journal of Criminology*, 9 (3): 276–289.

Kaase, Max. 1999. "Interpersonal Trust, Political Trust and Non-institutionalised Political Participation in Western Europe". *West European Politics*, 22 (3): 1–21.

Katsiaficas, George. 2013. *Asia's Unknown Uprisings, Volume 2: People Power in the Philippines, Burma, Tibet, China, Taiwan, Bangladesh, Nepal, Thailand, and Indonesia, 1947—2009*. Oakland, CA: PM Press.

Katsiaficas, George. 2018. *The Global Imagination of 1968: Revolution and Counterrevolution*. Oakland, CA: PM Press.

Kaufman Peter. 2003. "Learning to *Not* Labor: How Working-Class Individuals Construct Middle-Class Identities". *Sociological Quarterly*, 44 (3): 481–504.

Keefer, Phillip and Carlos Scartascini. 2022. *Trust: The Key to Social Cohesion and Growth in Latin America and the Caribbean*. Washington, DC: Inter-American Development Bank. https://publications.iadb.org/en/trust-key-social-cohesion-and-growth-latin-america-and-caribbean-executive-summary

Keele, Luke. 2007. "Social Capital and the Dynamics of Trust in Government". *American Journal of Political Science*, 51 (2): 241–254.

Kennedy, Liam. 2020. "Postwar Interpersonal Violence: Reflections and New Research Directions". *Aggression and Violent Behavior*, 53: 101429.

Khodyakov, Dmitry M. 2007. "The Complexity of Trust-Control Relationships in Creative Organizations: Insights from a Qualitative Analysis of a Conductorless Orchestra". *Social Forces*, 86 (1): 1–22.

Kim, Ji-Young. 2005. "'Bowling Together' Isn't a Cure-All: The Relationship between Social Capital and Political Trust in South Korea". *International Political Science Review*, 26 (2): 193–213.

Kinna, Ruth. 1995. "Kropotkin's Theory of Mutual Aid in Historic Context". *International Review of Social History*, 40 (2): 259–283.

Kip, Markus. 2016. "Solidarity" (pp. 391–398) in *Keywords for Radicals: The Contested Vocabulary of Late-Capitalist Struggle*, edited by K. Fritsch, C. O'Connor, and A. K. Thompson. Chico, CA: AK Press.

Kizito, Kalemba. 2017. "Bequeathed Legacies: Colonialism and State Led Homophobia in Uganda". *Surveillance and Society*, 15 (3/4): 567–572.

Klein, Naomi. 2007. *The Shock Doctrine: The Rise of Disaster Capitalism*. New York: Metropolitan.

Klein, Naomi. 2023. *Doppelganger: A Trip into the Mirror World*. New York: Farrar, Straus & Giroux.

Knapp, Michael, Anja Flach, and Ercan Ayboga. 2016. *Revolution in Rojava: Democratic Autonomy and Women's Liberation in Syrian Kurdistan*. London: Pluto Press.

Kohn, Marek. 2008. *Trust: Self-Interest and the Common Good*. Oxford: Oxford University Press.

Krastev, Ivan. 2013. *In Mistrust We Trust: Can Democracy Survive When We Don't Trust Our Leaders?* TED Talk.

Kropotkin, Peter. [1902] 2006. *Mutual Aid: A Factor in Evolution.* Mineola, NY: Dover.

Kunstler, James Howard. 1993. *The Geography of Nowhere: The Rise and Decline of America's Man-Made Landscape.* New York: Touchstone.

Ladhani, Noorin. 2011. "Egypt: First Cut Off the Internet!" *Social Policy*, 41 (1): 54–54.

Lalich, Janja A. 2004. *Bounded Choice: True Believers and Charismatic Cults.* Berkeley: University of California Press.

Lampe, David. 2014. *Hitler's Savage Canary: A History of the Danish Resistance in World War II.* London: Frontline.

Landry, Alexander P., Ram I. Orr, and Kayla Mere. 2022. "Dehumanization and Mass Violence: A Study of Mental State Language in Nazi Propaganda (1927–1945)". *PLOS One*, November 9.

Laursen, Eric. 2012. *The People's Pension: The Struggle to Defend Social Security since Reagan.* Oakland, CA: AK Press.

Lavin, Talia. 2021. *Culture Warlords: My Journey into the Dark Web of White Supremacy.* New York: Legacy Lit.

LeBon, Gustave. [1895] 1925. *The Crowd: A Study of the Popular Mind.* New York: Macmillan.

Lee, Matthew T. and Ramiro Martinez. 2009. "Immigration Reduces Crime: An Emerging Consensus" (pp. 3–16) in *Immigration, Crime and Justice*, edited by W. F. McDonald. London: Emerald Publishing.

Leier, Mark. 2006. *Bakunin: The Creative Passion.* New York: Thomas Dunne.

Lenard, Patti Tamara. 2008. "Trust Your Compatriots, but Count Your Change: The Roles of Trust, Mistrust and Distrust in Democracy". *Political Studies*, 56: 312–332.

Lerner, Gerda. 1986. *The Creation of Patriarchy.* New York: Oxford University Press.

Leval, Gaston. 2018. *Collectives in the Spanish Revolution.* Oakland, CA: PM Press.

Levine, Bruce. 2012. "Why Anti-Authoritarians Are Diagnosed as Mentally Ill". *Slingshot*, 110, Spring.

Levine, Bruce. 2018. *Resisting Illegitimate Authority: A Thinking Person's Guide to Being an Anti-Authoritarian—Strategies, Tools, and Models.* Chico, CA: AK Press.

Lewis, Avi and Naomi Klein. 2004. *The Take.* Documentary film. New York: First Run Films.

Light, Ryan. 2015. "Like Strangers We Trust: Identity and Generic Affiliation Networks". *Social Science Research*, 51: 132–144.

Lilley, Sasha, David McNally, Eddie Yuen, and James Davis. 2012. *Catastrophism: The Apocalyptic Politics of Collapse and Rebirth*. Oakland, CA: PM Press.

Lindenberg, Siegwart. 2000. "It Takes Both Trust and Lack of Mistrust: The Workings of Cooperation and Relational Signaling in Contractual Relationships". *Journal of Management and Governance*, 4: 11–33.

Lipka, Michael and Jessica Martínez. 2014. "So, You Married an Atheist…". Pew Research Center. www.pewresearch.org/short-reads/2014/06/16/so-you-married-an-atheist/

Lipsitz, George. 1994. *Rainbow at Midnight: Labor and Culture in the 1940s*. Urbana, IL: University of Illinois Press.

Liu, Elliott. 2016. *Maoism and the Chinese Revolution: A Critical Introduction*. Oakland, CA: PM Press.

Locke, John. [1689] 1988. *Two Treatises of Government*. Cambridge: Cambridge University Press.

Lofland, John. 1988. "My Turn: Interaction as Anarchism". *SSSI Notes*, 14 (3): 5–6.

Logan, John. 2002. "Consultants, Lawyers, and the 'Union Free' Movement in the USA since the 1970s". *Industrial Relations Journal*, 33 (3): 197–214.

Lorber, Judith. 2005. *Breaking the Bowls: Degendering and Feminist Change*. New York: W. W. Norton.

Lowry, Dennis T. Tarn Ching Josephine Nio, and Dennis W. Leitner. 2003. "Setting the Public Fear Agenda: A Longitudinal Analysis of Network TV Crime Reporting, Public Perceptions of Crime, and FBI Crime Statistics". *Journal of Communication*, 53 (1): 61–73.

Luft, Rachel E. 2008. "Looking for Common Ground: Relief Work in Post-Katrina New Orleans as an American Parable of Race and Gender Violence". *NWSA Journal*, 20 (3): 5–31.

Luhmann, Niklas. 1979. *Trust and Power*. New York: John Wiley & Sons.

Lynd, Staughton. 1967. *Class Conflict, Slavery, and the United States Constitution: Ten Essays*. Indianapolis, IN: Bobbs-Merrill.

Marable, Manning. 1983. *How Capitalism Underdeveloped Black America*. Boston, MA: South End Press.

Marcuse, Herbert. 2002. *One-Dimensional Man: Studies in the Ideology of Advanced Industrial Society*. New York: Routledge.

Mariette, Maëlle. 2022. "Spain, the Party That Tried to Please Everyone: Podemos and the Limits of Change". *Le Monde Diplomatique*, January. https://mondediplo.com/2022/01/02podemos

Martin, Brian. 1993. *Social Defence, Social Change*. London: Freedom Press.

Martin, Brian. 1996. "Democracy without Elections" (pp. 123–136) in *Reinventing Anarchy, Again*, edited by H. Ehrlich. Edinburgh: AK Press.

Martin, Brian. 1998. *Information Liberation*. London: Freedom Press.

Martin, Brian. 2008. "Expertise and Equality". *Social Anarchism*, 42: 10–20.

Marya, Rupa and Raj Patel. 2021. *Inflamed: Deep Medicine and the Anatomy of Injustice*. New York: Farrar, Straus & Giroux.

Mascarenas, Paul and Alejandra Valles. 2019. "American Red Cross and the World Trade Center". *Journal of Nonprofit Education & Leadership*, 9 (4): 360–377.

Massey, Douglas S. and Nancy A. Denton. 1988. "The Dimensions of Racial Segregation". *Social Forces*, 67 (2): 281–315.

Mastodon. 2024. "Mastodon Server Covenant". https://joinmastodon.org/covenant

Maté, Gabor. 2013. *In the Realm of Hungry Ghosts: Close Encountered with Addiction*. Mississauga, Ontario: Vintage Canada.

McKay, Iain. 2019. "Propertarianism and Fascism". *Anarcho-Syndicalist Review*, 75: 25–30.

McKay, Lawrence, Will Jennings, and Gerry Stoker. 2023. "What Is the Geography of Trust: The Urban-Rural Gap in Global Perspective". *Political Geography*, 102 (102863): 1–11.

Medsger, Betty. 2014. *The Burglary: The Discover of J. Edgar Hoover's Secret F.B.I.* New York: Alfred A. Knopf.

Medwinter, Sancha Doxilly. 2021. "Reproducing Poverty and Inequality in Disaster: Race, Class, Social Capital, NGOs, and Urban Space in New York City after Superstorm Sandy". *Environmental Sociology*, 7 (1): 1–11.

Merlan, Anna. 2019. *Republic of Lies: American Conspiracy Theorists and Their Surprising Rise to Power*. New York: Metropolitan Books.

Merriman, John. 2014. *Massacre: The Life and Death of the Paris Commune*. New York: Basic.

Messner, Michael A., Max A. Greenberg, and Tal Peretz. 2015. *Some Men: Feminist Allies and the Movement to End Violence against Women*. New York: Oxford University Press.

Mills, C. Wright. 1959. *The Sociological Imagination*. Oxford: Oxford University Press.

Milstein, Cindy. 2014. "Solidarity, as Weapon and Practice, versus Killer Cops and White Supremacy". https://cbmilstein.wordpress.com/2014/12/11/solidarity-as-weapon-and-practice-versus-killer-cops-and-white-supremacy/

Milstein, Cindy. 2015. *Taking Sides: Revolutionary Solidarity and the Poverty of Liberalism*. Oakland, CA: AK Press.

Mintz, Frank. 2013. *Anarchism and Workers' Self-Management in Revolutionary Spain*. Oakland, CA: AK Press.

Mohamed, Besheer. 2016. "A New Estimate of the U.S. Muslim Population". Washington, DC: Pew Research Center. www.pewresearch.org/fact-tank/2016/01/06/a-new-estimate-of-the-u-s-muslim-population/

Mohamed, Besheer. 2021. "Muslims Are a Growing Presence in U.S., But Still Face Negative Views from the Public". Washington, DC: Pew Research Center. www.pewresearch.org/short-reads/2021/09/01/muslims-are-a-growing-presence-in-u-s-but-still-face-negative-views-from-the-public/

Montgomery, Nick and carla bergman. 2017. *Joyful Militancy: Building Thriving Resistance in Toxic Times*. Chico, CA: AK Press.

Moody, Kim. 1988. *An Injury to All: The Decline of American Unionism*. London: Verso.

Morris, Brian. 2018. *Kropotkin: The Politics of Community*. Oakland, CA: PM Press.

Muirhead, Russell and Nancy L. Rosenblum. 2019. *A Lot of People Are Saying: The New Conspiracism and the Assault on Democracy*. Princeton, NJ: Princeton University Press.

Mullin, Gerald W. 1972. *Flight and Rebellion: Slave Resistance in Eighteenth-Century Virginia*. London: Oxford University Press.

Mumm, James. 2002. "Active Revolution: Organizing, Base Building, and Dual Power". https://theanarchistlibrary.org/library/james-mumm-active-revolution

Natapoff, Alexandra. 2009. *Snitching: Criminal Informants and the Erosion of American Justice*. New York: New York University Press.

Newburn, Tim, Rachel Deacon, Beka Diski, Kerris Cooper, Maggie Grant, and Alex Burch. 2018. "'The Best Three Days of My Life': Pleasure, Power and Alienation in the 2011 Riots". *Crime, Media, Culture: An International Journal*, 14 (1): 41–59.

O'Connor, Brendon. 2002. "Policies, Principles, and Polls: Bill Clinton's Third Way Welfare Politics, 1992–1996". *Australian Journal of Politics and History*, 48 (3): 396–411.

Offe, Claus. 1999. "How Can We Trust Our Fellow Citizens" (pp. 42–87) in *Democracy and Trust*, edited by M. E. Warren. Cambridge: Cambridge University Press.

Ogo, Drica Dejerk G. 2008. "Soma: An Anarchist Play Therapy". *Anarchy: A Journal of Desire Armed*, 66. https://theanarchistlibrary.org/library/ajoda-soma

Oliver, J. Eric and Thomas J. Wood. 2014. "Conspiracy Theories and the Paranoid Style(s) of Mass Opinion". *American Journal of Political Science*, 58 (4): 952–966.

Olson, Joel. 2004. *The Abolition of White Democracy*. Minneapolis: University of Minnesota Press.

Olson, Mancur. 1965. *The Logic of Collective Action: Public Goods and the Theory of Groups*. Cambridge, MA: Harvard University Press.

Omi, Michael and Howard Winant. 1986. *Racial Formation in the United States: From the 1960s to the 1980s*. New York: Routledge & Kegan Paul.

O'Rourke, Lindsey A. 2018. *Covert Regime Change: America's Secret Cold War*. Ithaca, NY: Cornell University Press.

Orwell, George. 1949. *Nineteen Eighty-Four*. New York: Harcourt, Brace, and Co.

Orwell, George. 1952. *Homage to Catalonia*. San Diego, CA: Harcourt Brace Jovanovich.

Ostrom, Elinor. 1990. *Governing the Commons: The Evolution of Institutions for Collective Action*. Cambridge: Cambridge University Press.

Osuna, José Javier Olivas, Max Kiefel, and Kira Gartzou Katsouyanni. 2021. "Place Matters: Analyzing the Roots of Political Distrust and Brexit Narratives at a Local Level". *Governance*, 34: 1019–1038.

Osuna, Steven. 2020. "Transnational Moral Panic: Neoliberalism and the Spectre of MS-13". *Race & Class*, 61 (4): 3–28.

Ovetz, Robert. 2022. *We the Elites: Why the U.S. Constitution Serves the Few*. London: Pluto.

Oxford English Dictionary. 2017. *Oxford English Dictionary Online*. Oxford: Oxford University Press.

Pager, Devah and Lincoln Quillian. 2005. "Walking the Talk? What Employers Say versus What They Do". *American Sociological Review*, 70 (3): 355–380.

Paley, Dawn. 2014. *Drug War Capitalism*. Oakland, CA: AK Press.

Palmer, Bryan D. 2000. *Cultures of Darkness: Night Travels in the Histories of Transgression*. New York: Monthly Review Press.

Parenti, Christian. 2000. *Lockdown America: Police and Prisons in the Age of Crisis*. London: Verso.

Parker, Suzanne L. 1995. "Toward an Understanding of Rally Effects". *Public Opinion Quarterly*, 59: 526–546.

Passett, Alex. 2023. "20% of American Households Now Have a Smart Video Doorbell". *IoT Evolution*. www.iotevolutionworld.com/smart-home/articles/457278-20-american-households-now-have-smart-video-doorbell.htm

Patel, Raj. 2010. *The Value of Nothing: How to Reshape Market Society and Redefine Democracy*. New York: Picador.

Paxton, Pamela. 2007. "Association Membership and Generalized Trust: A Multilevel Model across 31 Countries". *Social Forces*, 86 (1): 47–76.

Paz, Abel. 2011. *The Story of the Iron Column: Militant Anarchism in the Spanish Civil War*. Oakland, CA: AK Press.

Peng, Lü. 2013. "Political Confidence in the New Emerging Economies: A Comparative Analysis of the BRICS Countries". *Fugan Journal of the Humanities and Social Sciences*, 6 (2): 56–86.

Perry, Gina, Augustine Brannigan, Richard A. Wanner, and Henderikus Stam. 2020. "Credibility and Incredulity in Milgram's Obedience Experiments: A Reanalysis of an Unpublished Test". *Social Psychology Quarterly*, 83 (1): 88–106.

Pestana, Carla Gardina. 2013. "The Missionary Impulse in the Atlantic World, 1500–1800: Or How Protestants Learned to Be Missionaries". *Social Sciences & Missions*, 26 (1): 9–39.

Pettigrew, Thomas F. and Linda R. Tropp. 2006. "A Meta-Analytic Test of Intergroup Contact Theory". *Journal of Personality & Social Psychology*, 90 (5): 751–783.

Piven, Frances Fox. 2006. *Challenging Authority: How Ordinary People Change America*. Lanham, MD: Rowman & Littlefield.

Piven, Frances Fox and Richard A. Cloward. 1979. *Poor People's Movements: How They Succeed, How They Fail*. New York: Vintage.

Polletta, Francesca. 2002. *Freedom Is an Endless Meeting: Democracy in American Social Movements*. Chicago, IL: University of Chicago Press.

Poloma, Margaret M. and Ralph W. Hood. 2008. *Blood and Fire: Godly Love in a Pentecostal Emerging Church*. New York: New York University Press.

Polychroniou, C. J. 2016. "Syriza's Betrayal and the Selling of a Nation". *Al Jazeera*, June 7. www.aljazeera.com/opinions/2016/6/7/syrizas-betrayal-and-the-selling-of-a-nation

Portes, Alejandro and Min Zhou. 1993. "The New Second Generation: Segmented Assimilation and Its Variants". *Annals of the American Academy of Political and Social Sciences*, 530: 74–96.

Potiker, Spencer Louis, Dana M. Williams, and Jake Alimahomed-Wilson. 2022. "Anarchist and Anarchistic Anti-Systemic Movements in World-Systems Perspective: A Qualitative Comparative Analysis of Non-State Spaces". *Journal of World-Systems Research*, 28 (2): 188–218.

Potter, Will. 2011. *Green Is the New Red: An Insider's Account of a Social Movement under Siege*. San Francisco, CA: City Lights.

Power, Timothy J. and Diselle D. Jamison. 2005. "Political Mistrust in Latin America". *Comparative Sociology*, 4 (1–2): 55–80.

Price, David H. 2011. *Weaponizing Anthropology: Social Science in Service of the Militarized State*. Petrolia, CA: CounterPunch.

ProPublica. 2024. "Goodwill Industries International, Inc." https://projects.propublica.org/nonprofits/organizations/530196517

Purkis, Jonathan. 2022. *Driving with Strangers: What Hitchhiking Tells Us about Humanity*. Manchester: Manchester University Press.

Putnam, Robert D. 2000. *Bowling Alone: The Collapse and Revival of American Community*. New York: Simon & Schuster.

Quillian, Lincoln. 2006. "New Approaches to Understanding Racial Prejudice and Discrimination". *Annual Review of Sociology*, 32 (1): 299–328.

Rameau, Max. 2013. *Take Back the Land: Land, Gentrification and the Umoja Village Shantytown*. Oakland, CA: AK Press.

Rand, Ayn. 1992. *Atlas Shrugged*. New York: Plume.

Ratner, Carl. 2018. "Overcoming Pathological Normalcy: Mental Health Challenges in the Coming Transformation" (pp. 210–223) in *Health Care under the Knife: Moving beyond Capitalism for Our Health*, edited by H. Waitzkin. New York: Monthly Review Press.

Ratner, Margaret and Michael Ratner. 2000. "The Grand Jury: A Tool to Repress and Jail Activists" (pp. 277–286) in *States of Confinement: Policing, Detention, and Prisons*, edited by J. James. New York: St. Martin's Press.

Raudenbush, Danielle. 2016. "'I Stay by Myself': Social Support, Distrust, and Selective Solidarity among the Urban Poor". *Sociological Forum*, 31 (4): 1018–1039.

Raventós, Daniel and Julie Wark. 2018. *Against Charity*. Petrolia, CA: CounterPunch.

Reich, Gary and Jay Barth. 2017. "Planting in Fertile Soil: The National Rifle Association and State Firearm Legislation". *Social Science Quarterly*, 98 (2): 485–499.

Reichel, Philip L. 1975. "Classroom Uses of a Criminal Activities Checklist". *Teaching Sociology*, 3 (1): 81–86.

Reicher, Stephen. 2002. "The Psychology of Crowd Dynamics" (pp. 182–208) in *Blackwell Handbook of Social Psychology Group Processes*, edited by M. A. Hogg and S. Tindale. John Wiley & Sons.

Richards, Vernon. 2019. *Lessons of the Spanish Revolution, 1936–1939*. Oakland, CA: PM Press.

Rinaldi, Matthew and Keating, Kevin. 2004. *The Olive-Drab Rebels: Military Organizing During the Vietnam Era and Harass the Brass: Some Notes toward the Subversion of US Armed Forces*. Baltimore, MD: Firestarter Press.

Robbins, Blaine G. 2011. "Neither Government Nor Community Alone: A Test of State-Centered Models of Generalized Trust". *Rationality & Society*, 23 (3): 304–346.

Robinson, Adam. 2021. "Chico Teen Charged with Murder, Assault after Shooting Two Homeless Men Earlier This Month". KRCR. https://krcrtv.com/news/local/chico-teen-charged-with-murder-assault-after-shooting-two-homeless-men-earlier-this-month

Robinson, Adam. 2022. "Judge Dismisses Charges against Teen for 2021 Fatal Shooting at Teichert Ponds". KRCR. https://krcrtv.com/news/local/judge-dismisses-charges-against-teen-for-2021-fatal-shooting-at-teichert-ponds

Rodríguez, Dylan. 2007. "The Political Logic of the Non-Profit Industrial Complex" (pp. 21–40) in *The Revolution Will Not Be Funded: Beyond the Non-profit Industrial Complex*, edited by INCITE! Women of Color against Violence. Cambridge, MA: South End Press.

Rodriguez, S. M. 2017. "Homophobic Nationalism: The Development of Sodomy Legislation in Uganda". *Comparative Sociology*, 16 (3): 393–421.

Roediger, David R. 2005. *Working toward Whiteness: How America's Immigrants Became White*. New York: Basic Books.

Romer, Daniel, Kathleen Hall Jamieson, and Sean Aday. 2003. "Television News and the Cultivation of Fear of Crime". *Journal of Communication*, 53 (1): 88–104.

Rose City Copwatch. 2008. *Alternatives to the Police*. Portland, OR: Rose City Copwatch.

Rosenthal, Naomi Braun. 1984. "Consciousness Raising: From Revolution to Re-Evaluation". *Psychology of Women Quarterly*, 8 (4): 309–326.

Ross, Clifton. 2016. *Home From the Dark Side of Utopia: A Journey through American Revolutions*. Chico, CA: AK Press.

Rossides, Daniel W. 1972. "The Legacy of Max Weber: A Non-Metaphysical Politics". *Sociological Inquiry*, 42 (3/4): 183–210.

Roßteutscher, Sigrid. 2010. "Social Capital Worldwide: Potential for Democratization or Stabilizer of Authoritarian Rule?". *American Behavioral Scientist*, 53 (5): 737–757.

Rothbard, Murray. 2007. *The Betrayal of the American Right*. Auburn, AL: Ludwig von Mises Institute.

Rothschild, Joyce and J. Allen Whitt. 1986. *The Cooperative Workplace: Potentials and Dilemmas of Organisational Democracy and Participation*. Cambridge: Cambridge University Press.

Rothschild-Whitt, Joyce. 1979. "The Collectivist Organization: An Alternative to Rational-Bureaucratic Models". *American Sociological Review*, 44 (4): 509–527.

Rothstein, Bo and Dietlind Stolle. 2008. "The State and Social Capital: An Institutional Theory of Generalized Trust". *Comparative Politics*, 40 (4): 441–459.

Rothwell, Jonathan T. 2012. "The Effects of Racial Segregation on Trust and Volunteering in US Cities". *Urban Studies*, 49 (10): 2109–2136.

Rubinstein, Gidi. 2006. "Authoritarianism among Border Police Officers, Career Soldiers, and Airport Security Guards at the Israeli Border". *The Journal of Social Psychology*, 146 (6): 751–761.

Ryan, Ramor. 2011. *Zapatista Spring: Anatomy of a Rebel Water Project and the Lessons of International Solidarity*. Oakland, CA: AK Press.

Said, Edward W. 1979. *Orientalism*. New York: Vintage.

Sakai, J. 2014. *Basic Politics of Movement Security*. Montreal, Quebec: Kersplebedeb.

Sanders, Linley and Nicholas Riccardi. 2025. "Republicans' Trust in Accuracy of US Elections Jumps after Trump's Win, AP-NORC Poll Finds". *AP News*, January 3. https://apnews.com/article/voting-election-security-republicans-trump-ap-poll-6171a25bd64dbb47505b8c907d dcb037

Savage, Rowan. 2007. "'Disease Incarnate': Biopolitical Discourse and Genocidal Dehumanisation in the Age of Modernity". *Journal of Historical Sociology*, 20 (3): 404–440.

Schenwar, Maya and Victoria Law. 2020. *Prison by Any Other Name: The Harmful Consequences of Popular Reforms*. New York: New Press.

Schilke, Oliver and Laura Huang. 2018. "Worthy of Swift Trust? How Brief Interpersonal Contact Affects Trust Accuracy". *Journal of Applied Psychology*, 103 (11): 1181–1197.

Schneier, Bruce. 2015. *Data and Goliath: The Hidden Battles to Collect Your Data and Control Your World*. New York: W. W. Norton.

Schwartz, Shelly K. 2000. "Working Your Degree: Psychology Grads Often Work in Marketing, Social Work and Labor Relations". *CNN Money*, December 8. https://money.cnn.com/2000/12/08/career/q_degree psychology/

Schwarz, A. G. and Tasos Sagris. 2010. *We Are an Image from the Future: The Greek Revolt of December 2008*. Edinburgh: AK Press.

Scott, James C. 1999a. *Seeing Like a State: How Certain Schemes to Improve the Human Condition Have Failed*. New Haven, CT: Yale University Press.

Scott, James. C. 1999b. "Geographies of Trust, Geographies of Hierarchy" (pp. 273–289) in *Democracy and Trust*, edited by M. E. Warren. Cambridge: Cambridge University Press.

Scott, James C. 2009. *The Art of Not Being Governed: An Anarchist History of Southeast Asia*. New Haven, CT: Yale University Press.

Scott, James C. 2012. *Two Cheers for Anarchism: Six Easy Pieces on Autonomy, Dignity, and Meaningful Work and Play*. Princeton, NJ: Princeton University Press.

Secor, Anna J. and John O'Loughlin. 2005. "Social and Political Trust in Istanbul and Moscow: A Comparative Analysis of Individual and Neighbourhood Effects". *Transactions of the Institute of British Geographers*, 30: 66–82.

Semuels, Alana. 2023. "Private Security Guards Are Replacing Police across America". *Time*, May 2. https://time.com/6275440/insecure-private-security-replacing-police/

Shantz, Jeff. 2017. "Theory Meets Practice: Evolving Ideas and Actions in Anarchist Free Schools" (pp. 245–260) in *Out of the Ruins: The Emergence of Radical Informal Learning Spaces*, edited by R. H. Haworth and J. M. Elmore. Oakland, CA: PM Press.

Sharp, Gene. 1973. *The Politics of Nonviolent Action II: The Methods of Nonviolent Action*. Boston: Porter Sargent.

Shepard, Benjamin and Gregory Smithsimon. 2011. *Beach beneath the Streets: Contesting New York's Public Spaces*. Albany, NY: State University of New York Press.

Sherkat, Darren E. and Derek Lehman. 2018. "Bad Samaritans: Religion and Anti-Immigrant and Anti-Muslim Sentiments in the United States". *Social Science Quarterly*, 99 (5): 1791–1804.

Shirley, Neal and Saralee Stafford. 2015. *Dixie Be Damned: 300 Years of Insurrection in the American South*. Oakland, CA: AK Press.

Shutt, J. Eagle, J. Mitchell Miller, Christopher J. Schreck, and Nancy K. Brown. 2004. "Reconsidering the Leading Myths of Stranger Child Abduction". *Criminal Justice Studies*, 17 (1): 127–134.

Simmel, Georg. 1969. *Conflict and the Web of Group Affiliations*. Edited by Kurt H. Wolff. Glencoe, IL: Free Press.

Simon, Richard M. 2014. "The Foundations of an Anarchist Sociology: Max Stirner and the Alternative to the Collective Human Project". *Contemporary Sociology*, 43 (4): 473–478.

Sims, Amanda and Mary Grigsby. 2019. "Prepper-Worth Identity Work: A Cultural Repertoire for Constructing a Secure Self in an Insecure World". *Sociological Spectrum*, 39 (2): 93–115.

Sitrin, Marina. 2006. *Horizontalism: Voices of Popular Power in Argentina*. Oakland, CA: AK Press.

Sloman, Steven and Philip Fernbach. 2018. *The Knowledge Illusion: Why We Never Think Alone*. New York: Riverhead.

Smith, Andrea. 2007. "The Revolution Will Not Be Funded" (pp. 1–18) in *The Revolution Will Not Be Funded: Beyond the Non-Profit Industrial Complex*, edited by INCITE! Women of Color against Violence. Cambridge, MA: South End Press.

Smith, Christian. 1996. *Resisting Reagan: The U.S. Central American Peace Movement*. Chicago, IL: University of Chicago Press.

Smith, Sandra Susan. 2010. "Race and Trust". *Annual Review of Sociology*, 36: 453–475.

Smith, Tom W. 2009. "Trends in Willingness to Vote for a Black and Woman for President, 1972–2008". *GSS Social Change Report #55*.

Social Science Data Analysis Network. 2000. "Segregation: Dissimilarity Indices". www.censusscope.org/us/rank_dissimilarity_white_black.html

Solnit, Rebecca. 2009. *A Paradise Built in Hell: The Extraordinary Communities That Arise in Disaster.* New York: Viking.

Solnit, Rebecca. 2016. *Hope in the Dark: Untold Histories, Wild Possibilities.* Chicago, IL: Haymarket.

Spring, Joel. 1998. *Primer of Libertarian Education.* Montreal, Quebec: Black Rose Books.

Stanley, Jason. 2018. *How Fascism Works: The Politics of Us and Them.* New York: Random House.

St. Clair, Jeffrey. 2016. *Bernie and the Sandernistas: Field Notes from a Failed Revolution.* Petrolia, CA: CounterPunch.

St. Clair, Jeffrey and Joshua Frank. 2012. *Hopeless: Barack Obama and the Politics of Illusion.* Oakland, CA: AK Press.

Stephens, Nicole M., Stephanie A. Fryberg, and Hazel Rose Markus. 2012. "It's Your Choice: How the Middle-Class Model of Independence Disadvantages Working-Class Americans" (pp. 87–106) in *Facing Social Class: How Societal Rank Influences Interaction*, edited by S. T. Fiske and H. R. Markus. New York: Russell Sage.

Stirner, Max. 1963. *The Ego and His Own.* New York: B. R. Tucker.

Stjernø, Steinar. 2004. *Solidarity in Europe: The History of an Idea.* Cambridge: Cambridge University Press.

Stokes, DaShanne. 2009. "The Peace Corps and the American Empire: An Analysis of U.S. Cultural Imperialism". American Sociological Association annual meeting.

Suh, Hyungjun and Heidi Reynolds-Stenson. 2018. "A Contingent Effect of Trust? Interpersonal Trust and Social Movement Participation in Political Context". *Social Science Quarterly*, 99 (4): 1484–1495.

Tanaka-Gútiez, Yasushi Xavier. 2020. "'We All Came Together That Day': The 2011 English Riots as an Enactment of Solidarity" (pp. 210–234) in *Breaching the Civil Order: Radicalism and the Civil Sphere*, edited by J. C. Alexander, T. Stack, and F. Khosrokhavar. Cambridge: Cambridge University Press.

Tao, Ran, Dali L. Yang, Ming Li, and Xi Lu. 2014. "How Does Political Trust Affect Social Trust? An Analysis of Survey Data from Rural China Using an Instrumental Variables Approach". *International Political Science Review*, 35 (2): 237–253.

Tava, Francesco. 2023. "Justice, Emotions, and Solidarity". *Critical Review of International Social and Political Philosophy*, 26 (1): 39–55.

Taylor, Keeanga-Yamahtta. 2016. *From #BlackLivesMatter to Black Liberation.* Chicago, IL: Haymarket.

Taylor, Peter Leigh. 1994. "The Rhetorical Construction of Efficiency: Restructuring and Industrial Democracy in Mondragón, Spain". *Sociological Forum*, 9 (3): 459–489.

Templeton Anne, Maïka Telga, Enrico Ronchi, Fergus Neville, Stephen Reicher, and John Drury. 2024. "Understanding Crowd Responses to Perceived Hostile Threats: A Multidisciplinary Approach". *Crowd Dynamics*, 9 (A157): 1–10.

Terrell, Francis, Ivanna S. Terrell, and Susan R. Von Drashek. 2000. "Loneliness and Fears of Intimacy among Adolescents Who Were Taught Not to Trust Strangers during Childhood". *Adolescence*, 35 (140): 611–617.

Theoharis, Jeanne. 2018. *A More Beautiful and Terrible History: The Uses and Misuses of Civil Rights History*. Boston: Beacon Press.

Thome, Helmut. 1999. "Solidarity: Theoretical Perspectives for Empirical Research" (pp. 101–131) in *Solidarity*, edited by K. Bayertz. Dordrecht: Kluwer Academic Publishers.

Thomsen, Jens Peter Frølund and Arzoo Rafiqi. 2019. "Intergroup Contact and Its Right-wing Ideological Constraint". *Journal of Ethnic and Migration Studies*, 45 (15): 2739–2757.

Tilly, Charles. 2005. *Trust and Rule*. Cambridge: Cambridge University Press.

Tönnies, Ferdinand. 2001. *Community and Civil Society*. Cambridge: Cambridge University Press.

Traugott, Mark. 2010. *The Insurgent Barricade*. Berkeley: University of California Press.

Turan, Ömer and Burak Özçetin. 2019. "Football Fans and Contentious Politics: The Role of Çarşı in the Gezi Park Protests". *International Review for the Sociology of Sport*, 54 (2): 199–217.

Turner, Ralph. 1967. "Types of Solidarity in the Reconstituting of Groups". *Pacific Sociological Review*, 10 (2): 60–68.

Umoja, Akinyele Omowale. 2014. *We Will Shoot Back: Armed Resistance in the Mississippi Freedom Movement*. New York: New York University Press.

Urban, Hugh B. 2013. *The Church of Scientology: A History of a New Religion*. Princeton, NJ: Princeton University Press.

Uslaner, Eric M. 2011. "Trust, Diversity, and Segregation in the United States and the United Kingdom". *Comparative Sociology*, 10 (2): 221–247.

US News. 2020. "Jackson Lewis P.C.". https://bestlawfirms.usnews.com/profile/jackson-lewis-p-c/overview/1116

van der Steen, Bart, Ask Katzeff, and Leendert van Hoogenhuijze. 2014. *The City Is Ours: Squatting and Autonomous Movements in Europe from the 1970s to the Present*. Oakland, CA: PM Press.

Van Meter, Kevin. 2016. *Guerrillas of Desire: Notes on Everyday Resistance and Organizing to Make a Revolution Possible*. Chico, CA: AK Press.

van Stekelenburg, Jacquelien and Bert Klandermans. 2017. "In Politics We Trust... Or Not? Trusting and Distrusting Demonstrators Compares". *Political Psychology*, 39 (4): 775–792.

Vine, David. 2015. *Base Nation: How US Military Bases Abroad Harm America and the World*. New York: Metropolitan Books.

Visintin, Emilio Paolo, Jacques Berent, Eva G. T. Green, and Juan Manuel Falomir-Pichastor. 2019. "The Interplay between Social Dominance Orientation and Intergroup Contact in Explaining Support for Multiculturalism". *Journal of Applied Social Psychology*, 49: 319–327.

Vitale, Alex S. 2017. *The End of Policing*. London: Verso.

Vradis, Antonis and Dimitris Dalakoglou. 2011. *Revolt and Crisis in Greece: Between a Present Yet to Pass and a Future Still to Come*. Oakland, CA: AK Press.

Vysotsky, Stanislav. 2015. "The Anarchy Police: Militant Antifascism as Alternative Policing Practice". *Critical Criminology*, 23: 235–253.

Vysotsky, Stanislav. 2020. *American Antifa: The Tactics, Culture, and Practice of Militant Antifascism*. New York: Routledge.

Wagner, David G. and Joseph Berger. 1985. "Do Sociological Theories Grow?" *American Journal of Sociology*, 90 (4): 697–728.

Waller, Willard and Reuben Hill. 1951. *The Family: A Dynamic Interpretation*. Hold, Rinehart & Wilson.

Wallerstein, Immanuel. 2003. *The Decline of American Power: The U.S. in a Chaotic World*. New York: New Press.

Walsh, Jeffrey A., Jessie L. Krienert, and Cayla L. Comens. 2016. "Examining 19 Years of Officially Reported Child Abduction Incidents (1995–2013): Employing a Four Category Typology of Abduction". *Criminal Justice Studies*, 29 (1): 21–39.

Walz, Helga S. and Thomas E. Mitchell. 2007. "Adult Children and Their Parents' Expectations of Future Elder Care Needs". *Journal of Aging and Health*, 19 (3): 482–499.

Ward, Colin. 1996. *Anarchy in Action*. London: Freedom Press.

Ward, Kevin. 2015. "The Role of Anglican and Catholic Churches in Uganda in Public Discourse on Homosexuality and Ethics". *Journal of Eastern African Studies*, 9 (1): 127–144.

Way, Lori Beth and Ryan Patten. 2013. *Hunting for "Dirtbags": Why Cops Over-Police the Poor and Racial Minorities*. Boston, MA: Northeastern University Press.

Weber, Max. 1958. "The Three Types of Legitimate Rule". *Berkeley Publications in Society and Institutions*, 4 (1): 1–11.

Wells, Jonathan Daniel. 2020. *The Kidnapping Club: Wall Street, Slavery, and Resistance on the Eve of the Civil War*. New York: Bold Type Books.

Werner, Emmy E. 2004. *A Conspiracy of Decency: The Rescue of the Danish Jews during World War II*. Boulder, CO: Westview.

Williams, Dana M. 2011. "Why Revolution Ain't Easy: Violating Norms, Re-socializing Society". *Contemporary Justice Review*, 14 (2), June: 167–187.

Williams, Dana M. 2017. *Black Flags and Social Movements: A Sociological Analysis of Movement Anarchism*. Manchester: Manchester University Press.

Williams, Dana M. 2018. "Happiness and Freedom in Direct Action: Critical Mass Bike Rides as Ecstatic Ritual, Play, and Temporary Autonomous Zones". *Leisure Studies*, 37 (5): 589–602.

Williams, Dana. 2019. "Hope Springs Forth from Fire: Mutual Aid and Disaster Response to California's Deadliest Wild Fire". *Fifth Estate*, 404: 4–5.

Williams, Dana M. 2020. "Relationships of Horizontalism and Hierarchy: Exploring Divergent Forms of Socio-Political Trust". *Social Science Quarterly*, 101 (3): 1150–1164.

Williams, Dana M. 2021. "'But It's Honoring! It's Tradition': The Persistence of Racialized Indian Mascots in Sports" (pp. 155–167) in *Getting Real about Race*, 3rd ed., edited by Stephanie M. McClure and Cherise A. Harris. Los Angeles, CA: Sage.

Williams, Dana M. 2023. "How Do Political Opportunities Impact Protest Potential? A Multilevel Cross-National Assessment". *International Journal of Comparative Sociology*, 64 (4): 350–374.

Williams, Dana M. 2024a. "Global Confidence in Police: An Analysis of Anarchist Possibilities" (pp. 15–35) in *Towards Anti-Policing: Prefiguring Possibilities beyond the Thin Blue Line*, edited by Simon Springer and Richard J. White. Lanham, MD: Lexington Books.

Williams, Dana M. 2024b. "The Uncivil Sphere and Anti-Authoritarian Movements: Problems of Status Quo Violence, Internationalist Militancy, and Non-State Civil Society". *Theory in Action*, 17 (2): 1–37.

Williams, Dana M. 2025a "Political Representation" in *Inequality around the World: Understanding the Rich–Poor Divide from America to Zimbabwe*, edited by Deric Shannon. New York: Bloomsbury.

Williams, Dana M. 2025b. "Social Movements" in *Inequality around the World: Understanding the Rich–Poor Divide from America to Zimbabwe*, edited by Deric Shannon. New York: Bloomsbury

Williams, Dana M. and Suzanne R. Slusser. 2014. "Americans and Iraq, Twelve Years Later: Comparing Support for the Bush Wars in Iraq". *The Social Science Journal*, 51 (2), June: 231–239.

Williams, Kristian. 2015. *Our Enemies in Blue: Police and Power in America*. Oakland, CA: AK Press.

Williams, Kristian. 2018. *Whither Anarchism?* Oakland, CA: AK Press.

Wilson, William Julius. 1987. *The Truly Disadvantaged: The Inner City, the Underclass, and Public Policy*. Chicago, IL: University of Chicago Press.

Wimberly, Dale W., Pallavi Raonka, Talitha Rose, Sofia Sabirova, and Sasha Gheesling. 2024. "The US Student Antisweatshop Movement's Presence and Success at the Campus Level: Impacts of Collective Identity Strength and Network Density". *Sociological Inquiry*, 94 (3): 627–654.

Witoszek, Nina. 2019. *The Origins of Anti-Authoritarianism*. London: Routledge.

Wolfe, Alan. 2012. "The Ridiculous Rise of Ayn Rand". *Chronicle of Higher Education*, September 7: B2.

Woodall, Denise. 2017. "Interrupting Constructions of a Criminalized Other through a Revised Criminal Activities Checklist Classroom Exercise". *Teaching Sociology*, 45 (2): 161–167.

World Health Organization. 2024. "WHO COVID-19 Dashboard: Weekly COVID-19 Cases and Deaths by Date Reported to WHO". https://data.who.int/dashboards/covid19/data

Yamane, David, Sebastian L. Ivory, and Paul Yamane. 2018. "The Rise of Self-Defense in Gun Advertising: The American Rifleman, 1918–2017" (pp. 9–27) in *Gun Studies: Interdisciplinary Approaches to Politics, Policy, and Practice*, edited by J. Carlson, K. Goss, and H. Shapira. London: Routledge.

Yates, Luke. 2015. "Rethinking Prefiguration: Alternatives, Micropolitics and Goals in Social Movements". *Social Movement Studies*, 14 (1): 1–21.

Yu, Tianlong. 2006. "Challenging the Politics of the 'Model Minority' Stereotype: A Case for Educational Equality". *Equity and Excellence in Education*, 39 (4): 325–333.

Zheng, Hui. 2015. "Losing Confidence in Medicine in an Era of Medical Expansion?" *Social Science Research*, 52: 701–715.

Zibechi, Raúl. 2010. *Dispersing Power: Social Movements as Anti-State Forces*. Oakland, CA: AK Press.

Zimbardo, Philip. 2007. *The Lucifer Effect: Understanding How Good People Turn Evil*. New York: Random House.

Zimmer, Kenyon. 2015. *Immigrants against the State: Yiddish and Italian Anarchism in America*. Urbana, IL: University of Illinois Press.

Zinn, Howard. 1995. *A People's History of the United States, 1492–Present*. New York: HarperCollins.

Zinn, Howard. 1997. *The Zinn Reader: Writings on Disobedience and Democracy*. New York: Seven Stories Press.

Zuboff, Shoshana. 2020. *The Age of Surveillance Capitalism: The Fight for a Human Future at the New Frontier of Power*. New York: PublicAffairs.

Zuckerman, Phil. 2009. "Atheism, Secularity, and Well-Being: How the Findings of Social Science Counter Negative Stereotypes and Assumptions". *Sociology Compass*, 3 (6): 949–971.

Zuesse, Eric. 2017. "Polls: U.S. Is 'The Greatest Threat to Peace in the World Today'". Centre for Research on Globalization. www.globalresearch.ca/polls-u-s-is-the-greatest-threat-to-peace-in-the-world-today/5603342

Index